VASTU SCIENCE FOR
21ST CENTURY

Vastu Science with its application in designing of built environment to enhance the quality of life can help you in your day-to-day activities. For architects this science based on Vedantic knowledge is a must. *Vastu Science for 21st Century* is a sequel to the author's earlier essays to bring closer home secrets that have hitherto been ignored.

The series of books written by Prof. Puri provides an excellent background for developing a curriculum incorporating the knowledge of Vastu Science for Architecture, Town Planning and Engineering Colleges and Universities and for the general public with faith in Vastu Shastra.

Vastu Science for 21st Century

To Enjoy the Gift of Nature

B.B. Puri

New Age Books

ISBN: 81-7822-107-1

First Edition: 2003

© 2002 B.B. Puri

Published by
NEW AGE BOOKS
A-44 Naraina Phase-I
New Delhi-110 028 (INDIA)
Email: nab@vsnl.in
Website: www.newagebooksindia.com

Distributors
MOTILAL BANARSIDASS PUBLISHERS PRIVATE LIMITED
41 U.A., Bungalow Road, Jawahar Nagar,
Delhi - 110 007

Printed in India
at Shri Jainendra Press
A-45 Naraina Phase-I, New Delhi-110 028

Acknowledgement

I wish to express my heartfelt thanks to my readers and friends for the wholehearted support and inspiration given to me for writing this book.

My gratitude to Dr. P.S. Rana, Director, HUDCO, New Delhi for writing a very encouraging Foreword for this book.

I also thank Er. Pankaj Agrawal, Secretary, The Institute of Vastu Science, India, for his personal encouragement in this project.

I wish to give my blessings to Ms. Anubha (M.Phil.) for taking special pains in computer typing and editing the manuscript.

I also thank the publisher M/s New Age Books for bringing out this book with state-of-art technology. I am grateful to Shri Rajeev Prakash Jain, Director, Motilal Banarsidass Publishers Pvt. Ltd., Delhi, for giving personal attention in the production of this book.

Last, but not least, I offer my sincere thanks to all my clients, students, staff and faculties of Vastu Research Centre, Vastu Kala Academy, members of The Institution of Vastu Science (India) and Board of Trustees of Research Institute of Vedic Culture for their co-operation and support.

B.B. Puri

Foreword

'Vastu Science for 21st Century' is the latest contribution by the author, Prof. B.B. Puri, after an overwhelming response to his earlier books titled *Vedic Architecture and Art of Living, Applied Vastu Shastra in Modern Architecture* and *Vastu Shastra for Mass Housing.* Vastu Shastra is not merely an art but a definite science in itself. This book has made an excellent effort to establish this fact. The knowledge of Vastu is based on Vedic literature and is derived from the fundamental principles of Vedantic knowledge.

Prof. B.B. Puri is a well-known architect, having a vast experience in the field of architecture. He is the founder of *Vastu Kala Academy,* the School of Architecture and Interior Designing. He is also the founder of *Vastu Research Centre.* He has brought out in clear terms that the knowledge of modern architecture is incomplete without Vastu science. The Vastu principles have been formulated keeping in view the cosmic influences of the sun, the direction of the wind, the position of moon, the earth's magnetic field and the influence of the entire cosmos on our planet.

Prof. Puri's attempt to highlight the principles of Vastu science and its application in designing of built environment is commendable. It is highly desirable that all our young architects are equipped with this knowledge and they make use of it in their day-to- day design activities. To achieve this objective, it would be necessary to incorporate the knowledge of Vastu science in the curricula of Architecture, Town Planning and Engineering Colleges and Universities. The series of books written by Prof. Puri provide an excellent background for developing such a curriculum and encourage other scholars of Vastu to record their experience and knowledge in this field.

I pray the Almighty to bless Prof. B. B. Puri to continue his efforts in spreading the knowledge of Vastu science.

Dr. P.S. Rana
Director (Corporate Planning)
HUDCO

Date: 28ᵗʰ September, 2001
Place: New Delhi

Contents

Preface

As a practising architect with 40 years of experience in the field and 20 years research of Vastu Shastra, I compiled my conclusions in *Vedic Architecture and Art of Living*, which was foreworded by President, Council of Architecture and was released by then President of India Dr. Shankar Dayal Sharma. It was well received by the readership.

After research in Vedic Vastu, I attempted to find out the solution on how to apply Vastu principles in modern living in a sequel titled *Applied Vastu Shastra in Modern Architecture.*

I am convinced that the time has come when Vastu vidya and Vastu vigyan come to take their place in human affairs. With this vision in mind, I founded *Vastu Kala Academy*, Delhi, in 1992, a college of Architecture and Interior Designing, which is now affiliated to Indraprastha, Guru Nanak University, Delhi and is conducting a course leading to B. Arch. Degree in Architecture. Side-by-side, I founded *Vastu Research Centre*, where I started teaching Vastu gyan and organizing Vastu workshops, seminars as well as conducting further study of literature containing tenets of this science. On 12th Feb. 2000, the Institute of Vastu Science, India was set up to spread Vastu knowledge uniformly in India and other parts of the world.

In this book, I have tried to justify that Vastu principles are based on scientific logic and Vastu itself is a science much in need in the 21st Century in view of rapid advancements man is making in other fields without compensating on ecology front, which forms the basis of Vastu.

I have already discussed in detail the orientation of building, plot, cut plot, set back, basement and height of building, Mandalas, slope, the permanent recommended position of open space, water bodies, Agni (Fire) and air directions etc. in my earlier books.

I have since received lots of questions from readers on whether Vastu is a science and if its application is universal. A science eveloved thousands of years ago can still be useful and effective in 21st Century in the modern life and changing styles of Architecture. In the present text I take up these and other issues with reference to wider concern of balance and harmony with Nature that is uppermost in the minds of those who know how things stand with this planet.

In the 21ˢᵗ Century, a growing concern about environment has introduced a new dimension to demographic studies. The crisis of human settlement is no less acute than the crisis of population explosion, and the need for optimising human settlements is as great as that for controlling population growth. Of late, however, rapid urbanization, increasing rural-urban migration and the consequent ecological disaster have put immense strain in the minds of people and has compelled demographers to turn their attention to Vastu gyan.

 The first need is to study Vastu Science based on Nature. But one could argue with equal force that "the first need is to take the strain off rural areas the strain of continued poverty, conditions of unemployment and economic and social stagnation."

It is important to bear in mind that throughout the world young people migrate from rural areas to big cities and metropolitan centres and not always for economic reason. Unless the frame of rural areas is improved, rural development alone will not be effective to discourage migration. The search for a more satisfactory and peaceful habitat has led to the advocacy of small towns with growth protential which, it is argued, could serve as a bridge between Vastu (habitat) and Nature.

There are serious complications of air pollution, water pollution, traffic congestion, inadequate housing, and noise in all the urban areas. On the other hand, the problem of maintaining social, economic and cultural traditions are being aggravated in rural areas with dearth of population. Taking into account the urgency of ensuring the people's health and welfare and the necessity of rationally using the extremely limited land surface, a new comprehensive environment development plan must be devised. A view has been expressed that urban housing receives higher priority than rural housing in developing countries in spite of the fact that "rural housing cannot be ignored if Governments wish to reduce the drift of a large number of people from rural to urban areas." But the trend of rural-urban migration does point to strong pull of cities in spite of acute housing shortage in cities.

It is doubtful if improved rural housing alone will make a significant change in the rate of rural-urban migration. It is well known that young men and women are reluctant to stay in villages and they are the first to look outside. It is clear there are other factors. Basic security, entertainment avenues and relative privacy. Primarily, it can also be seen as a cultural problem, or apathy with traditional family structures.

Again, unless there are adequate employment opportunities in rural areas, the drift to towns and cities is inevitable. In India, in the very First Five-Years Plan period (1951-1956), an experiment was made in remodelling an entire village because it was felt that in the rural environment sanitation, water supply and disposal of human waste were more important than the mere construction of houses. This experiment was not successful and it was realized that improvement in housing conditions has to be related to the improvement of the economy of the village. The villagers found it difficult to repay the loans advanced by the Government because "the general productivity and especially that of agriculture has not increased."

Coming back to the topic, Vastu architecture is an art. It provides an aesthetic object. Like other arts, it cannot be simply judged out of its context, from the outside. To judge a building, one must get into it or be shown what is behind its outer walls, with relation to inner as well as its surrounding landscape.

Computers and robots have moved into Vastu/architect's offices and the building industry to reduce mental and physical strain on man. Machines are not regarded as being in conflict with man. Man has developed machines which are humanised though man himself has to a certain extent become 'machinised'. We must use science and technology for progress, but never become their slaves. The Year 2001 and onwards will be symbolic of tomorrow, a time that will critically surpass today's designs in living environment. We must now ask what kind of sketches of architects of the present will correspond with those of Vedic times.

The highest purpose of a good city is to provide better life and growth to the individual and the family and the mission of those of us who are called to work with the city planning was two-fold:

1. To relieve the congestion of existing cities and give the outgoing populations the space and opportunity to regenerate themselves.
2. To effect an economic recovery against a declining agricultural or industrial base.

What has caused a great tension in the past decade is that the new towns have been immensely successful on one hand in leading to economic growth and providing homes and associated facilities for the new generations and, on the other hand, the conditions in the main cities have continued to decline. Violence, homelessness and congestion have got even worse until the point has now reached when people by and large are preferring to move out of the cities into rural environment. The new towns and cities are designed to decongest these overpopulated cities.

In any further planning, the location of such towns is of prime importance. They should have facilities for self-employment and must not become dormitories of large cities, where pressure on existing infrastructure increases. The plan of new towns must be strategic to allow expansion as well as change of land use as and when required. The new towns, new city centres can have better working conditions and the process of providing better houses, schools, religious buildings and leisure facilities in a new urban environment must be handled carefully so that it can develop into a well designed and attractive habitat. It should provide for the growth of the individual and the family. The issues concerned are serious and in case of housing, the task is still stupendous considering shifts in population concentration due to migration.

Does development mean raising of high-rise buildings? Since ancient Vedic times, the life span of human being has increased, man has become more intelligent and smart but also, and as a consequence, he has lost the charm of living and the opportunity of being an honest human being. Worldwide tolerance and love have been replaced by hatred, jealousy and bitterness.

Today, nobody knows what is community living. People either live in buildings one on top of the other or in huge houses distant from each other. In Vedic period clusters of houses were built around an open space common to all the houses, known as Brahma Sthan, which not only provided ventilation across the clusters but was a platform for the families of clusters to interact with each other. Learning, sharing of problems and living as one big family was a common practice. Today, more and more towns have been converted into industrial centres, with their entire population solely working on pecuniary interests. This has had the result of converting men into the very machines they work, with a dangerous trend, if any.

If we want to see the real city based on Vastu principles, we do not confine our view to the great skyscrapers, we look at the dwellings of the common people. We see how people live, their mode of livelihood, their streets and milieu of homes, the environment in which they raise their families, the children who will grow up to be fellow countrymen and neighbours of their children a generation removed.

Buildings located in parallel lines along each side of a street did not provide the same privacy for living areas nor quiet for sleeping rooms. The next step in Vastu planning technique was the placement of all buildings at right angles to the streets. The space between buildings was thereby free of traffic. This arrangement provided privacy for all living units, safety for play and recreation areas and uniform orientation for all dwellings.

Research in Vastu planning techniques has led to a rational consideration of orientation, sunlight and other such factors significant in every room as a rule, and orientation of the buildings to provide East and West exposure becomes mandatory. The preferable exposure is western light for living rooms and elderly couple and eastern light for young children's bedroom.

Here, theoretical and practical aspects of these problems have been discussed. An attempt has been made to give a compound solution to the problem of Vastu-based planning that is to describe in an intercorrelated manner with the five elements as to how human being is a part of the nature and how to enjoy through Vastu the gifts of Nature with all of the social, architectural, topological and technical aspects taken into consideration.

B.B. PURI

Chapter 1

Vastu Principles and Logic

Vastu: A Vedic Knowledge

Vastu offers a multi-disciplinary approach designing enhanced living. Vastu Shastra, provides a framework for good, peaceful and healthy standards of living. The shape of a building, for example, should merge with the surroundings, the environment and the topography of that area. One should also consider the climate of that area. As per Vastu Shastra, the shape of the building—the proportion of the length, breadth and height, the entrance and the open spaces—play a very important role in life. It is not wise to ignore architectural and/or environmental principles at the same time. It is advisable that practitioners or a Vastu consultant must possess a good knowledge of architecture before experimenting with Vastu principles.

While designing any building, Vastu advises us balancing of the five elements: Earth, Water, Fire (Sun), Air and Space (as explained in Chapter 3) in their proper place and proportions to keep the occupancy of that place in harmony and to allow one to enjoy happiness and peace in the dwelling and/or working place.

The orientation of the building or plot towards the directions or level of the existing ground, burial or cremation places, hills or slopes, highways, stationary or running water, rivers, ponds, streams, nullahs, wells, places of worship, temples, garbage dumps and other public places, high tension wires etc. influence the Vastu of that site with negative/positive energies.

The points of energies allow people to work or rest, to sleep or to plan their future. They are driven energetic and innovative because of their enterprising attitudes, with positive thinking and sincere, hard work.

When we build a structure in an open space on the Earth, the space where various types of energy fields flow, the equilibrium is affected. This is explained in chapters 8, 10, 12, 13 and 14.

Vastu helps in designing the structure of the building to ensure a harmonious flow of energy and equilibrium. Vastu considers the interplay of various forces of nature involving the five elements and nine planets (as discussed in Chapter 15) to maintain equilibrium as these elements and planets influence, guide and change the living/life styles of not only human beings but every living being on the earth. Thus, they influence our behavior, style, growth, deeds, luck and other basics of life.

If the profession of Architecture, Engineering or Vastu consultant has to be equipped to meet the challenges in the 21ˢᵗ Century, They must examine the forces that are now transforming the building techniques and the art of living within the framework of Vastu principles.

In this book, the Author has presented an in-depth study of Vastu principles and logic.

There are three main protections for human comfort. The first protection is provided by the nature (our skin) since birth. The second protection we choose depending on climatic condition, customs and religions with the clothes we wear. The third protection we discuss in this book is 'shelter' from elements. Shelter protects us from the worst and extreme forms of Nature while enjoying the same.

Vastu principles are applicable universally and have relation to motions of planets rather than caste and creed of people. It is secular, it is holistic and is universal. Its application however changes with orientation, geography and climatic conditions of a place.

Vastu science is complete in itself and this science can bring peace and happiness to the whole world, and to enjoy full life on the earth by leading four types of happiness are deluxe comfort, peace, rightful living, fulfilment of desires and liberation from disease.

Happiness and health are not gained by chance or luck. They can be chosen. We are suffering because we have drifted away from nature. Ignorance about Vedic knowledge, gifted by the nature as Rig Veda, Yajur Veda, Sama Veda and Atharva Veda bring misery in life. Historical facts and authentic stories mentioned in Puranas called the fifth Veda enlighten on the Vastu issues having relation to life.

Some of the Vedic literature that have a bearing on Vastu are as below:

- Ayurveda— Holistic Medicine Science taught by Lord Dhanvantari.
- Dhanurveda— Military Science taught by Maharishi Bhrigu.
- Gandharvaveda— Art of Music, Dance and Drama.
- Sthapatyaveda— Science of Architecture (Vastu Shastra).
- Artha Shastra— Science of Government (Politics).
- Manu Smriti— Laws of Dharma Sutras.
- Kaam Shastra, Paak Shastra and so on.

Vedas, Vedanta Sutras, Brahmanas and *Upanishads* were all considered to be *Shruti* (the original revealed knowledge, *Mahabharata, Ramayana, Bhagawad Gita* and other *Puranas* are called *Smriti.* Persons who possessed the complete knowledge of *Shruti* and *Smriti* were called *Aryans.*

This Earth is the only planet which is having life, because of existence of five elements (Earth, Water, Air, Fire and Space), so we take a healthy birth with the balance of these five elements and grow with the aid of our five senses and develop our knowledge within Zenith and Nadir.

Zenith represents *Aakash* (Space), and Nadir represents *Pataal* (The Earth). *Aakash* represents the cosmic energy and *Pataal* (Earth) represents Geo-Energy. It is the effect and harmony of the geo and cosmic energies which bring in mental and spiritual well-being of the man and keep the body, mind and soul healthy.

Unfortunately, the science behind Vastu postulates cannot be readily deciphered. Since the original text itself is not available *in toto,* this situation is being exploited by many. Keeping this in view this situation, I have tried to dig out the facts and made an honest attempt to present my findings on the science behind the basic postulates of Vastu shastra.

A few important basic scientific explanations have been covered in my earlier books, the first volume titled 'Vedic Architecture and Art of Living' which was well-received by the public and the experts gave me the encouragement to write a second volume 'The Applied Vastu Shastra in Modern Architecture'.

It can readily be considered that the postulates of Vastu science as annunciated by our rishis and munis are absolutely correct and scientific, but they are applied with due regard to the geography and climate. Cardinal directions are absolute in nature. They do not change. However, importance of their effect needs a subtle modification depending upon the Latitude and Longitude of a place, which in turn contribute in a big way in deciding the building orientation and in meeting the needs of the people in the 21st Century.

Keeping with the times, I have tried to give to my readers in this third volume in comprehensible details an analysis of the scientific explanations with logic and the importance of Vastu in comprehensive details.

Chapter 2

Vedic Fundamentals and Vedantic Thoughts

A man of perfection will love to live and love to die. His life will be a song. For him there is no distinction between life and death.

Light of Knowledge

- The Light of knowledge is the ultimate thing. When one dies in awakened state, it means he chooses if he wants to be reborn or not.
- When someone becomes capable of being conscious, wakeful and aware in the sleep state, he will be free of the three bodies.
- When a person is born, he comes from the deep sleep state. He is carrying with him all the results and carry over of past actions, influences and conditioning of the past lives. He came carry over to the dream state and then to the waking state and a new life due to his previous past actions (Karma). He is born in the darkest ignorance and his Spiritual Master (Guru) opens his eyes with the touch of knowledge. One has to suffer for his ignorance. One has to pay the price for his mistakes.
- Vastu is the foundation of architecture, if the foundations is not strong, good results cannot be expected. An architect should be intellectually aware of the highest truths formulated in religion. The subject of architecture is one among the several sacred sciences derived form the highest metaphysical principles. So the architects/Vastu consultants should put in all their sincere efforts to acquire this comprehensive, far-sighted and timeless wisdom.
- An architect/Vastu consultant should exhibit his skill by overcoming the difficulties and differences between the principles laid down in Vastu Shastra and the present day requirements, keeping in mind the original relation between

man, material and nature and to find acceptable solutions to get positive results.

- We have entered the 21ˢᵗ century. The challenges before professional architects are to examine the forces that are now transforming the building activity and architectural thoughts of the people and the high tech advance technology needed in 21ˢᵗ Century.

Vastu of Relationships

In a man's life there are three types of relationships:

1. Relationship of intellect (between a teacher and a student) which cannot be very deep.
2. Relationship of love which can be deeper than the intellect the relationship between a mother and a child, between brothers, husband and wife. They arise from the heart.
3. A deeper relationship, arises from the navel called friendship. They go deeper than even love. Love can end. Friendship almost never ends.

Friendship

The relationship of friendship arises from the navel, chakra.

Love—Binds   Friendship—gives Freedom.
Love—Possesses   Friendship—spreads Universal.

Lovers insist that the other should not love anyone else One can have friends, and friend. It arises from the deepest cenret of life. Friendship ultimately becomes the greatest way to take us towards the divine, because his relationship is taking place with everyone's navel center and one day he becomes related to the navel center of the universe. Similarly, Vastu is secular and Universal, Vastu is a bridge between nature and man based on the five elements.

Five Yoga Mudras by our finger elements

The hand and the five fingers of our body also represent the five elements, and they act accordingly:

1. The Thumb represents FIRE (Agni).
2. The Index Finger represents AIR (Vayu).
3. The Middle Finger represents SPACE (Shunya).
4. The Ring Finger represents EARTH (Prithvi).
5. The Little Finger represents WATER (Jal).

As in Vastu, we have discussed and studied that when all the five elements are in proper balance in our building design, in relation with the climate of the country and are blended with weather condition, then we claim that our house/building is healthy and the occupants of that building enjoy good health, possess wealth and stay in peace. Similarly, when these five elements are in balance in our body, we experience good health and balance of mind.

However, if there is an imbalance of elements, one suffers corresponding ailments. To cure and balance, one can practise "Yoga Mudras" i.e. following five mudras:

1. *Varun Mudra* : Join the tips of little finger and the thumb together. This helps in curing skin disease and bring lusture to the dry skin and makes it smooth.

2. *Prithvi Mudra* : Join the tips of ring finger and the thumb together. This helps in curing weakness of mind and body. Gives positive energy and injects life-force in the body.

3. *Gyana-Dhyana-Mudra* : Join the tip of index finger and the thumb together. This helps in the case of loss of memory, sleeplessness and lack of concentration.

4. *Surya Mudra* : Put the ring finger at the base of thumb and press gently. This helps in reducing excess cholesterol in blood.

5. *Hridaya Mudra* : Put index finger between the point at the base of the thumb and keep the tips of both middle and ring fingers on the tip of the thumb. This helps in *asthama*, breathing problems and heart palpitation.

These above five Yoga Mudras by our five finger elements are easy to practice. To get the effective result one must do the mudra practice twice a day for 20/30 minutes at a stretch.

Sloka

> *Serve Bhavantu Sukhinah Serve Santu Niramaya*
> *Serve Bhadrani Pashyantu Ma, Kashchid Duhkhs*
> *Bhagbhavet II*

Meaning: The voice of Vedas says—"Let all the people in the world prosper and be happy. Man always discovers how to live in peace and happiness."

Our sages and saints always wanted to ensure happiness and prosperity not only to the mankind, but to every living being in this world. They showed their serious concern about the happiness and welfare of everyone, with a view to ensuring that all people live in peace and harmony with prosperity and enjoy health and wealth in their life.

They discovered various codes and systems for our living which are contained in Vedas and Upanishads etc. One of the system they discovered and explained is 'Vastu Shastra, the Art of Living.' Our sages and Saints could see thousands of years ahead. They knew various mysterious and mystical elements of this Universe even before western scientist could start finding them out.

According to Mayamatam, 'Vastu Shastra' is an ancient art and science, containing principles and practices of designing and constructing buildings which ensure harmonious balance between Man, Material and Nature.

Various texts on Vastu Shastra finds its origin in Mayamatam, Maya Vastu, Vishvakarma, Shilpa Shastra, Shilpa Ratana, Shilpa Prakash, Vasturatnakara, Manasara etc.

I was born in the darkest ignorance and my spiritual master opened my eyes with the touch of Vastu knowledge.

Chapter 3

Vastu Purusha Mandala and the Eight Directions

The Vastu Purusha Mandala, a grid of square and regarded as a perfect figure is conceived to be a fundamental form in architecture. All other shapes are derived from it.

The square is oriented to the eight cardinal directions; it makes space comprehensible, and therefore, it is looked upon as an all-encompassing symbol of the world. Tradition prescribes 32 types of mandala. The simplest one is square. It is called *Sakala* (Diagram Number 1) or one

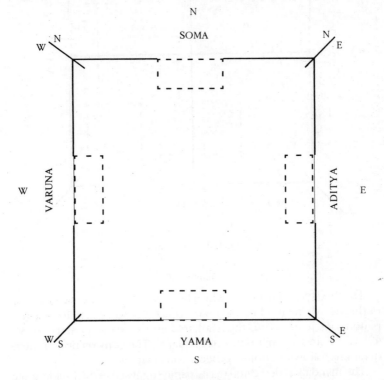

Sakala Mandala

Diagram 1

which has no parts and is prescribed for an ascetic's seat. It was a simple enclosure around sacred fire and was never used as a site for building.

The next one called *Pechaka* (Diagram Number 2) contains four squares presided over by demonic powers. It was meant for the worship of Shiva in his terrifying form.

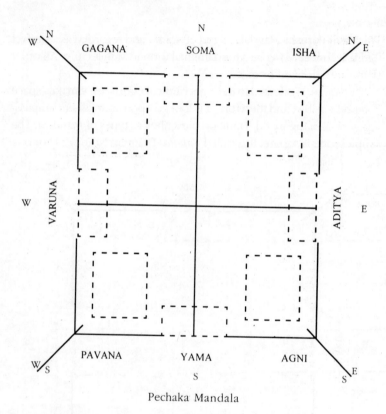

Pechaka Mandala

Diagram 2

The third type of mandala which has nine squares, is known as Pitha or throne. All the rest are expanded version of squares to form a grid pattern of squares. Thus the resultant figures are composed of 9, 36, 49, 64, 81, and so on, up to 1,024 squares. The construction of these diagrams follows a gnomic progression, a Greek method.

The mandala is dedicated (as its name suggests) to the building site or Vastu. The earth is the primal Vastu, since it forms natural support to buildings. In its far spread, the site is marked out; that too, is known as Vastu.

In India, religious and artistic continuities survive. The theme of depicting the Universe as a cosmic Purusha is used as a telling metaphor to describe creation. The universe of the Hindus is portrayed as a colossal Purusha as the mandala whose micro-cosmic body contains the world. The bounds of this anthropomorphized being constitute the regions of earthly and cosmic space.

The word Vastu means the ultimate particle in the micro-cosmic universe, or the egg, as well as the subtlest particle in the microcosm. It is believed that this Vastu is the organ of creativity in both the universes, existing as it does as the infinite unchanging particle. Brahma or primal energy is an integral part of this particle. All that is represented on the earth is called Vastu. Hence, building and images, and other manmade objects are included in Vastu. In short, the Vastu Brahma stands for the primary subtle substance, while the Vastu is the tangible representation.

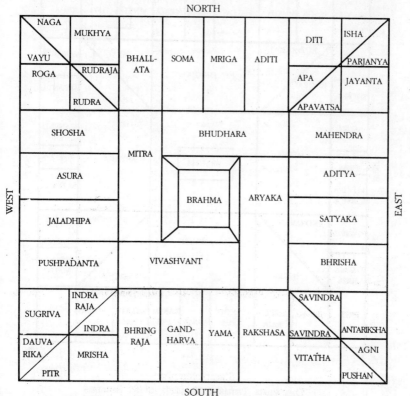

Manduka : The Vastu Purusha Mandala of 64 Squares

Diagram 3

The spirit of energy of the earth is called Vastu Purusha. In bhoomi puja this energy is invoked to give the desired benefit so as to make man's life on earth peaceful.

Sculpture and architecture may be seen as part of a total divine experience. The primary sculpture or shilpa in the form of Natraja expresses endless creativity of the primary energy. The primary architecture is the Garbhgriha, a cubicle that encloses the primary energies. Thus, architecture becomes that enclosure which is capable of enclosing vibrant energy, and sculpture is the representation of this energy in morphic form.

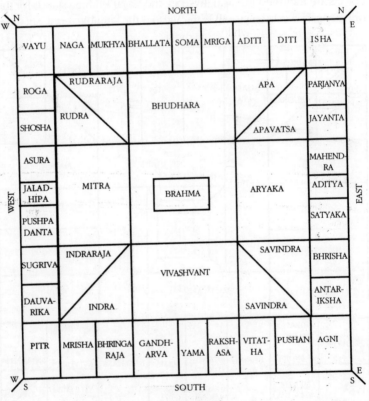

Paramashayika
The Vastu Purusha Mandala of 81 Squares

Diagram 4

Where architecture is concerned the order is maintained through the adoption of a modular planning technique called *Pada Vinyasa*. The land is divided into grids with Sutras running North-South and East-West axis that runs through the centre of a Vastu is called the Brahma Sutra and the North-South as Soma Sutra.

The plot may be divided into even or odd number of Padas. The central point is called the Brahma Sthan, the outer rings as Brahma Pada, and Pechaka Pada.

This order is carried out in the both individual building as well as in the layout of villages and towns. In the case of temple layout of villages and towns, the modules, is divided into smaller units so as to facilitate adoption of rhythmic modules in the horizontal and vertical plans in the wall or in the projection of the basement.

To be able to achieve rhythm and order in the entire Vastu Shastra and sculpture piece, the shilpi uses the above principle in an extremely simple manner. The rhythm gives rise to a visual order and structural rigour. The understanding of materials gives rise to marvels such as the musical pillar and the bell in the lion's mouth. The perfection of joints and finish comes from disciplined work of ethic and community ethos. Flashes of genius and evocative beauty grow out of strict adherence to a social belief and the adoption of grammar of design.

Vastu Mandala

Mandala means configuration, enclosure or network. Energy networks of desired objectives are also expressed graphically in the matrix form in square, triangular, hexagonal or octagonal grids. The square grid is the most common. (Astrological matrix of the donor or deity, the number combinations, the Yantra and also Mantra symbols are inscribed in specific configurations responding to respective network). Mandala is particular to time, place, person and purpose. It is a composite operative programme chart of all necessary overlays as explained below.

To sum up, the Mantra, Yantra and Mandala are science, technology and management techniques for discipline of mind for specific persons. They are in the holistic tradition of Vedic science and thought.

Vastu Purusha-Mandala

Purusha and Mandala are associated with Vastu (Site). Vastu means site, the site for building a house, or a dwelling, Vastu encompasses the house with site and its environment.

According to the Vedic thought Purusha is not only the cause and life behind all Prakriti, but also behind all creations of man. Since mind

VASTU PURUSHA MANDALA 81 SQUARES (YOGINI)

Vastu Purusha Exists in Each and Every House
Suggested Placement of Different Activities

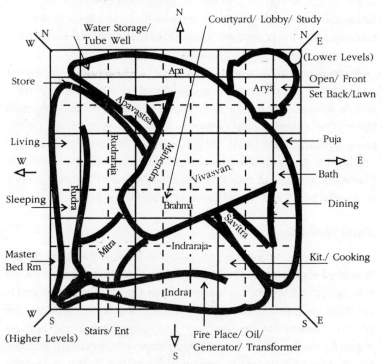

Main Door Position as Per Birthsign of Head/ Owner of House

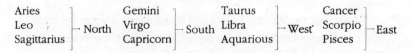

Aries		Gemini		Taurus		Cancer	
Leo	North	Virgo	South	Libra	West	Scorpio	East
Sagittarius		Capricorn		Aquarious		Pisces	

Vastu Purusha : The Demi God

Daigram 5

in its State and form represents Purusha and mind is the Lord or author of all creations of Man-Psychic as well as physical creations.

Any tool developed through human will, mind and efforts is extension of man himself. Whether as producers, receivers and users, men enjoy or suffer the development or limitedness of human intelligence or skill. So, the concept is that the manmade products are the projections of man's own personality (material, emotional, intellectual, vital and bliss). The object made by him also has Purusha (Atman or Prana).

Vastu Purusha (The Demi-God)

The house is ruled by a demi-God the Vastu Purusha. If not appeased, he would destroy the house and bring adverse conditions for the house

BRIHAT SAMHITA

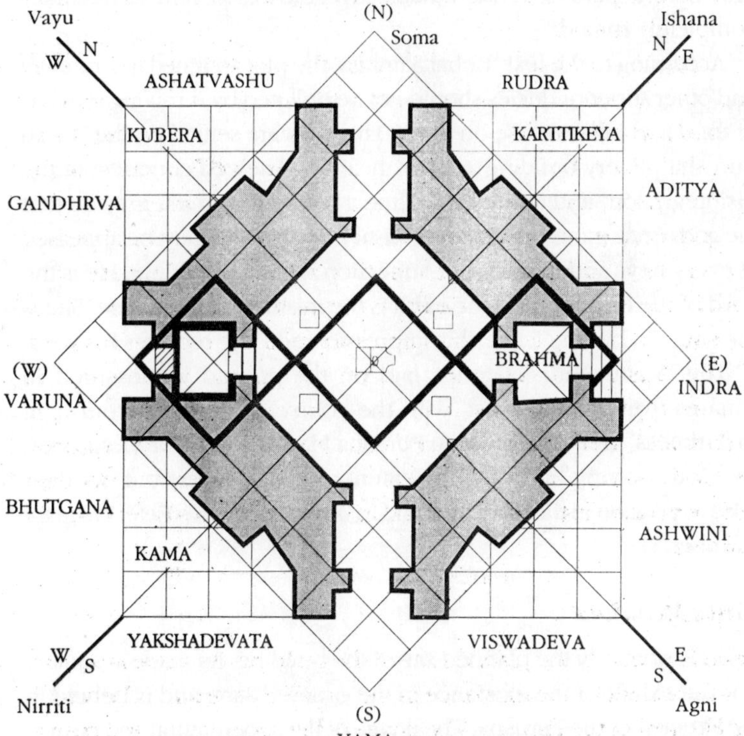

Vastu Purusha Mandala 64 Square (Pada)

Diagram 6

holds. To appease him, one must follow the sacred ceremonies at every step religiously.

The rituals give sanctity to the entire process. The rituals and fasting to be followed by the architect help him gain full control over his mind, body and soul.

According to text 'Mayamatam' "It should be known that the spirit of the building (Vastu Purusha) has six bones, a single heart, four vulnerable points and four vessels and that he lies upon the ground, his head towards the North-East". He, who, is present in every human dwelling, is responsible for good and for bad fortune, that is why the wise must avoid tormenting his limbs with the limbs of the owner of the house. Thus, the sage must always spare the body of the spirit in the course of construction through ignorance of the architects, if any of its several parts be rendered defective, the master himself becomes completely ruined.

According to the text 'Brihat Samhita' the plot assigned to Brahmah and other superior deities should not be polluted by throwing remains of food and other refuse on them. The gods are settled on the 'Vastu Purusha'. Every building activity means a renewed conquest of the disintegration, and at the same time a restitution of integrity so that the gods once move the limbs of 'Vastu Purusha' and must be appeased at every new undertaking in connection with the building, He is the Lord of the building and the earth is the mistress of the house. She is the soil. On her, he leaves his impression and she receives his seed.

The 'Vastu Purusha' once laid on the ground is measured in squares from east to west, with the course of the sun, from light to darkness, their total is Vastu Purusha Mandala of 64 or 81 squares. 45 Gods occupy his body, the extent of which differs but not their relative position in the plan, so is said in 'Brihat Samhita'. (Refer Diagram Number 5)

Vastu Mandala

Vastu is primarily the planned site of the building. Its shape is square. It is the extent of the existence in the ordered state and is beheld in the likeness of the Purusha. The image of the supernatural and cosmic man, the Purusha is congruous and identical to the planned site. Purusha, cosmic man, the origin and source of 'Apara Prakriti' (existence) is

VASTUPURUSHA MANDALA (YOGINI)

For Vastu Kala

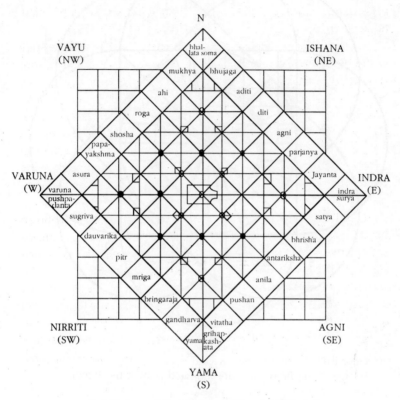

Ambiguity and Certainty in a Plan for Vastukala

Diagram 7

instrumental or efficient cause. The plan makes the site of the building in his image, which is his form. The plan of the building is in the likeness of the 'Purusha', or the totality of the manifestation. Mandala denotes any closed polygon. The form of 'Vastu Purusha Mandala' although a square can be conceived as triangle, circle, hexagon, octagon of equal area. (Refer Diagram Number 3, 4, 6, 7 and 8)

Through Vastu Purusha Mandala, man also incorporates these aspects in the building. Thus, the Vastu Yantra and Vastu Purusha Mandala are the creative conceptual diagrams which program the building

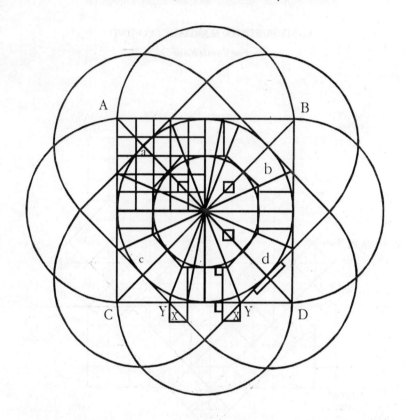

Octagonal Plan Using Circles. A Grid is indicated in The Upper Left
Quadrant; Entry Piers are indicated only at the Bottom

Diagram 8

activity and render protective aspects. Its language is symbolic. (like
any computer program diagram or matrix). Since, Vastu Purusha Mandala
is specific to time, place function and owners of the project, it is
developed on a case-to-case basis and site, location and town.

The Vastu Mandala tries to overlay these various conceptual sieves
on one Mandala. It is possible to cut such elaborate Mandalas for modern
architecture with the help of the science of computers (artificial intelligence). The human mind is potentially the most original efficient and
creative computer. The schools of creative arts and sciences in India

have a storehouse of knowledge at their disposal, both for training of creative and productive minds as well as development of thought process and method to produce eco-culturally appropriate living environment.

Man above all, is a tool making animal. He communicates and expands beyond his physical frame through mind, spirit, skills and instrumentations. The quality of man needs to be guided for positive co-existence. His various faculties be trained and disciplined for the highest efficiency, positive co-existence and creative efforts.

Now, let us understand the nature-man-architecture transfer process. If man is reflection of nature, architecture reflects man and his total personality (Purusha). If human body and the mind complex are instruments which communicate, expand and get consumed in the nature, architecture and habitat also pulsate, absorb, expand and get consumed into man. Nature, man and architecture (habitat) are the natural evolutionary extension of the another forming a complete whole of Vastu Purusha.

The Eight Directions

Before planning any building weather residence, temple, palace, commercial building, school shopping centre, villages or city. They make Mandala and draw squares according to the size of plot which we call as *Yogini*. According to the orientation of the site in respect of North, they allot each Mandala i.e. square to God of nature by dividing the site into eight direction i.e. North, North-East, East, East-South, South, South-West and North-West. All these directions have been controlled by the respective Gods (refer Diagram 9).

1. East   :   Is controlled by Lord Indra.
2. Agni   :   i.e. Lord of Fire in East-South.
3. Yama   :   the God of Death in South.
4. Nirriti :   the God who protects us from evil or enemies in South-West.
5. Varuna   :   the God of Rains in West.
6. Vayu   :   the God of Air in North-West.
7. Kubera   :   the Lord of Wealth in North.
8. Isha   :   the God/Ishwar in North-East.
9. Space   :   In the Center the Brahma, the creator of Universe open to Sky.

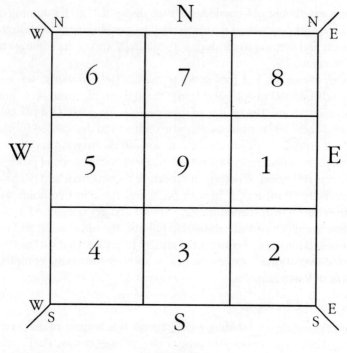

Diagram 9

According to the use and requirement as well as the activity of the user they allot the different areas and rooms to make healthy house and to get peace, wealth and pleasures of life.

According to Mayamatam and Shastras, if we worship and respect the Lords of these eight directions, they shower their blessings on us:

- Earth is mother, she gives you everything and recycles everything for the benefit of humans.
- Sun gives you Energy for the life source (Pran-Shakti).

When you sleep head towards these four magnetic directions it is interesting to know how these directions behave in your attitude:

- East direction: Attachment, Love, Peaceful Life and Entanglement.
- South direction: Lust and obsession.
- West direction: Greed and Jealousy.
- North direction: Arrogance and Anger.

Chapter 4

Vastu for Planning

Architecture drawn up under Vastu can regulate the relations between man, nature and his environment. Physically, architecture constitutes one of the most important aspects of the environment, and if the semi-architectural elements such as roads, squares and gardens etc. are taken into consideration, it is connected with practically all human activities. Vastu, ideally, participates in these activities by forming a practical frame, an adequate psychological background and by expressing all that which takes place of importance to the community. Originally, all these aspects were unified in a general demand for protection and survival of the species. In the earliest civilizations, it was impossible to distinguish between the practical and the religious. Thus, the idea of seeing the symbolical as a derivation of the practical is a modern understanding. The primitive forms of building resulted from the need of our protection from the elemental as well as social and cultural aspects. Physical protection and social stability were a new problem in the first civilization, this magical synthesis, for the modern man is becoming more and more difficult especially in the 21st Century.

The fundamental expression of the building in the early civilizations were man's attempts at mastering his environment. Later, the building task became more specialized, a development which has reached a peak of all time, without, however, resulting in any visual order. Modern architecture aims at scientifically controlling the environment in order to make interaction and collaboration between elements possible. This control has several different aspects. The most elementary is the creation of an artificial climate which is a physical aspect controls. Another factor is participation of buildings in human action, in his physical milieu and it falls under the functional frame. The actions, however, are socially determined and the physical objects participating, therefore, manifest social meanings. Finally, architecture today, may represent cultural conceptions like religious, philosophical or cosmological. This cultural symbolization, together with the social aspect could be termed as symbolic milieu.

Physical Control

Physical control is dealt with with a high scientific precision in today's world. Acoustics, illumination, heating and air-conditioning have become highly developed specialities where the architect only in part is competent. According to the functions of the building, the needs for heating, illumination etc. changed. An architect, therefore has to study climate. Control required for a particular function is under consideration. As the physical control is co-related with functional factors and as the functional factors are dependent upon social and cultural issues, it remains an abstraction to study physical control as a separate problem.

The architect must investigate the ability of the building materials to insulate against heat, noise, humidity etc. This would involve a study of filter to heat and cold, and barrier to light. Doors and windows have the character of switches, because they can stop or connect at wall. All conditions of physical control entering the building task can be analyzed to arrive at a clear definition of the need for connecting and separating elements.

The physical control not only influences the inner organization of a building and its technical solution, but also reflects its orientation relative to sunlight and wind. In hard climate, the physical influences determine regional character of the people. The importance of this aspect is especially great in "utilitarian" buildings. Therefore, the architect must thoroughly study Vastu principles in relation to the five elements.

Functional Frame

The building is determined by the actions which take place within its walls. In overtime, the functions have become complex due to the fundamental changes in our lifestyles. Every action requires a certain space. Sometimes, this space can be accurately measured, at other times it may vary within more or less determined units. In most cases, we can specify the minimum measures needed for an action. Maximum measures are also valid in city planning. The centre of a city, for instance, ought to be planned on the pedestrian scale and the size of a neighborhood is amongst the issues determined by the maximum distance between the homes the place of work or school, to determine the model parking in 21ˢᵗ Century and traffic problems.

The functions not only prescribe the size of the spaces, but generally also their form. The form is often determined by the fact that most functions are a series of actions which are connected with different places. The functional frame has to adapt itself to such action complexes.

The functional frame should represent action-structure by manifesting the spatial, topological and dynamic characteristics of the functions. To render an account of the functional aspect of the building such action-structures have to be described. They may be classified in rows (series), clusters, and group of actions. In the first case, actions follow each other in linear succession; a processional road with stations is a characteristic example. Clustered actions are instead actions that take place close to each other without necessarily having defined inter-relations. A shopping center may have certain cluster structure; certain shops chould be situated together, without a determined order. The term 'Grouped Functions' designates an organization where the character and position of each element is precisely determined.

The functional theme can never be studied in isolation. Its functions will always be related to the functional aspects of the surroundings. From the smallest utensil to the most encompassing geographical environment, their exists a functional continuity.

A reinterpretation of a functional theme may be due to a wish to improve the solution on a purely practical basis, but more often it stems from a shift in the very conception of what is functional. Such a change, again, depends upon social and cultural factors.

Social Milieu

As mentioned earlier, artifacts and buildings participate in social situations. While defining the building task, we have to take this into consideration and render an account of the social factors which should enter the architectural concretization. The social purpose of a building may be the expression of a status, a role, a group, a collectivity or an institution; and a collection of buildings may represent society as a whole.

In a democratic society, it may not be right to express difference in status, but it is surely still important to represent different roles and institutions. Our individual roles should probably not show themselves too much in the dwellings, as this would contradict the democratic equality. The personal expression of a dwelling at least has to be kept within certain limits: Our places of work should be differentiated to show that the individual roles participate in the varying phenomenal contexts. The surgery by a physician should not only be practical, it must also appear clean and sanitary. In this way, it calms down the patient. The office of a lawyer on the contrary, should soothe the worried client by appearing friendly, confident and inspiring, at the same time as it expresses, that the lawyer is an able man. Today, the need for an architectural characterization of the different institutions requires a study in consultation with Vastu advisor.

The idea of expressing roles and institutions is relatively new in the present day architecture. In general, one may say that buildings and cities both decide and bring together human beings and milieu fitted for different public or private activities.

In the past, cities were civilizations themselves, the native soil of thought, art and craft. The individual could draw from experiences of others, and inspite of feudalism and political bondage, social life was in many ways richer than what avails in the present confusion. While this confusion is mechanized and passivating, the cities of the past show that human intercourse with surrounding has a stimulating effect, and must be considered the main prerequisite for cultural development. A culture is characterized by the common institutions which result from human interaction. The idea of differentiating the environment according to the social structure has unconsciously determined most of the urban organism of the past, and also the individual buildings. To solve the stressing need for an adequate (relevant) expression, it is necessary that the architects incorporate psychological and sociological information in the definitions of building, by balancing man and material with nature. Vastu is the bridge between man, material and Nature.

Cultural Symbolization

Vastu Shastra itself is a cultural subject at the same time. As the social structure is based upon common values and symbol systems, it is evident that the cultural symbolization is closely related to the formation of society. In the symbol-milieu, which comprises both aspects, the social milieu mediates cultural objects such as common values, empirical constructs, philosophical ideas, moral codes, religious beliefs, ideological convictions and economic conditions. A culture is also characterized by being transmitted inspite of the existing social situation. Therefore, any social milieu indirectly symbolizes cultural objects, while the cultural symbolization can also take place directly by letting particular forms designate particular cultural objects.

Only recently the demand for cultural symbolization has again come to life because we understand that modern architecture needs this dimension to create a meaningful environment. Only through cultural symbolization, architecture can show that the daily life has a meaning which transcends the immediate situation and forms a part of cultural and historical continuity. We, therefore, need a better understanding of the cultural symbolization and its role in Vastu. It is not enough to render an account of the 'meanings' of the forms; we also have to understand why certain meanings are preferred at certain times. Vastu has to serve the desired meanings, but it also reacts to the user or the client not only within themselves, but the entire society.

Functions at Human Levels

Thus, all four dimensions introduced are interrelated. The physical control is interconnected with particular functions, and the functions on the other hand are determined by social conditions and presuppose the existence of cultural objects.

The differentiation of the building activity becomes always more necessary as the complexity of the civilization increases. The demand is not arbitrary but follows from contemporary sociological insight. Architecture plays a colossal role of not only forming a frame around existing activities, but also creating new activities. Only by means of full understanding of the role of modern architecture, we may find solutions. It is more important for the result to put correct questions than to find correct answers to wrong questions.

Sloka

   shastrenanen Servasya Lokasya Param Sukham I
   chaturvarga Phalapraptisrallokashch Bhaveddhruvam II
   shilp Shastra Parigyan nmartyoapi suratam Vrajet I

paramanand Janakasya Devanamidmiritam II
shilpamvinah Na hi Jagattrishu Lokeshu Vidyate I
jagadvina Na Shilpam cha Vertatae Vasav Prabho II

Meaning: Because of Vastu Shastra, the whole Universe receives benediction good health, happiness and all-round prosperity. Human beings attain divinity with this knowledge. Followers of Vastu Shastra not only get worldly pleasures but also experience bliss.

Sloka

sukham Dhanani Budhimsch Santati Servadanrinam I
priyanesham cha Sansidhim Servasyat Shubhalakshanam II
yatra Nindit laxmatra tahitesham vidhakrit I
athservamupadeyam Yabhdavet Shubhalakshanam II
deshah purniwashch Sabhavisam Sanani Cha I
yadyadidrisamanyashch Tathashreyaskaram Matam II
vastushastradritetasya Na Syallaxannirnayah I
tasmat Lokasya Kripya satmetbhaduriyate II

Meaning : properly designed and pleasing house will be an abode of good health, wealth, family peace and happiness. Negligence of canons of architecture will result in bad name, loss of fame, sorrows and disappointments.

Design is a learning process. Man, surroundings and methods are integral to each other. Therefore, any design or action is relative and requires holistic, meditative and creative processes, within the law of the Nature.

One struggles to find answers to the vital questions like what was the beginning of life, how did the Universe evolve; what is the real constitution of a human being; what is the ultimate aim can Vastu help in the 21st Century living condition etc.

In the Vedic period, people built homes, temples, hermitages with a view to having peaceful living, offering prayers and living in general harmony. But, in the modern world, people build concrete clusters, mainly for a high rate of pecuniary return. After the Second World War, the architectural practice has turned into a race towards so-called modernization. Adopting bureaucratic values have resulted in worlwide pollution, environmental and ecological problems, and no substantial peace of mind to humans in any kind of shelter.

It is a misconception that 'Nature' is hostile to man. If approached in true harmony, its secrets can be revealed and its energies can be harnessed for the benefit of the living. Nature, man and product are within evolutionary network guided by performance standards. Beauty is to be seen, felt, perceived, experienced and perhaps be rendered gratitude. The 'Moderns' are looking to the Orient for the desired peace of mind. India is one source: The fountainhead of the vast ancient Vedic knowledge available on the planet is relatively unknown, when the Vedic concept is presented modern hightech and technological expression, the sublime information becomes available to a surprised new society. The new outlook in the world of Vastu Science for the 21st Century, is to let the world know how to enjoy the gifts of nature.

Chapter 5

Vastu Design for 21st Century

Everyday, a man spends $1/3^{rd}$ of his life in his bedroom, $1/3^{rd}$ in the other portion of his house and $1/3^{rd}$ outside, on his work/job/business etc. He develops his family life and the next generation within the four walls of his house. A house or a shelter, thus, becomes a vital part of the very process of living. Spatially, shelter is the largest single user of land in an urban environment. In terms of financing and the application of human resources, shelter probably is the largest single item of investment. Not only does shelter represent an enormous economic activity—its socio-psychological effect on human welfare has never really been measured. Shelter, therefore, rightly finds a place of great importance in any planning exercise.

There is great quality difference between rural shelter and urban shelter. One common factor in all these codes is that every cultivator, agricultural *laborer* and village artisan is entitled to a free housesite in the village habitation. One of the best terms used for habitation site is 'abadi'. Basically, the entitlement to a free housesite means that every villager, whether he is a landowner or not is given the opportunity to build his own shelter which he then owns as on right. The pattern of habitation in a village is that almost all houses are owner- built and self-occupied. Shelter design tends to be traditional and the building materials used are those that are locally available. Thus, timber, bamboo, mud and locally excavated stones, brick and tiles fired by the local potter are the main building materials and their use provides employment to local artisans. There has, of course, been some change at the upper income levels in villages, with modern building materials substituting the local. Much of village housing is still built of mud and even where more permanent materials are used, mortar and plaster still tend to be of local clay. Because the material used is affected by moisture and wind action, the houses have to be kept under constant maintenance.

The renewal of mud and dung plaster and flooring is an on-going village exercise, with the women folk acting as the principal agents of renewal and maintenance of housing. Such constant maintenance is possible because materials are available free of cost and there is an incentive to keep the structure in good order because it is owner-occupied. Traditional village architecture has evolved over centuries to suit the local climate condition and, whilst much of village housing would be unacceptable to the architect trained in modern techniques, it certainly serves a strongly utilitarian purpose in the village environment.

An urban area, especially a large city, presents a totally different picture of shelter. A great deal of the urban population is mobile and there is a greater degree of movement of people between cities within cities and between localities.

Quite often, there is greater shift of residence on rented housing in a city than in a rural area. Because rented accommodation is almost never repaired by the tenant and very seldom by the owner, it becomes necessary to construct housing with materials which have a long life and are less amenable to weathering than mud. The very first qualitative difference between urban and rural housing, therefore, is in the material used. Much more brick and mortar is used in an urban setting than in the rural one.

In a town, there is no automatic entitlement to a housesite, both because of the growing population pressure and because land itself is not subject to the dual alternative uses of agriculture and residential site, but has a multiplicity of use option. There is a scarcity factor in operation in the matter of land availability. This automatically calls for the achievement of relatively high urban densities and, therefore, there is a shift away from the rural homestead with elbow room, into housing which is either built in ribbon form or is stacked one above the other. The architecture of the urban shelter and its engineering is equally different.

Unfortunately, our cities are witnessing an increasing emergence of precisely such shelters, which has virtually destroyed not only the city's aesthetic looks but even its minimum hygienic requirement.

The second major constraint is the availability of financial resources for housing for a growing population. Durable housing in the requisite quantity, using the existing materials and technology, simply cannot be built because we do not have the physical resources. Unless a major breakthrough is made in materials and building techniques, there does not seem to be any possibility of our being able to meet the housing needs of urban India. Maybe the answer lies in recycling waste materials. The fourth major constraint can be generically termed as the problem of human resource. Lumped together, human resource would include architectural and technological input in the matter of design and labor input in the matter of construction skills. It has earlier been stated that urban housing consists of two distinct types, the durable, designed, engineer-built housing and the haphazard, self-designed and self-built squatter housing. Because the engineering and architectural skills are directed towards durable housing, material and financial resources for which are not available in sufficiency, the human resource input into housing may be deemed to be wholly inadequate for the purpose. Even if there is sufficient availability of skilled architects and engineers who are willing to apply a design input to non-formal squatter housing, there would still be a critical shortage of skilled craftsmen if the housing program were geared up to overcome the shortage. As it is, even the workers in the basic skill areas of masons, carpenters, electricians, plumbers are in short supply and this is one reason why house construction is slow, expensive and of poor quality.

Unless there is a major change in building techniques, materials availability and management, imparting skills in construction technology and a vast expansion in the availability of skilled craftsmen, the shortage of trained manpower alone could cripple any efforts at solving the housing problem. The above analysis would indicate that the vast majority of city dwellers are shelterless. No doubt, we have a substantial number of pavement dwellers who are wholly without shelter. The fact still remains that human ingenuity has worked out ways to overcome the problem of urban shelter.

For the homeless in urban areas occupying any odd piece of open land that may be available, regardless of its suitability for construction is a normal practice. Low lying banks of city drains, areas subject to flooding, hidden corners which a municipal or revenue inspector is likely to over- look, incomplete roads, open land earmarked for a particular purpose but not so used, land around high rise buildings left unbuilt to provide light and air are some of the spaces occupied by squatters.

The resultant out settlements are extremely unhygienic and uncomfortable so far as the squatter is concerned, but they are better than nothing and represent a deliberate choice where freedom from detection is the paramount felt need. If the squatters were to occupy more valuable land, he would be given shortshrift. The squatter also seems to have overcome the non-availability of proper building materials by ingenious recourse to junk. There is a great skill displayed in the construction of hut. Structurally, it consists of a frame or load bearing walls. The latter would generally be mud, rubble or discarded brickbats. Such construction will normally be found in an area where the squatter feels he has some permanency and where there is a little extra space available for a dwelling unit with thick walls. The frame structure is likely to consist of wooden poles, very often the discards of the scaffolding and centering material used by the average Indian building contractor. Even though the poles are of uneven length and poor quality, they are erected into a frame by clever use of bracing and an understanding of what the material will tolerate. The roof would be made by odd wooden poles acting as rafters, with purlins made out of bits of bamboo, rejected length of steel or wooden scantlings. The favorite materials for the roof is beaten out coal tar drums. They are relatively strong because of the thickness of the sheet and resistance to corrosion because they have a coating of asphalt. Other alternative materials are packing cases, sheeting beaten flat from kerosene tins, country-tile, thatch and plastic sheeting salvaged from garbage.

Rags layered together and bits of tarpaulin could also be used. The walling might be of any material, including air itself if mats, mud and rubble, wooden platings from cases etc., are some of the walling materials used. There may or may not be any doors and windows. Thus, from the detritus of society, from flotsam and jetsam, the urban man builds a house for himself in circumstances where his better educated, skilled and trained compatriots—the politicians, bureaucrats, architects and engineers have thrown in the sponge. Verily, squatter housing is representative of human genius in its smartest form, with man building something virtually out of nothing. This is a fact which very few planners have learnt to appreciate or improve upon !

The squatter also seems to have overcome resource constraints in terms of finances and human skill. A squatter house is as near a zero cost shelter as we can achieve. Similarly, not being possessed of construction skills, the average squatter evolves a house form which requires almost no specialized skills for constructions. The instinct which enables a bird to design and build a nest seems to be at work in such housing. To that extent, the shelter that one finds in these 'colonies,' could be equated to the nest of a bird. However *untidy* a nest, one never hears a nature lover condemning its aesthetics. Why can city planner not learn to appreciate the human effort represented by the hut of a squatter? Why are squatter colonies invariably looked down upon as inimical settlements to be eradicated or, more euphemistically, relocated and improved upon? These are questions which are rarely posed by the Indian planner to himself and even more rarely answered.

The constraints are likely to remain constant or even aggravate and, therefore, the need to build shelter at the lowest possible cost will persist. The very first issue to be tackled, therefore, would be where such a shelter should be located. This automatically leads to one of the issue of land for shelter.

A planning approach which tries to optimize the existing land use would make available substantial land areas for housing development, especially low cost housing. Additional land accruals could take the form of serviced sites, located close enough to work center to make it convenient for the poor, and earmarked specifically for the construction of self-built housing, which initially could take the form of temporary shelter. Intelligent land use planning, which aims at providing rather than preventing, could go a long way in eliminating the present haphazard growth of squatter colonies in places which should really be left open. This is not to state that all such new housing sites for the poor should come up only on the periphery of the towns. The first objective of the planner has to be convenience of the location, which also means convenience in reaching place of work.

Having provided land for shelter, the planner, architect and engineer should not shy away from involvement in the construction of structures, or at least in their designing. The problem, however, must be approached not from the angle of making a durable house cheaper, but by taking the squatter's hut as the basic housing unit and then trying to make it upwardly mobile towards an acceptable, durable urban house. Every planner and architect, and every school of architecture, must begin by analyzing the Materials, Structural and Architectural Designs and Construction Methodology of the squatter tenements.

Having mastered the analyzing of improving the existing squatter

housing, there could then be research input into the development of
building materials which are more durable than junk, can be standardized and would permit the construction of a proper house at really
low cost. Whether construction should be on the basis of pre-fabrication,
partial prefabrication of materials which are assembled *in situ*, or there
is *in situ* construction with basic components which may be factory
produced, is a matter of details. Even the method of production of
components would have to be designed from scratch because what
we are looking for is not simply a cheaper brick but durable construction
material which is a substitute for junk and can compare with it in cost.

It is not only brick and mortar which have to be substituted. Much
of the squatter housing has no door as understood in the traditional
sense. There is an opening to cover over which there might be flap
of jute sacking, bamboo matting or a piece of tin hanging on make-
shift hinges.

With a new design approach and the development of appropriate
building materials which could permit large-scale construction of really
cheap housing it would be necessary to develop new construction skills.
Much of the new construction would have to be self-built, with little
or no external assistance from skilled craftsman.

This is because the average urban dweller of the low income
category would still seek a house which, in cash terms, is very near
to zero cost. He, therefore, cannot afford the services of skilled
craftsman. Both the design and the materials would have to be engineered to permit a relatively unskilled person to build his own house.
Even where the recourse is to hire craftsman, they would have to be
trained in really speedy construction with new materials so that the
time of hire is kept to an irreducible minimum. This would be the cell
for the development of a whole new set of skills and the imparting
of training which would permit a craftsman to do his job with the
minimum of delay. The training would be vocational, but because it
is directly involved with shelter design, the training format would
form a part of city planning. The development of the human resource
which would create urban shelter in mass, thus, becomes a part of the
total city planning process.

Housing for the poor forms perhaps the most important single
component of urban shelter. There are, however, other elements. If
urban India concentrates the poor in a city, it is also the home of a

growing middle class. The middle class could itself be split into two, income and social strata. The upper income group would form the upper middle class and the lower income group the lower middle class. The latter group is largely salaried, subject to transfer and has a preference for ready-built housing on easy credit terms. The upper middle class, on the other hand, has the income and leisure and can command the services of others, which would permit it to undertake custom built housing scheme. There is also the class of the very rich, for whom money and land offer no constraint. The housing needs of these three categories, the lower middle class, the upper middle class and the very rich are totally different from those of the urban poor. With the increasing strength of the professional and trading classes in cities, any housing strategy would necessarily have to cater to the needs of these people also. The middle class is the one which generally prefers to built accommodation.

Mass public housing by housing boards and development authorities regardless of lip service to provide housing for the poor is generally aimed at this class of people. The worst atrocities in architecture perpetrated on our cities is not by slum housing but by the mass public housing which has created an almost endless sea of box-like, look-alike structures stretching up to the far horizon. The avarice and corruption of engineers and contractors have further compounded the problem by use of poor quality material for housing, the design of which has already been ruined by the incompetence of non-thinker architects. The sheer poor quality of design, looks and construction of much of our public housing is an abiding blot on the urban scene. There is a real need to construct mass housing for those who prefer built accommodation. There is an equally real need to apply design aesthetics to such housing which, together with squatter colonies, constitute about 70 percent of the entire built environment of any major city.

Mass public housing, because of the scale of construction, does offer scope for prefabrication. Even if total modules are not factory manufactured for assembling on site, it should be possible to produce structural and roofing members, sanitary modules, filler material, wood work, electricity system packages, etc., of standardized design and quality. The cost of mass housing can be reduced and corruption of *in situ* construction of even the smallest items checked controlled if partial prefabrication is widely adopted. This would not only build up a large building materials industry, it would also enable research components to develop because production would now be on an industrial scale.

The resistance of engineers to such changes is partially for conservation and partially because their source of lucrative illicit gain would be cut off. This must be overcome in the interest of speedy, economical and standard quality middle income housing.

Shelter is such a vital human requirement that a great deal of resource can be mobilized from private savings for its fulfilment.

In fact, even without state intervention, there is very substantial investment in shelter. Non-availability of land, uncertainity of tenure, rent laws which act as disincentive to housing activity and maintenance, public policy which makes the shortage of essential materials chronic, and planning laws which almost force people into unauthorized constructions, are some of the factors which hinder resource mobilization for housing. The decrepit rundown look of much of our city housing speaks volumes for the manner in which the rent laws have operated against any meaningful investment in housing repair. They are also one of the major causes of the slight rate of investment in rental housing.

There is a basic, fundamental difference between urban and rural settlement which demands the imposition of order on a town. A rural settlement is still largely homestead-based and tends to be auto-serviced. This means that even where systems of water supply, drainage and conservancy do not exist, the village survives because either there are household-based water supply systems, centering on a well, or water is drawn by hand and carried from a community source. All waste water is diverted into the 'abadi bari', or kitchen garden. Garbage is composted for use in the fields. The house-owner is the manager of his own city services. An urban settlement, however, is neither homogeneous nor does it provide an independent home for every citizen. There is greater concentration and, with high density, it becomes necessary to service the area. The rural employment cycle is clock-based and there is less time for loitering. Because the town is not auto-serviced at household level, municipal services have to be organized. They should be organized even in a village, but in their absence the rural settlement would still survive.

There is a profound environmental and ecological logic which demands that areas of dense population concentration should be planned in detail. Cities pollute and large cities pollute in great measure. The pollution may be industrial or domestic, of water, air or land.

The environmental hazards of pollution are not confined to the city area because there is a far reaching downstream effect. A rural settlement, with an economy closely knit with land, does not pollute because it follows a more natural cycle and rhythm. It is absolutely essential to plan collection, treatment and disposal of the waste generated by an urban settlement so that the environment remains protected.

Urban settlements are wasteful users of land. Because a village is agriculture based, its inhabitants try and reserve all arable land for cultivation, with abadi or habitation sites being confined to non-agricultural waste lands. Cities, on the other hand, gobble-up all the rich agricultural land on the periphery. There is not even an attempt to re-cycle builtup areas because it is easier to acquire virgin land than to demolish and reconstruct constructions on occupied land.

The environmental and ecological logic for ensuring that cities use land sparingly and as per carefully thought out design is irrefutable. Actually, urban planners need neither Dutch courage nor a string of justifications for the planning of cities. Vastu planner advises that unless the discipline of planning is injected into urban India on a universal scale, there is likely to be an increasing chaos in our cities and towns.

Modular Design

The theory of Vastu for Modular Design is the necessity of the fast development in the architectural field as well as the habits of the people and changing standards of living, towards the so-called Modernization. Manpower and craftsmen are being rapidly replaced by machines and the automatic systems with advanced Technology. So that the movement of man and material is faster today.

Vastu as an art of living provides authentic objectives. Like other arts it cannot be simply judged from the outside. To judge a building one must get into it and see behind its outer wall with relation to inner space as well as surrounding landscape etc.

The architects generally have been trained within rules of modern architecture. Modern rules and building by-laws are universally recognized. The application of science and technology in architecture is a very wide subject.

Prefabrication, the use of material, both old and new, structures, energy, computers and robots are some of the fields in which advances are being made. These advances influence the way the architects design, the way buildings are constructed, used and maintained.

What is interesting, however, is that the end product of modern science and technology, at least in architecture, is not always hightech or futuristic. Instead, old or conventional forms and customs are often perpetuated. That is to say, innovative uses of science and technology have been in process. What we end up with are often very familiar looking buildings that reveal age-old concern. Thus, despite tremendous progress in science and technology, humans have not changed all that much. We are conservative creatures and can easily be disturbed by a change, though our life-style has changed, and living standards have become modern.

Computers are also used to determine the plans best suited for a client. More uses of computers are foreseen, particularly in estimating, cost and quantities and in structural design. The actual houses, however, are quite conventional in design. Outwardly, the houses are constructed by more ordinary methods. New materials, such as advanced ceramic and carbon fibers, are being introduced as a revolution in industry. There are various factors in architecture design, the length of the construction period and construction cost, that hamper the introduction of such materials. Nevertheless, the building trade is beginning to take an active interest in the application of new methods and materials, more particularly in multi-storey and high-rise buildings.

Computers and robots have moved into architect's offices and the building industry to reduce man's mental and physical efforts. Machines are not regarded as being in conflict with man. Man has developed machines which are humanized though man himself has to a certain extent become mechanized. We must use science and technology for progress but never become their slaves. The 21ˢᵗ Century will be symbolic tomorrow, a time that will critically surpass today's design. We must now ask what kind of sketches architects of the present will have to make to correspond with those of Vedic times.

Mass Scale Housing

Perhaps the answer lies with climatically based Mass Scale Housing with right orientation in line with Vastu principles on modular design buildings and new townships for 21ˢᵗ Century the mass housing have the following objectives.

1. To relieve the congestion of existing cities and to give them the space and opportunity to regenerate themselves.
2. To generate economic recovery for a declining agricultural or industrial base.
3. Major Urban development requires the creation of a special agency with a clearly defined task.
4. Any long-term development plan must commit the minimum of resources and have a high degree of flexibility to accommodate future changes.
5. In all planning and implementation people come first. Too often urban development is concerned with pretty pictures for glossy magazines and neglects providing for the aspiration and dynamics of the community living.
6. The implementation plan is an essential ingredient to focus the energies and resources of a variety of individuals on achievable objectives.
7. Cities and towns last a long time and we must not take short cut on quality.

Prefabrication System

The answer perhaps lies in prefabrication system based on modular design. This system has been being introduced long ago and adopted by all other developed countries around the world. It is time that we must develop and do more research with the high technique modular concept suitable for given climatic conditions.

High-Rise Buildings

Does development mean bringing up of high-rise buildings? From ancient times until now it may be that the lifespan of a human beings has increased or that man has become more intelligent and smart, but he has lost the charm of living and of being a clean, honest human being.

Worldwide, tolerance and love have been replaced by hatred, jealousy and bitterness. When things start changing outside, internationally, a parallel change takes place inside, extremely affecting the way we relate to other people, to things, to the entire Universe, arts and values. To understand what is happening to us as we move into the age of super industry, and modernization, we must analyze the process of man's upbringing, his environment and his psychology. Why until now we have never given a serious thought to it and how could such a vast problem relating to the whole of mankind be solved is a serious issue.

This indeed is not a medical problem that doctors could answer or set things right for future generations. It is a problem created by modern architecture. Only Vedic architects in consultation with Vastu science, town planners and environmetalists can bring about change to ensure a proper future for generations to come. More people were killed in homes than on the road. Even now the figures are very comparable. Death due to house accidents account for 60 percent. A house does not mean just a shelter for the night. It is a place where man comes back from work exhausted to rest and recharge himself for the next day. A house is where a person brings up his family and the children grow up to become the future adult one day.

Now with the increasing of population, the life-styles have changed to fast made. Man has no time or passion, the manual manpower is being replaced by mechanized systems. On the construction site, labour has been replaced by machines. In an architect's office the draftsman has been replaced by computer, and indigenous/individual design building is being replaced with the modular structure.

The Basic Principle of Modular System

The basic of modular method in component sizing is mentioned from joint center line to center line using a multiple of standard model. This place in which grid lines are as one model. Thus, multiple of each model on the basic model or can be extended towards expansion on all or any required direction. The plot or site should be first marked with the required equal girdings and the required proposed covered area should be designed in such a manner that every dividing wall is on the gridlines. This mean modular based design and can easily be given extension towards required directions and right orientation.

In Vedic period, the Vedic architecture had also adopted the same girding system which was called mandala and each mandala was given a specific direction or areas keeping in view of the orientation.

Chapter 6

Vastu for Interiors

History of Interiors Design

Interior Decoration is Profession

The profession of 'Interior Design' did not exist before 20th Century. Traditionally, the Carpenters or the Storekeeper used to advice the arrangement of interiors for their clients. Until the first World War, Interior Decoration was closely related to the trade of antiques. The social and economic situation during the 20th Century increased the importance of an interior decorator. Interior decoration still remains a luxury available only to the upper classes of the society. Certain status is attached in society in taking professional advice on the appearance of home or work place.

The role of interior decorator is always advisory because of the consultative nature of the work. It is one of the professions in which women do very well. In America, women have tried to establish economic independence through working for interior decoration of existing building or rooms.

Interior Decorator is mainly responsible for selecting suitable textiles for floor and wall coverings, and furniture, lighting and color schemes for rooms. Interior decoration has never enjoyed the status of architecture and the interior decorator is really responsible for structure alteration. It is regarded as a branch of fashion design because in interior decoration very few schemes remain intact for a long time. Interior decoration gained importance with the publication of book 'The Decoration of Houses' by novelist Edith Wharton and Architect Ogden Codman in 1897. They identified the principles of proportion and harmony for the planning of interior schemes. The criteria of 'Good Taste' dominated the profession.

Importance of Vastu Professional for Interior Designing and Decoration

The status of an interior designer did not improve further due to the Second World War shortages. Then the emergence of Interior Designer with professional qualification started to dominate the interiors. These designers worked on non-domestic interiors because the commercial sector realized the worth of good interior design. During and after the second world war, modernization was developed in America. Mies Van Der Rohe, designed the exposed steel frames and brick and glass infills. Different functional areas were delimited by storage units not reaching the ceiling. Many of the technical innovation of Post-War interior designs are widely used in the interiors.

Modern Interior Design Features for 21ˢᵗ Century

Let us discuss some important interior design features in modern buildings. The false ceiling of each floor conceals services such as air conditioning and electric cables. They can be easily accessible for maintenance through the false ceiling. The interior working space was opened with rows of desks and small partitions replacing corridors and office rooms. The concept of an open office was developed during the 1950's with large floor areas divided by partitions, desks, filing cabinets and plants. The working environment is totally controlled with air conditioning and artificial lighting. The natural elements are introduced with floor carpets, indoor plants and the use of skylights. Another interior design feature is to leave interior brickwork and concrete exposed.

New techniques for moulding and gluing plywood were discovered by American manufacturers during the War for the navy. These are used for furniture design like plastics with fiber-glass reinforcement. Plastic shell chairs on metal legs, wire chairs, stacking plastic chairs, bent plywood chairs and black leather upholstery, open shelving drawers, cupboards and desks replaced partition walls. Thus, a good interior design was defined as 'Item in which the design was simple of good proportions and without dust collecting features with stress on good construction'. Manufacturers were allowed to produce their own designs and there was public demand for ornaments and periodic design features. Certain features of modern interiors are indoor plants, built-in furniture, animal skins as floor coverings, Venetian blinds, open storage space and smooth organic forms. There is a tendency to use different textures and patterns, free-standing lamps replaced wall and ceiling lamps. The garden is integrated with the living space by a sliding glass door. The discovery of new building materials led to many more innovative interior design concepts.

Basic Design Composition

It is divided into two Groups :

1. The Basic Elements :

    (a) Line   (b) Form
    (c) Texture   (d) Pattern
    (e) Color   (f) Light

2. The Basic Principles :

    (a) Balance   (b) Emphasis
    (c) Rhythm   (d) Proportion
    (e) Unity or Harmony.

VASTU: The main source of Design Language

Nature + Man + Materials = Creations

The main source of design has for man and his creations. From nature many aspects have been picked up for various designs To communicate these thoughts, there is a need to develop a Design Language. Broadly, we can divide them into two groups:

1. *The Elements :* These are basically visual components used in creating an object or composition. They can be classified into:

    (a) Line   (b) Form
    (c) Texture   (d) Pattern
    (e) Color   (f) Light

2. *The Principles :* These principles help us in determining an object, whether it is artificially good or bad in appearance. They can be classified into:

    (a) Balance   (b) Emphasis
    (c) Rhythm   (d) Proportion
    (e) Unity or Harmony.

Let us discuss the 'Elements' in detail:

(a) *Line:* Line is the basic design elements. Too many lines of different nature in a room create an impression of visual chaos like too many beams, paneling on walls etc. Lines should be restricted to the minimum. Equal height in furniture bring in the impression of Unity in the space. Vertical lines create the impression of height and, similarly, horizontal lines are obtained by tables, chairs, bookcases etc.

(b) *Form:* It is also referred as shape, area or mass. Forms are closely related to lines. Forms unite with lines to achieve overall design of a given space. A long rectangular table or sofa helps in creating a Line of Unity in the room, but at the same time too many shapes or forms of furniture create an impression of chaos.

(c) *Texture:* Surface characteristics of any object are known as texture. Texture of surfaces ranges from smooth to rough. A rough texture absorbs light and a smooth surface reflects light. Small and dark rooms should have smooth texture and large rooms can have rough texture, if needed. Textures can be used for wall finish, woodwork furniture etc.

(d) *Color:* We react emotionally to different colors in different ways. Our national flags and political party flags are good examples of our attachment to various colors. We all know that colors are an integral part of our religion and culture. So, the choice of colors is very important and relative to the functional use of space. Light is intimately linked with colors because light is the source of all colors in nature. Bright color should be used in dark areas and dark colors can be used in lighted areas. There is wide variety of colors for interior surfaces. A careful and thoughtful use of color is very essential for attractive interiors.

(e) *Pattern:* Pattern is kind of surface enrichment. Any room will look dull without pattern. In interior design, there are three types of motifs or units of design.

- *Naturalistic Motifs,* which look like picture of flowers, fruits, animals or scenes.
- *Stylized Motifs,* which depend upon the material as well as purpose of the articles. Ferns and leaves are the most commonly used pattern models for fabrics and other decorative articles.
- *Geometrical Motifs,* which are based on forms of circle, rectangle etc., stripes, dot and checks are the most commonly seen geometrical motifs in interiors.

(f) *Light* : Light is an art and utilitarian element. Light is closely related to color and texture. Daylight is very important in the overall appearance of a room, Artificial lighting has become common in interior design today due to the lack of natural light in the interiors. There are many reasons for this. Many designers prefer artificial light for dramatic effect of interior. However, a good combination of natural and artificial lighting will save energy consumption. Artistic placement of lights can bring out important areas and keep subordinate areas in shadow. There are several types of artificial lighting appliances available today for interior designers.

Introduction to Building Materials

1. Stone,
2. Clay,
3. Cement,
4. Mortar,
5. Concrete,
6. Plywood and related products,
7. Plastics and related products,
8. Timber,
9. Glass and related products,
10. Paints and related products,
11. Ferrous and non-ferrous materials,
12. Gypsum and related products
13. Adhesives.

Buildings are made of different kinds of materials. It is very important to know these building materials. The knowledge of different building materials, their properties and uses help in achieving economy and efficient use of materials. The cost of materials in the construction of a building ranges from 60 to 70 percent of the total cost. Some essential building materials are described below. Many new building materials are combination of these materials or further innovations of these materials. However, there are many other new building materials in the market, so it is also necessary for the interior designer to get acquainted with them for creative interior designing.

Vastu Science suggests only natural and local material to be used.

Stone

There are many varieties of stone available in nature. They can be broadly classified as below:

(i) *Sandstone:* It is very easy to dress and work. It is extensively used in general building construction and ornamental carving.

(ii) *Limestone:* Limestone slabs are used for flooring. It is also used for general building purpose and manufacturing of lime.

(iii) *Slate:* Slates are used as a roofing and flooring material. Harder slates are used for damp-proofing and steps of staircases.

(iv) *Marble:* It is extremely suitable for ornamental and superior types of building work. It is also used for flooring and other decorative work.

(v) *Granite:* It is very hard and durable stone suitable for bridge abutments, piers etc., it is not suitable for carving.

(vi) *Laterite:* It is normally used for inferior type masonry work.

(vii) *Basalt:* It is hard and compact and hence very expensive to work with. It is used in foundations of structures and superstructures also, but not used for ornamental work.

Stone Aggregate

Aggregate is a general term applied to all inter-materials which when bonded together with cement form concrete.

General Properties

(a) A good building stone should be hard, tough, compact grained and uniform in texture and color.

(b) Stone absorbing less water is stronger and more durable as it rain water will have less action on it.

(c) Stones should be properly seasoned by exposure to the air before they are put in a structure.

(d) They should be small enough to be lifted and placed by hand.

(e) Length should be three times the height and breadth.

(f) All stones should be put into soft water before use for a minimum of 24 hours.

Chapter 7

Creation Through Vastu Science

Prakriti (Nature)

Man's vital energy and health depend in large measure on the direct effects of his environment and a clean environment depends on Nature. It is well-known that in certain climatic areas, where excessive heat and cold prevail, energy is diminished by the biological strain of adaptation to the extreme conditions. Physical and psychological factors result from this struggle for biological equilibrium.

The creation is the main instrument for fulfilling the requirements of comfort. It modifies the natural environment to approach optimum conditions of livability. The desirable procedure, to work towards such requirements, would be to work with and not against the forces of nature. The structure which in a given environmental setting reduces undesirable stresses, and at the same time utilizes all natural resources favorable to human comfort would be climatically balanced. The natural cover of the terrain tends to moderate extreme temperatures and stabilize conditions through the reflective qualities of various surfaces. Plants and grassy cover reduce temperature by absorption through insulation, and cool by evaporation. Conversely, cities and manmade surfaces tend to elevate temperatures as the materials used are usually of absorptive character.

The natural environment, however, can be made livable by careful selection of building materials, layout and space planning according to the solar and wind conditions, shading devices, vegetation and water bodies. The Vastu consultant, however, has to remain alert to regional variations.

The Mind (Purusha)

The early man was bound religiously to the solar cycle. Later, however, man no longer reacted to the Sun mainly as a symbol; his interest turned to its therapeutic and psychological effects. The total problem in Vastu science for buildings to be dealt with five elements are factors like local topography, the requirements of privacy, the pleasures of a view, reduction of noise apart from the climatic factors of wind and solar radiation. Additional problems in 21ˢᵗ Century are excess radiation induced by electrical and electronic gadgets and equipment, Electromagnetic (EFM) and other radio and communication transmissions etc. which I have discussed in other chapters.

The age-old problems of controlling the reception of solar radiation in buildings have been sharply enlarged by modern developments in architectural planning and construction.

Traditional massive bearing wall which combined the function of support with protection from light and heat have been supplanted by clear structural members devoted to load-bearing and covered with curtain walls. It is generally agreed that air, temperature, wind and sound are best controlled within the wall itself, while light is easier to control inside the building shell, and heat radiation is most efficiently halted before it reaches the building environment.

The materials of the building 'skin' play a decisive part in the utilization and control of solar rays. The use of shading devices is a fundamentally sound method and effective for interception of sun-rays before it attacks the building. In this way, the obstructed heat is reflected and can dissipate into the outside air. In addition, the sun breaker can express a strong spatial character, add new elements to the Vastu vocabulary, and phrase a truly regional consciousness.

The materials which provide a screen between man and the natural environment offer rich possibilities for visual expression. Many materials elaborate the surface, others invite a play of light and shadow or add to the spatial composition, while some constitute their own architectural entities. To their plastic appearance, they add visual ties of rhythm, light, color and texture from the power of lines and circles.

Desirable air movements should be utilized for cooling in hot periods and during times of high absolute humidity. Adaptation for wind orientation is not of great importance in low buildings, where the use of windbreaks, the arrangement of openings and low pressure areas, and the directional effect of the window inlets can help to ameliorate the airflow situation. However, for non air-conditioned high-rise buildings, such as apartment houses, office buildings, or hospitals where surrounding trees and landscaping has little effect on the upper storeyes careful consideration has to be given to wind orientation.

Large air masses cannot be altered in their motion which is dictated by differences of air pressure. However, velocities near the living or ground level can be controlled to a certain extent. The frictional drag of vegetation and the resistance and obstruction created by trees can cause diversions in the air flow, which may be utilized beneficially.

Besides their aesthetic and shade-giving properties, the value of trees, windbreaks, lies in their ability to reduce wind velocities and noise barrier. This mechanical effect brings perceptible changes both in the temperature and humidity of the air.

The Medium of Creative Tools (Technology)

Tips on Vastu Principle:

Stairs

- Stairs of R.C.C. is recommended in South, South-West or West.
- The steps should be in odd numbers and never in even numbers.
- Steps should be clock-wise for upwards.

Beams and Columns

- Inverted or hanging beams, particularly in living room should be avoided.
- Never sleep or sit below any load bearing beams.
- No column should be placed on Brahmasthan and North-East Mandala as shown in *diagram*.
- Avoid beam also in center of Brahmasthan and North-East Mandala as shown in *diagram*.

Temple in the House

If you plan a temple or puja place in the house, follow the following advice:

- For a proper temple with *sthapana* of deities of your choice, select a peaceful corner in WEST side of your house, no wall adjoining with the bath or kitchen. There should not be any living room particularly, W.C. or kitchen, service/maintenance staff room.
- The platform should be raised minimum 1' 6" or 1/2 meters and the deities' face should be towards East.
- If you want only a prayer or puja room or corner place, it should be on the North-East corner of the house and you should sit facing East.

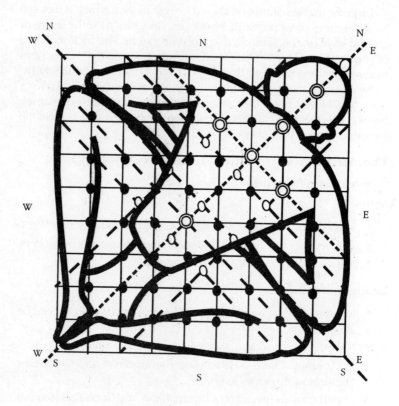

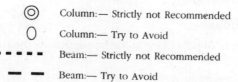

Column:— Strictly not Recommended

Column:— Try to Avoid

Beam:— Strictly not Recommended

Beam:— Try to Avoid

Vastu Purusha Mandala of
Columns and Beams

Diagram 1

Basement

- Basement should be planned or constructed maximum on North, North-East or East side of the plot.
- Basement should not be used for sleeping purpose or as a bedroom, particularly for growing children.
- The stairs from basement to Ground floor upward should be designed from East to West or North-East to South-West.

Dampness or Moisture

- The dampness or moisture on the walls or ceiling or floor should be avoided and stopped immediately.

SETBACK AND ROOMS PLANNING

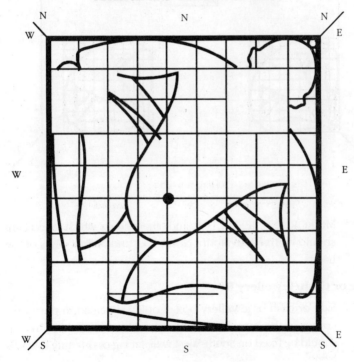

Vastu Purusha Mandala with
four corners

Diagram 2a

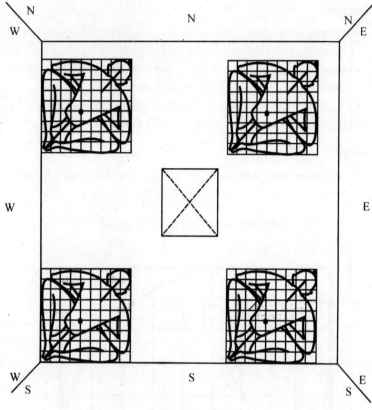

Diagram 2b

- MIRROR AND REFLECTOR and other objects which reflect light should be fixed on North, North-East and or East walls of the house.

Safe or Cash/Jewellery Box

- Safe or cash or jewellery box should be placed in the North corner of the house but if the safe is heavy, made of iron, it should be fixed on South-West wall, facing or opening towards North.

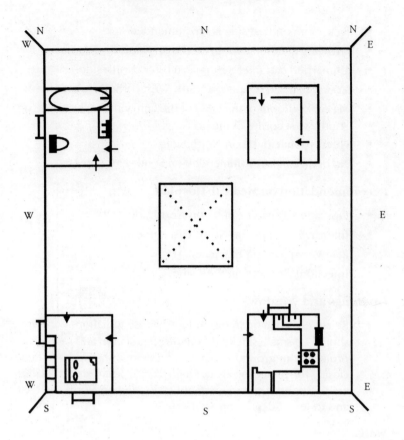

Diagram 2c

Children and Study Table

- Children's table and study table should be placed on East wall and the child should sit for study facing East.

Plants

- If you want to keep many plants they should be kept in North-East corner and water for plants should be changed every alternative day.

Rooms for All

- Delivery room for new born baby room should be selected from one on East side.

- Sick room on East side is recommended.
- Growing children's room can be on North-East corner.
- Unmarried daughter's room can be on North side.
- Young married couple on North-West corner.
- Master bedroom or the head of the family room should be on South-West corner of the house.
- Guest room can be on North Side.
- No bedroom is recommended on South-East corner.

Recommendation on Medical/Hospital

- Operation Theater can be on North side.
- Intensive care unit on North-East corner.
- Recovery room on East side.
- Infectious diseases on West side.

Openings and Windows

- Relatively small openings reduce intense radiation. Windows should be small, shielded from direct radiation and set high to protect from ground radiation. Openings should have tight closing for protection against high diurnal heat. External shades are preferred. Openings should be located on North and East and to lesser degree on South sides.

Walls

- Walls of daytime living areas should be of heat storing materials; walls of night-use rooms should be of materials with light heat capacity. South and West walls should preferably be shaded. High reflective qualities are desirable for both thermal and solar radiation.

Roof

- Generally, heat insulation is best, which uses the fly-wheel effect of out-going radiation for daily heat balance. However, a shaded, ventilated roof is also applicable, primarily over largely used rooms. Water spray or pool on roof is effective. High solar reflectivity is a basic requirement, emissivity is essential for long wave radiation.

Material

- Required insulation value relative to South is: East – 1.1; West– 1.2; North–1.0; roof –1.6.
- High heat capacity walls are essential necessary time lags for internal heat balance are: East – 0 hours; South – 1.0; West – 1.0; North – 0 hour, roof – 12 hours.

Shading Devices

- Devices should be separated from main structure, and exposed to wind convection.

Mechanical Equipment

- Equipment should have high operating efficiency in heat producing devices, such as those for cooking.

Site Selection

- On North, North-East, East slope exposure, lower portions existing water bodies are preferred, where cool air flow effect can be utilized and controlled. High altitudes on South-West, and locations with evaporative possibilities are advantageous.

Town Structure

- The walls of houses and garden should provide shade to outdoor living areas similar to the effect of horizontal " egg crate" devices unit dwellings or groups should create patio-like areas: concentration is desirable. The town structure should thus, react against heat with a shaded and dense layout.

Public Spaces

- There should be a close connection between public spaces and residential areas; half and full shade protection is desirable; paved surfaces should be avoided. Pools of water and landscaping are beneficial.

Landscape

- As vegetation is generally sparse concentration of plants and grass covered areas in the manner of an oasis is desirable.

Vegetation

- Vegetation is desirable both as a radiation absorbant surface and for its evaporative and shade-giving properties.

Chapter 8

Vastu for Natural Climatic Conditions and Solar Efficient Building Design

Vastu Concepts, Techniques and Applications

Introduction to Climatology

The traditional building forms of the rural tropics often include solutions to climatic problems. But it deserves a careful study. The surroundings provide the building materials in the humid tropics—timber, bamboo and thatch; in Arid zone—stone, earth and bricks; and in composite climates, organic and inorganic compounds.

Western style of architecture is copied in all parts of the world. But the problems of the Tropics cannot be solved by their use, in altogether different climatical conditions, different cultures and different economic conditions. It seems so obvious that housing types and building materials from cold climate cannot solve the problems of cities where heat is high and humidity is in excess. So it is the duty of the Vastu consultant to determine according to the climatic conditions prevailing in that particular region.

The climate presents a challenge to the Vastu adviser that he should build the shelter in such a way so as to bring out the best of the natural possibilities, of balancing the five Elements in line with Man, Material and Nature.

Climatic Primed Planning and Designing Input

The energy requirement of a building depends upon various factors like comfort requirements location of building, usage of building etc.

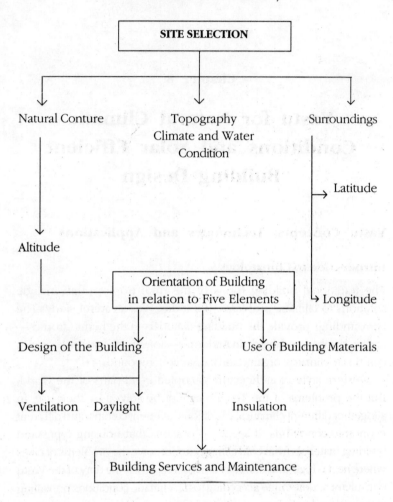

Diagram 1

Climatology and its Effect on Men, Building and Building Material

Man's energy and health depend in large measures on the direct effects of his environment. It is well-known that in certain climatic areas, where

SKY CONDITIONS

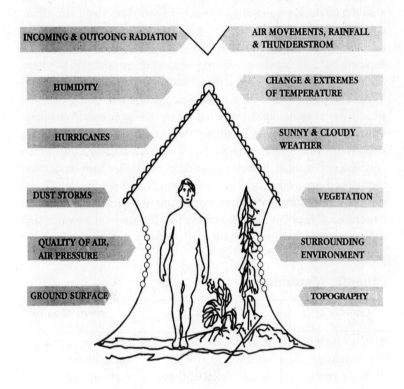

INCOMING & OUTGOING RADIATION

AIR MOVEMENTS, RAINFALL & THUNDERSTROM

HUMIDITY

CHANGE & EXTREMES OF TEMPERATURE

HURRICANES

SUNNY & CLOUDY WEATHER

DUST STORMS

VEGETATION

QUALITY OF AIR, AIR PRESSURE

SURROUNDING ENVIRONMENT

GROUND SURFACE

TOPOGRAPHY

Site Climate/ Micro Weather

Five Elements of Climate which Affect Human Body
Comfort & Use of Building/ Shelter

Diagram 2

excessive heat or cold prevails, energy is eliminated by the biological strain of adaptation to the extreme conditions. Physical and psychological strain result from this struggle for biological equilibrium. The design, which in a given environment setting reduces undesirable stress, and at the same time utilizes all natural resources favorable to human living comfort would be considered responsive to climate.

In Vedic period, the Vastu Shastra suggested that the environment was made livable by careful selection and orientation of the building, including placement of openings, thermal efficiency of building materials, layout and space planning according to the solar and wind conditions, shading devices, vegetation and water bodies. The Vastu consultant, therefore, has to remain alert to regional variations and pay attention to examples of vernacular architecture in various climatic zones of India. Building industry consumes vast resources of energy through all phases of development, starting from the production of building materials to its use and maintenance. Besides the scarcity, and their rising cost, their negative environmental impacts has shifted the emphasis from energy utilization to energy conservation. The need today in 21ˢᵗ century is to draw from the experiences of the past to refashion it with the modern concepts and realities, in creating buildings, which are harmonious with the natural environment. This is the only Vastu pattern which will sustain. It modifies the natural environment to approach optimum conditions of livability. The desirable procedure to work towards such requirements would be to work with and not against the forces of nature.

Climatic Parameters

Climate	Weather	Micro Weather
Average weather over a period of many years.	Integration variables atmosphere for a brief Period of time.	Integration variables atmosphere for a particular place for a brief period of time.

These parameters are:
- Solar Radiation
- Air Humidity
- Air Temperature
- Wind Speed and Direction
- Wind Pressure
- Precipitation

These are the parameters which have an effect on the building design.

Settlement and Habitation at Comfort Zone

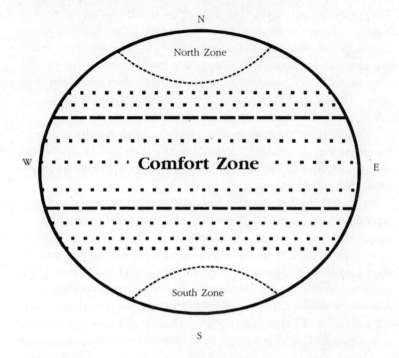

Diagram 3

It is generally agreed that air, temperature, wind and sound are best controlled within the wall itself, while light is easier to control inside the building shell, the heat radiation is most efficiently halted before it reaches the building environment. The materials of the building skin play a decisive part in the utilization and control of solar rays. The thermal efficiency of different material accounts for the variation in indoor climate with similar building skins. A good understanding of the thermal behavior of building materials is essential for any energy efficient planning. The total problem of orientation for buildings other than the thermal consists of optimisation factors like the habits of people living in a particular topography which are an important indicator of how they have been facing the vagaires of nature.

Climatic Efficient Building Design

The conventional sources of energy are rather limited and the present known sources are depleting fast. Generally, at the planning stages buildings are designed and constructed with the initial cost as the primary consideration. Little attention is paid to ensure low energy consumption. Efficient energy management is the need of the day. New buildings should be planned and existing modified to reduce the energy requirements to the optimum levels.

Vernacular architecture in various climatic zones of India such as in Jaipur, Amber palace, Hawa Mahal, Udaipur, Lake palace, North and South block, Sansad Bhawan with shaded balcony corridor around show how optimisation has been achieved.

In the 21ˢᵗ century, modern building industry with its significant achievements in housing is providing comforts to a growing populatioin, unfortunately it is highly dependent upon the easy availability of energy. Building industry consumes vast resources of energy through all phases of development, starting from the production of the building materials, to its use and maintenance. In view of recent energy crisis all over the world, importance of utilization of solar energy and other natural means of heating and cooling of buildings are being explored and adopted. The solar passive systems have been used and tested with encouraging results. Hence, now a time has come that such means based on Vastu principle be considered and adopted while designing buildings that help in the conservation of energy.

The answer perhaps lies in understanding the principles of Vastu, the nature and its cycle like the early man who was bound religiously to the solar cycle. There is a major challenge before the Vastu professionals, architects, planners and engineers, to find out the solution for a sustainable development in Vastu and climatically efficient building design environment for the people to enjoy and not rue the fruits of 21ˢᵗ century technology.

Sun is the source of life of this planet and is an inexhaustible source of energy. In the broadest sense, all fuel systems in use today are based on solar energy. Fossil fuels store solar energy over millions of years. Natural gas, coal and petroleum are stored solar reserves and if exhausted cannot be renewed in our planet's lifetime. Wood fuel store solar energy for hundreds of years and can be renewable energy resource if used with careful reforestation. Considering the renewal aspect, Vastu energy, which is renewable even on daily basis, can be developed.

Solar Passive System

The solar passive system is a gift of five natural elements i.e. Sun (heat or light), Air, Water, Space and Earth to use them properly and utilize them and, thereby, architectural media is called Passive Solar Architecture. There are two solar passive systems:

1. Solar passive heating in cold climatic zone.
2. Solar passive cooling for hot climatic zone.

In *Solar passive heating*, we have to study the

- Direction of flow.
- Rate of flow.

The direction of heat flow is always from hot to cold. In winters, heat flows from inside to outdoors, whereas in summer, the flow reverses and travels from hot outdoors towards cooler interior. The speed and rate of flow depends on difference in temperature. Heat transfer is accomplished in three basic ways—Conduction, Convention and Radiation.

In *solar passive cooling*, the first step in the design system is to reduce the unnecessary heat load into the building, like

- Exterior loads due to climate.
- Internal loads due to people, machines, appliances, cooking, lighting load and orientation and proper ventilation.

DIRECT GAIN

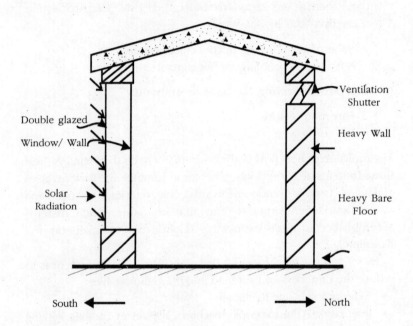

This is the most common Passive Solar System for Heating Building
Interior in Cold Climate since the South face is exposed to a Maximum
amount of solar energy in the cold winter months
When the sun angle is low.

Diagram 4

INDIRECT GAIN TROMBE WALL

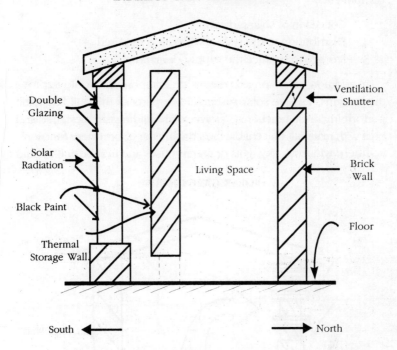

The Wall is built heavy masonry (Trombe Wall) with Usually
Black Paint Which Store the heat Energy in cold winter.

Diagram 5

The thermal load enters into building by three major ways:

1. Penetration of sunlight beam.
2. Conduction of heat through walls and roof.
3. Infiltration of outside air.

The design and the system must be chosen very carefully as every
system has specific design limitation and use which satisfies most of
the design criteria in relation to its thermal needs and space.

To briefly dwell on the technicalities, any solar system has three basic components:

1. Collection of solar radiation.
2. Distribution to the region where it is required.
3. Storage to balance the supply-demand.

In addition, retention and regulation components would improve the systems. Passive solar systems have parts of the building itself performing these functions. Passive solar buildings are designed and built with materials that enable the structure to perform these functions. Southern windows, skylights or greenhouses and trombe walls could

SOLAR GREEN HOUSE

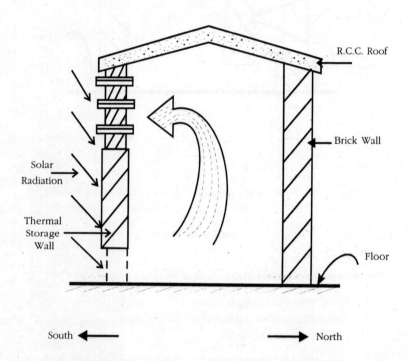

This combines the features of direct gain and thermal storage wall techniques. The green house does not require very good temperature control.

Diagram 6

serve as collectors and masonry walls, roofs or floors for storage. Although they seem simple, they do work. Passive systems are generally integrated into the architectural scheme of the structure. Properly designed, these systems can be highly cost effective, a natural way to reduce energy consumption. The age-old problems of controlling the reception of solar radiation in buildings have been sharply enlarged by the modern development in architectural planning and construction walls. Traditional massive bearing walls, which combine the function of support with protection from solar radiation and heat have been proposed.

ROOF SPACE COLLECTOR

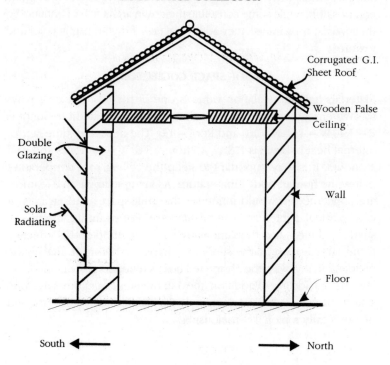

We collect the solar passive heating during the day from the
G.I. sheet roofing and gradually release to the
interior space when needed.

Diagram 7

SOLAR GREEN HOUSE

It is generally agreed that air, temperature, wind and sound are best controlled within the wall itself, while light is easier to control inside the building shell, and heat radiation is most efficiently halted before it reaches the building environment. The materials of the building skin play a decisive part in the utilization and control of solar rays. The thermal efficiency of different materials accounts for the variation in indoor climate with similar building skins. A good understanding of the thermal behavior of building materials is essential for any energy efficient planning. Many materials elaborate the surface; others invite a play of light and shadow or add to the spatial composition, while some constitute their own architectural entities. To their plastic appearance, they add visual ties of rhythm, light, color and texture.

ROOF SPACE COLLECTOR

Materials having insulation value is one of the cost effective ways to save energy, the required insulation value in relation to South is E – 1:1, W – 1:2, N – 1:0 and Roof – 1:6. The necessary time lag for internal heat balance is E & N – 0 hours, S & W – 10 hours and roof 12 hours. It is very important to keep the ceiling/roof temperature below the human body temperature. As far as solar passive features are concerned, it would influence the built spaces and facades. It is of particular interest to architects here. For example, the use of shading devices is a fundamentally sound method and is effective if the interception of the sun's rays happens before it attacks the building. In this way, the obstructed heat is reflected and can dissipate into the outside air. In addition, the Sun breaker can express a strong spatial character, add new elements to the architectural vocabulary, and phrase a truly regional consciousness.

RAINFALL

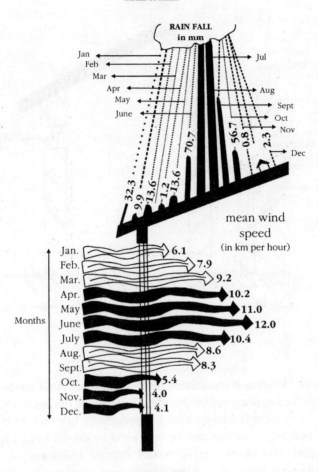

RAIN FALL
in mm

Jan ←
Feb ←
Mar ←
Apr ←
May ←
June ←

Jul →
Aug →
Sept →
Oct →
Nov →
Dec →

56.7 0.8 2.3

32.3 9.9 13.6 1.2 13.6 70.7

mean wind
speed
(in km per hour)

Months		
Jan.		6.1
Feb.		7.9
Mar.		9.2
Apr.		10.2
May		11.0
June		12.0
July		10.4
Aug.		8.6
Sept.		8.3
Oct.		5.4
Nov.		4.0
Dec.		4.1

CLIMATE

The amount of rainfall is very important in design consideration. Rainwater penetrating into the walls and roofs will cause dampness in structure. Water penetrates into the wall through capillaries between the mortar joint. They are liable to crack and their impermeability is likely to cause rapid evaporation of water.

The rainfall data assists at the time of selecting the nature of roof.

The figure shows extreme rainfall and wind speed.

This data shows north Indian climate.

Diagram 8

SOLAR CHIMNEY

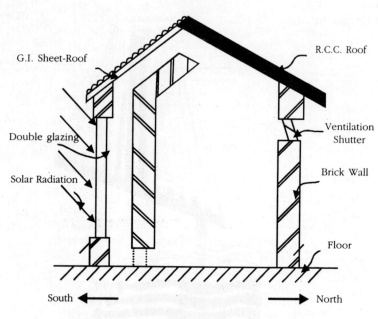

Diagram 9

Outdoor heating is transmitted into buildings through the walls, so that the heat is not transferred to the main structure through the shading devices. Good wall and roof insulation reduces the heat and radiant input to a building. This can also be tempered by the building's thermal capacity. Traditional thick-walled domed buildings of Jaipur and those of other parts of the country are one example—they cool off at night and heat up slowly during the day, reducing day-night temperature fluctuations. In an improvement on this traditional principle some recent buildings have been designed with thermal masses that are cooled by the night air and protected from solar radiation during the day by mobile screens. The best examples you can see are the Delhi South and North block or balcony around Sansad Bhawan. Windows can be protected from the solar radiations by various kinds of shading devices. A system now being tested is thermochromic glass—a 'sandwich' enclosing a thin transparent film that becomes opaque when it reaches a certain temperature, thus, drastically cutting short input. Metalized reflecting film is another way to reduce solar input.

EARTH-AIR TUNNEL

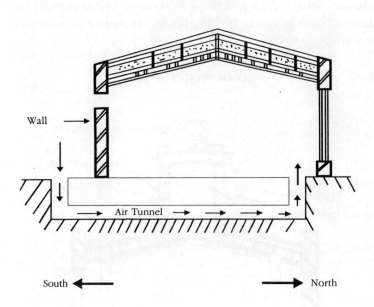

Air tunnel constructed inside the ground exploits the earth storage potential to be effectively used for cooling the building.

Diagram 10

Isolation can also be reduced by increasing the building's albedo and also the vegetation around, for, besides providing shade, plants transpire creating a surrounding area of coolness, as when the water evaporates, it removes heat from the surrounding air. Dispersing heat into the ground is another method of passive cooling that can be done by convection when the air in the building and is forced to circulate and cool the underground ducts, or by direct conduction. These methods of reducing heat input can be combined with methods for cooling the air indoors, a principle that has been applied since antiquity in some places of Rajasthan. Ventilation is another essential way to increase thermal comfort. It is important for the architect/Vastu consultant to know the speed, direction and frequency pattern of prevailing winds at the building site. Urban planners can try to arrange building areas so as to enable air movement and cool outdoor spaces. Building design can also use air movement to provide coolness.

COOL WIND TOWER

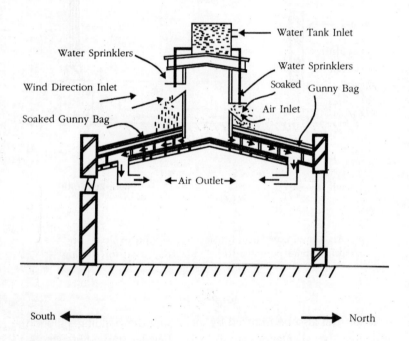

To cool down the summer winds and
circulate them through the building.

Diagram 11

The above points in the design of buildings have been taken from my own book titled *Mass Scale Housing for Hot Climates* published by, Oxford & IBH Publishing Co. Pvt. Ltd. in 1993. These are just a few tips for climate responsive passive designs in warm places.

Therefore, I would like to advise my fellow Vastu consultant to make a careful study of the total problem of orientation of buildings. With the applicability of the principles of solar efficient design, it will help in improving living standards at little cost and in improving energy source availability.

In the last, I would like to refer to my book *Vedic Architecture and Art of Living,* wherein I have mentioned in-depth about the inexhaustible solar energy, a free gift from nature. This energy must be properly utilized. My another book titled *Applied Vastu Shastra in Modern Architecture* in which I have discussed in detail the importance of orientation of building in relation to the Vastu system to achieve the best results. For more details, refer to my book titled *Mass Scale Housing for Hot Climates.*

Elements of Climate and Our Environment in 21st Century

We live on earth which is a unique planet in the solar system. Its uniqueness lies in that its environment is favorable for all forms of life. Our environment is dynamic in nature. Both physical and biological elements of the environment change in the course of time. The sun is the main source of energy, which causes changes in the environment. We are familiar with the day-to-day changes in weather and seasonal changes in climate. These changes are a result of differences brought in the heating of the earth and its atmosphere by the sun. The nature of the land forms in an area sets certain limitations to its use by men. For example, a hill slope can be cultivated only when it is terraced at considerable expense. Construction of houses and highways has to be in conformity with the topography of the region. Thus, the pattern of land use in a region depends on the nature of land forms, besides economic and cultural factors. An understanding of the processes at work in shaping the land forms in a region is essential for planning proper use of land.

Ventilation in Shops/Factory

As very small space creates obstruction, a huge span of shops supersede the penetrating power of natural blows. Apart from this keeping 15 air changes in mind a mechanical ventilation system has to be provided as on some occasions, when there is no wind the required air changes can be achieved. This is provided with the means of top exhaust system i.e. natural ridge ventilators throughout the bay and mechanical fans in exhaust hood by combining the openings at lower levels.

VENTILATION SYSTEM

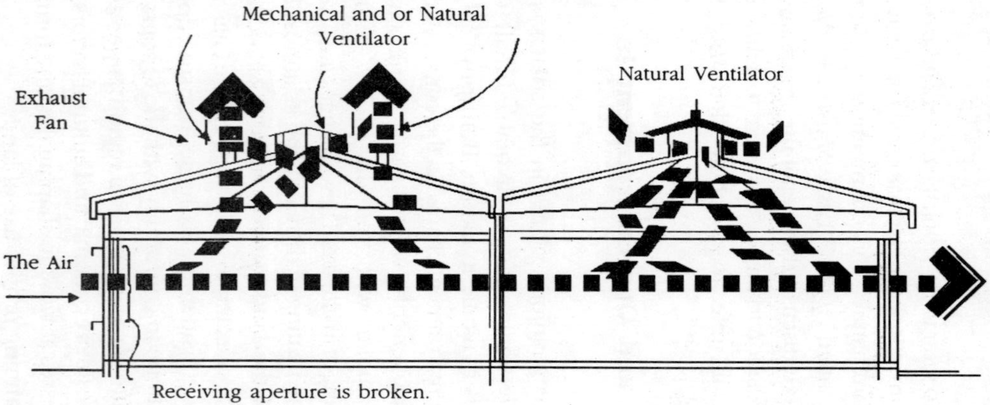

Natural Ventilator

Mechanical and or Natural Ventilator

Exhaust Fan

The Air

Receiving aperture is broken.

Natural and Mechanical Ventilation

Diagram 12

The surface of that land is rarely uniform in height or appearance over large areas. Mountains, plateaus and plains are major land forms on the continents. Land forms vary in size and shape not only from place to place but also change with the passage of time. Wind action is dominant in arid and semi-arid regions. The absence of vegetation cover enables the winds to blow freely near the surface of the land and removes easily and dries particles of sand and dust. The temperature of a place is modified by prevailing winds. In winter, land winds lower the temperature while sea winds increase the temperature. In summer, land winds increase the temperature and sea winds lower the temperature. Winds blowing from low altitudes are warmer than those blowing from middle and high latitudes. The effect of such winds may be felt only for a few days, as wind direction may change.

Weather and Climate

Weather is a composite picture of the various elements at a particular time at a place. A variety of weather conditions may be experienced at a place depending on the season of the year. Weather conditions may vary at intervals of a few hours or a few days.

Climate is different from weather. It refers to the general features based on average values of several elements of weather. The climate of a place may be considered as an integrated or synoptic picture of weather conditions over a long period of time such as a season or year. While weather may refer to a particular place, climate refers to the atmospheric conditions over a large area. The atmospheric condition at any place is a combination of several elements such as temperature, pressure, winds, humidity, precipitation, sunshine and cloudiness.

Climate and Humans

Climate of a region affects man directly and indirectly. Changes in temperature are directly felt and man adapts himself by wearing clothes appropriate to the season. Woollen clothes worn in winter protect us from cold. Cotton clothes are preferred in the hot summer as they absorb sweat and allow air circulation. People living in colder regions use tight-fitting clothes, while those living in tropical regions wear loose garments, which permit movement of air so that the body is kept cool. Exposure to extremes of temperature during heat waves or extreme cold may cause death. Climatic changes resulting in droughts and floods affect man directly.

Houses built by humans are adapted to the climatic conditions. In India, for example, in regions of heavy rainfall like Kerala, and the North-East state of Assam, houses have steeply sloping roofs to drain off the rainwater. Flat roofs are commonly found in deserts. In cooler regions, houses have glass panels for doors and windows to allow more sunlight and heat. In warmer regions, houses have broad verandahs to protect them from direct sunlight. Windows are large to allow greater circulation of air so that the inside of the house remains cooler than the outside. In mountain regions like the Himalayas, South-facing slopes are preferred for construction of houses as they are exposed to sunlight. Humans are now using mechanical devices like fans, air-conditions, heaters, humidifiers etc., to overcome adverse climatic conditions and to live in comfort. Such devices however consume large quantities of scarce energy.

Study of Local Environment

The local environment around a place may be studied by making field trips. Observations may be made about land forms, rivers, source of water supply, drainage, land-use, crops cultivated etc., covering both natural environment and cultural aspects. Examples of environmental pollution may also be noted.

Weather

Weather is our most common topic of conversation. Hardly a day passes without weather-phenomenon claiming headlines in newspapers or news broadcasts. These may include reports of heavy floods causing breach and damage, with considerable loss of life and prosperity, in squalls or hailstorm or lightning strikes.

Meteorology

It is the branch of science, which deals with earth's atmos-phere and the physical processes in it. It includes the study of the changing atmos-pheric conditions such as rain, wind, thunderstorm, snow, fog, which go to make up our weather. Meteorology is compa-ratively a young science. Meteorologist attempts to forecast future weather over a place or region on the basis of a large number of actual weather observations recorded at fixed time at meteorological observations.

Value of Weather Knowledge

Weather plays an important part 'in all aspects of human life, be it personal, social or economic. It is thus, an inescapable phenomenon in human life. Weather plays vital and intimate role in architecture. It is only the knowledge of the weather elements that can enable Vastu advisor to design with maximum efficiency and comfort.

Atmosphere

The atmosphere is the shallow skin or envelope of gases surrounding the surface of the earth. If the earth is compared to a baseball, the atmosphere's thickness of the gaseous envelope or skin is still a matter of argument. What is known is that there is no sharp limit to it, and is somewhere between 200 and 600 miles up.

Composition of Air

Although extremely light, air has weight and is highly elastic and compressible. It is a mixture of gases, with many gases entering into its composition. The chief are Nitrogen (comprising 78 percent of the volume of the dry air) and Oxygen (comprising 21 percent), Argon, Carbon dioxide, Hydrogen, Neon, Helium, Krypton and Xenon are also present in very small quantities. Besides these fixed components, the atmosphere also contains water vapor in variable amounts.

Air envelopes the entire surface of earth on which we live. Although it is not visible to us but we can always feel it. When we run fast, it opposes our motion and when it is in fast motion, it can uproot even big trees. A fast moving air body is called storm. Air is absolutely essential for life. No living being, plant or animal can survive without it. It gives us energy and plants get their food from the carbon dioxide present in it. Water vapor in air helps to produce rains. The quantity of water vapor in air varies from place to place. The desert air is dry, whereas the air in the areas adjoining the sea contains considerable amounts of water vapor. This is why it rains heavily in places near the sea.

Presence of Water Vapor

Although an invisible gas, water vapor is a very important constituent of the atmosphere, under certain conditions water vapor can condense into the millions of tiny droplets of water or crystals of ice which constitutes fog near the frond and clouds. Clouds produce rain, snow or thunderstorm and also partially prevent, radiation of heat from the Sun from reading the ground. It is, therefore, necessary to know something about the importance of water vapor in the atmosphere.

Humidity and Saturation

The amount of water vapor in the air is called humidity. There is a limit to water vapor content of the air at any temperature. As only a certain amount of sugar will dissolve in a cup of tea and if more is added the surplus remains in the bottom of the cup. Similarly, air at a given temperature in contact with a flat surface of pure water (or ice) can take only a limited amount of water vapor. The higher the temperature, the more water vapor it can contain. Air is said to be saturated at a particular temperature when it contains the maximum possible quantity of water vapor.

Relative Humidity

Relative humidity is a term used to express the degree of saturation of air. It is the percentage ratio of the amount of water vapor actually present in the air to the amount, which would be needed to saturate it at that temperature. When air can hold more water than cold. When the air with a given amount of water vapor is warmed, its relative humidity decreases. If it is cooled, the relative humidity goes up. Normally, the relative humidity of the air is highest at the time of sunrise when the surface temperature is minimum and decreases as the temperature goes up.

Now the question comes, what is the source of moisture in the air. Moisture is always present in the air in the form of water vapor, but we are unable to see it. The amount of water vapor present in the air varies from place to place. Even the air in big deserts contains some amount of water vapor. As we know, about 70 percent of the earth's surface is covered with water. Due to solar heating, water from the seas, rivers, lakes and ponds evaporates and mixes with air. And thus constant supply of water vapor in the air is maintained. In scientific language, the water vapor content present in the air is called humidity. It varies from season to season. The amount of humidity is more during the summers than in winters. This is because large quantities of water from the seas, rivers, ponds etc. gets converted into water vapor due to the higher atmospheric temperature during summer. Also, the air expands due to heating and is capable of accommodating more water. When it rains, the humidity increases tremendously because a very large portion of the earth's surface is covered with water, which goes on evaporating into atmosphere.

It is the water vapor present in the air that causes the formation of dew, fog, frost, snow etc. We get a lot of information about the weather by studying the variations in humidity. The instrument, which measures humidity, is called 'Hygrometer'. High humidity indicates the possibility of rains. Cotton mills require humid atmosphere because the presence of moisture in the atmosphere prevents the breaking of cotton threads. Thus, we see that the study of humidity helps us in many ways.

Winds

Wind is defined as air in horizontal motion. Although the atmosphere has both horizontal and vertical motions of air, the horizontal motions have, in general, larger speeds, and their measurement both near the ground and at upper levels can be made with a much greater degree of accuracy than in the case of vertical motions. Like any other fluid, air has got a natural tendency to move from a region of air surplus (high pressure) to one of air deficit (low pressure). This movement is the primary cause of wind. The speed of movement is proportional to the "gradient of pressure", i.e. the rate of change of pressure from high to low. Thus, if the pressure gradient were the only force, we would expect the wind to blow directly from high pressure to low pressure. It is the mixture of oxygen, nitrogen, carbon dioxide, water vapor and dust. Air in motion is known as wind.

When the sun's rays heat up any spot on the earth, the air of that place gets heated. Due to this heating, the air expands and hence, its density decreases and it becomes lighter. The hot air due to its lightness a goes up in the atmosphere. And this causes a decrease in atmosphere pressure in that area. Under such a condition air from high-pressure cool area rushes to that place to restore balance. This movement of air is called the 'blowing of the wind'. In the area adjoining the sea, the earth becomes hot during the day. Due to this, air becomes lighter and goes up in the atmosphere. To fill up the void so caused, cold air from the sea blows towards the land, during the night. A reverse movement takes place; that is, the earth becomes colder than the seawater and as such the air moves from the land towards the sea. It is very hot in the regions surrounding the equator. So, there is a constant upward movement of hot air from these regions. The hot air flows out to the north and south. The rotation of the earth on its axis considerably effects the directions of the winds. The westerly winds are the direct result of the earth's rotation from West to East. The spinning of the earth makes all the winds in the Northern Hemisphere deflect towards the right and in the Southern Hemisphere towards the left. The presence of mountains also influences the wind direction. The mountains obstruct the winds and change their directions. The instrument used for measuring the wind velocity is called as 'Anemometer'.

Buys Ballot's Law

Buys Ballot's Law states that in the Northern Hemisphere, if an observer stands with his back to the wind, the lower pressure is to his left. In the Southern Hemisphere the reverse is true. From Buys Ballot's law, it follows that the wind circulation around a low, in the Northern Hemisphere is anti-clockwise, and around a high, clockwise.

Diurnal Variation of Winds

It is common observation that surface wind strengthens during the day time and becomes light or even calm during night. This is very well-marked on a clear summer day. Mixing processes taking place within the frictional layer during day time bring about this change. The insulation sets up convection currents which are strongest in the afternoon. These up-currents are accompanied by compensating descending currents, This vertical mixing leads to the strengthening of surface wind and the upper wind movement is retarded. During night, the cooling of the bottom layer leads to stability and mixing is inhibited. The upper wind remains undisturbed and the ground wind becomes light and reaches a minimum value around early morning.

Katabatic and Anabatic Winds

These are characteristic of hilly areas. At night, the ground on a hill slope cools rapidly with result that the temperature at any point close to the hill is less than that of free air at the corresponding level. Air close to the hill slope is thus heavier and slides down the slope to give rise to a wind as "Katabatic Wind". During the daytime, the reverse processes take place and as up-slope wind known as "Anabatic Wind" occurs.

Fohn Winds

This is a local name in the Alps region for a warm dry wind on the leeward side of the mountains, but has now become a general term for winds of this nature.

Valley Winds

When a mountain is broken by a valley, the wind tends to blow along the valley at a speed appreciably greater than in neighbouring areas on either side. Such winds are known as valley winds. When wind travels in one direction for a long distance, its moisture gets dried up due to heat. This dry wind absorbs all the moisture of the area which it passes. The result is that the soil starts getting dried up. Plants and trees also whither away due to lack of moisture and the soil becomes sandy and loses its fertility. Then that area is gradually converted into a desert.

Hot and dry deserts are generally found near equator. There is great heat around equator and hence there is no dampness in the soil and it becomes sandy like a desert. Deserts can be formed away from the equator. If there are many mountain ranges between the sea and that area, the damp air from the sea cannot cross the mountain ranges and it rains only on one side of these mountains. The other side of the mountains remains dry and with passage of time becomes desert area.

Rain

Rain falls from clouds. Every cloud is made of water droplets or ice crystals. The growth of a cloud droplet to a size enough to fall out is the cause of the rain and other forms of precipitation. This important growth process is called coalescence. Coalescence occurs in the following ways:

- Droplets in clouds are of different sizes. Big drops move more slowly in turbulent air and in path differ from the path of the small droplets. Bigger, heavier drops are not whipped around so rapidly. So drops collide, become bigger, and finally come down as rain. This is probably the main cause of rainfall from other low clouds.

- The most important type of coalescence occurs when tiny ice crystals and water droplets occur together (as near the middle of cumulonimbus clouds). Some water droplets evaporate and then condense on the crystals. The crystals grow until they drop as snow or ice pellets. As these drop through warm air, they change into raindrops.

- Lightning discharges in a thunderstorm form oxides of Nitrogen that are extremely hygroscope (water absorbing). These oxides are added to the atmosphere and become one of the kinds of nuclei for future condensation and eventual coalescence and rainfall. But the two processes mentioned above are the rain and perhaps the only cause of coalescence and hence precipitation. Research may show other possibilities.

Differences between Drizzle, Rain and showers

Drizzle —Fine drops diameter less than 0.5 mm.
Rain — Drops with diameter more than 0.5 mm.
Showers—ain generally of short duration with sudden commencement or cessation.

The highest rainfall of the world takes place at Cherapunji (Assam) in India. The average annual rainfall of this place is 1200 cm. In 1861, the total rainfall recorded here was 2175 cm.

It is a seasonal wind of South Asia that blows in summer from the ocean towards the land and in winter from the land to the ocean. In summer, the wind blowing from the ocean towards the land spells the possibilities of rains, whereas in winter, blowing from the land towards the ocean is indicative of dryness. In south Asia, the wind from the Indian Ocean blowing towards the shore is the monsoon wind. This wind indicates the chances of rains. Monsoons are of two kinds: South-Western or summer monsoon and North-Eastern or winter monsoon. These winds advance from the Indian Ocean towards the shore in mid-June and after being obstructed by the Himalayas cause rains in the plains. Contrary to this, in the winter, in the Central Asia and North India, very cold, dry and strong winds blow offshore. They are called winter monsoon or the retreating monsoon. They cause some rain in the coastal areas.

It is interesting to see how the monsoon winds change the coastal weather. It is a scientific truth that big sub-continents warm up or cool off much faster than the seas adjoining them. The areas of central and South Asia start warming up in the spring and by the summer become very hot in comparison to the Indian Ocean in the South and the Pacific Ocean in the East. Due to high temperature, there is a reduction in the air pressure on the land and consequently winds start blowing from the sea to the shore. This is the summer monsoon. With the onset of autumn, entire Asia starts cooling fast and by the winter, the temperature is much less than that of the adjoining oceans. This increases the atmospheric pressure and as such in the winter, monsoon winds start blowing from the dry shore to the seas. South and East Asia have a monsoon climate because of their large landed area.

Climate and Micro-Climate

The combined climatic conditions of a region small in area or the parts of a region which characterize the micro-climate are: temperature, humidity, means radiation temperature, velocity of air movement and level of light intensity and distribution. Micro-climate is considerably affected by the terrain of the place (North or South slope, valley or upland), ground and soil conditions, plant life, the building pattern of the town, degree of air pollution, etc. The micro-climate of an urban territory is thus regarded as the result of the interaction of natural and town planning factors such as water impounding, landscaping, asphalt paving, buildings density, etc.

Climatic factors operate constantly throughout the year and hence the process of adaptation of people living, for example, in the tropics does not proceed in the same way as in regions with clearly defined seasons where the human's organism changes its protective properties to respond to the changes in weather. We are inclined to think of the climate as a certain uniformly pattern distributed over a large area. This impression is partly because weather data are collected at points where "undisturbed conditions" prevail, and partly because large-scale maps depict equal mean temperatures in a few smooth lines. However, at ground level multifold minute climates exist side by side, varying sharply with the elevation of a few feet and within a distance of a mile. Plants are sensitive indicators of favorable circumstances. This effect is well known to farmers who prefer southern slopes for growing grapes or cultivating orchards. Further, every elevation difference, character of land cover, every water surface, induces variations in a local climate. These effects within the large scale "macro-climate" form a small-scale pattern of "micro-climates." Deviations in climate play an important part in architectural land utilization. First, in site selection, favorable locations should be considered. Second, a less favorable site may be improved by windbreaks and surrounding surfaces that induce an advantageous reaction to temperature and radiation impacts.

Human Life and Shelter

Given same environment man encounters the same stresses as the other fauna. From Aristotle to Montesquieu, many scholars believed that climate had pronounced effects on human physiology and temperament. More recently interest has centered on human energy in relation to his environment. Climate ranks with racial inheritance and cultural development as one of the apparently live factor in any region where man can obtain food, has strictly limited conditions under which his physical and mental energies (and even his moral character) can reach their highest development. Optimum climate conditions for human progress are:

1. Average temperature from somewhat below 40° F in the coldest months to nearly 70° F in the warmest months.
2. Frequent storms or winds to keep the relative humidity quite high, except in hot weather and provide rain in all seasons.
3. A constant succession of cyclonic storms which bring frequent moderate changes in temperature but are not severe enough to be harmful.

Man's inventiveness enables him to defy the rigors of his environment with fire for warmth and with furs for clothing. When the weakling among the animals substituted Promethean inventiveness for the physical adaptation of other species, shelter became his most elaborate defence against hostile climate. It enlarged the space of biological equilibrium and secured a favorable milieu for productivity. As the elaboration of shelter evolved, accumulated experience and ingenuity diversified it to meet the challenges of widely varying conditions of climate and other factors.

The Effects of Climate on Man

Man's energy and health depend in large measure on the direct effects of his environment. It is a common experience to find that on some days the atmospheric conditions stimulate and invigorate our activities, while at other times they depress the physical and mental efforts. It is also well-known that in certain climatic areas, where excessive heat or cold prevails, energy is diminished by the biological strain of adaptation to the extreme conditions.

The measurement of climatic effects has been investigated in many ways. Here two methods of evaluation may be mentioned. One method describes the negative effects of climate on man, expressed as stress, pain, disease and death. The second defines the conditions in which man's productivity, health, mental and physical energy are at their highest efficiency. Both approaches may be combined, to show coinciding and complementary relationships, in defining desirable or disagreeable atmospheric and thermal conditions.

Effect of Weather on Human Body

Our daily life cycle comprises states of activity, fatigue and recovery. It is essential that mind and body recover through recreation rest and sleep. The mental and physical fatigue result from activities of the day. Unfavorable climatic conditions and the resulting stress on body often hinder the cycle of recovery and mind causes discomfort, loss of efficiency and may eventually lead to a breakdown of health. The effect of weather on man is therefore a factor of considerable importance. It is the task of the designer to strive towards an optimum of utilisation of available resources. He has to consider both the physical as well as the emotional aspects of his environments.

Human thermal control is the dominant problem in tropical climates. Human response to the thermal environment does not only depend upon air temperature but also upon humidity, radiation and air movement. To understand the effect of these factors, it is necessary to examine briefly the basic thermal processes of the human body also i.e. heat gain and his methods of heat loss in main.

The body continuously produces heat. Most of the bio-chemical processes involved in tissue building, energy conversion and muscular work are exothermic i.e. heat producing. All energy and material requirements of the body are supplied from the consumption and digestion of food. Of all the energy produced in the body, only about 20 percent is used while the remaining 80 percent is 'surplus' heat and must be dissipated back to the environment e.g. solar radiation or warm air that also has to be dissipated. The body can release heat to its environment by convection, radiation and evaporation and to some extent by conduction. Conduction depends on the temperature difference between the body surface and the object the body is in direct contact with.

Elements of Climate

The designer is interested in those aspects of climate, which affect human comfort in the use of the buildings. It includes average changes and extremes of temperature, the temperature differences between day and night, humidity, sky conditions, incoming and outgoing radiation, rainfall and its distribution, air movements—thunderstorms, dust storms, hurricanes. It is the desiner's job to analyse climatic information and present it in form that allows him to provide features, which are beneficial to the occupants of that building.

Vegetation

The elements of climate are incomplete without considering the character and abundance of plant life. Although generally regarded as a function of climate, vegetation influences the local or site climate. It is an important element in the design of outdoor spaces, providing sun shading and protection from glare. For this we need a study and survey of native plants and trees —their shape and color and also their preferred orientation and situation. Factors governing the climate of a zone, which may cause local deviation, are:

1. Topography — i.e. slope, orientation, exposure, elevation, hills or valleys at or near the site.

2. Ground Surface —Whether natural or manmade, its reflectance, permeability and the soil temperature as these affect vegetation which in turn affects the climate (woods, shrubs, water, grass etc.)

3. Three dimensional objects:— Such as trees, or tree belts, fences, walls and buildings as these may influence air movement, may cast a shadow and may sub-divide the area into smaller units with different climatic features.

In general, the steps for climatic method of planning comprise of :

1. Climate Data of a specific region should be analysed with the yearly characteristics of their constituent elements, such as temperature, relative humidity, radiation, and wind effects. The data, if necessary, should be adapted to the living level. And the modified effects of the micro-climate conditions should be considered.

2. Technological solutions may be sought, after the requirements are stated, to intercept the adverse and utilize the advantageous impacts at the right time and in adequate amount. This necessary function of a balanced shelter should be analyzed by calculative methods :

    • In site selection most of the factors are variable. In general, sites, which show better characteristics in the winter— summer relationship, are more viable.

- In orientation, the sun's heat is decisive both positively (in cold periods) and negatively (in hot periods). A balance can be found between the "underheated period", when we seek radiation, and the "overheated period", when we want to avoid it.

- Shading calculations are based on maximum protection throughout the year, when the structure is underheated to get sunshine and when the structure gets heated up to prevent sun's rays. A chart of the sun's path, plus geometric and radiation calculations can describe the effectiveness of shading devices.

- Housing forms and building shapes should conform to favorable or adverse impacts of the thermal environment; accordingly, certain shapes are preferable to others in the given surroundings.

- Air movements can be divided into the categories of winds and breezes, according to their desirability. Winds occurring at underheated periods should be intercepted, cooling breezes should be utilized in overheated periods. Indoor air movement should satisfy bioclimatic needs.

3. Architectural application of the building must be developed and balanced according to the importance of the different elements. Climate balance begins at the site, and should be taken into consideration for individual dwelling units.

Shelter and Environment

The physical environment consists of many elements in a complex relationship. One can try to describe the environmental constituents as: light, sound, and climate, space, and all animated beings. They all act directly upon the human body, which can either absorb them or try to counteract their effects. Physical and psychological reactions result from this struggle for biological equilibrium. Man strives for the point at which minimum expenditure of energy is needed to adjust himself to his environment. Conditions under which he succeeds in doing so can be defined as the "comfort zone", wherein most of his energy is freed for productivity.

The shelter is the main instrument for fulfilling the requirements of comfort. It modifies the natural environment to approach optimum conditions of livability. It should filter, absorb, or repel environmental elements according to their beneficial or adverse contributions to man's comfort. Ideally, the satisfaction of all psychological needs would constitute the criterion of an environmentally balanced shelter. Here, however, only one element will be analyzed—the feeling of thermal balance. Without it, any definition of comfort is impossible.

The major elements of climatic environment which effect human comfort can be categorized as: air temperature, radiation, air movement and humidity. (There are others too, such as chemical differences, physical impurities, electric content in the air. They act on man in a complex relationship, the means by which the body exchanges heat with its surroundings which can be classified into four main processes: radiation, conduction, convection and evaporation. It is estimated that radiation accounts for about 2/5 of the heat loss of the body, convection for 2/5 and evaporation 1/5. However, these proportions change with variations in the thermal conditions. The actual relative magnitude of body heat production and heat interchange with the environment may vary within wide limits. The vital processes of the body are accompanied by considerable energy exchange. This energy is derived from the oxidation of foodstuffs and is utilized with a gross efficiency of the order of 20 percent; the remaining 80 percent of the energy is expended as heat. Even when the body is completely at rest and in warm surroundings its heat production does not fall below a certain minimum level to allow the basal metabolism.

The architect's problem is to produce an environment which will not place undue stress upon the body's heat-compensation mechanism. The approach should be rephrased in terms of comfort; the presentation should be in graphic form; and, to be easily applicable, the data should derive from the empirical findings available to the practising architect. Desirable air movements should be utilized for cooling in hot periods and as a relief from vapor pressure during times of high absolute humidity. Conversely, air movement should be blocked and avoided by a bioclimatic analysis for the region, which divides the year into overheated and underheated conditions during the cold season. The yardstick for evaluating wind movements is provided by the bioclimatic analysis. Before investigating possible arrangements that will give wind protection or will utilize air movements beneficially, it is necessary to consider the orientation of the building.

All external heat impacts must pass through the building shell material; the process is comparable to the absorption of moisture by a porous material. Successive layers of the structure become 'saturated' with heat until finally the effect is felt on the inside surface. Anyone who has entered a large stone built church on a hot summer day may have experienced its comforting coolness. In such structures the large mass of the masonry material absorbs and reflects the coolness of the previous night, resulting in a delayed temperature approximating a seasonal average. A similar effect is evident in such 'cryptoclimatic' examples as the pyramids, where the interior space is negligible in relation to the immense mass of heavy material. The interior of the tomb chamber will constantly be close to the yearly average outdoor temperature. In the subterranean homes of the Troglodytes, analogous conditions prevail, since the mass of earth keeps temperature near isotherm conditions. Historic houses sturdily built of heavy wall materials for reasons other than the thermal stability nevertheless react well from this standpoint. By comparison, the structures of today are extremely light and thin and the question of temperature balance arises urgently. Under many conditions light structures are quite undesirable, being at the mercy of external forces just as light boats are tossed about on the sea. The aim of this inquiry is to define the material requirements for an opaque shell, which, by damping and distribution, will balance the external thermal impacts of various regions and exposures. These qualities may be determined by investigating the processes and properties that allow for surface control, touching briefly the related problems of moisture and deterioration.

Climatic Analysis for Vastu Basic Design

The average condition of the weather at a particular place over a long period constitutes the climate of that place. The climate of a place has an intimate relation to the living, civilization, culture and economic development of that place. It depends upon its temperature, rain, atmospheric pressure, wind directions, mountains, height from the sea level and latitude of that place. Different kinds of climate are found in different parts of the world. Different instruments i.e. thermometer, barometer, rain-gauge etc. are used to study the climate, atmospheric pressure, wind directions, rains, clouds, humidity etc. Mainly, five kinds of climate are found all over the world. These are Tropical climate, Sub-tropical climate, Mid-latitude climate, High-altitude climate and High-latitude climate.

Tropical Climate

This is found in regions between 30°C North and 30°C South Latitudes. In the middle, there is the equatorial climate. These places are very hot. These places have considerable rain, but places near the equator are deserts because of high temperatures. Since India is also near the equator, its climate is tropical.

Sub-tropical Climate

It is found at places with latitudes between 30°C and 40°C, both North and South. These places are very hot and dry, but never very cold. In all seasons, there are heavy rains, as such jungles are in abundance. Places with Sub-tropical climate include mainly South-East America, Brazil, Australia and South-East Africa.

Mid-latitude Climate

This climate occurs between 40°C and 60°C, North and South Latitudes. The average annual temperature in these areas is less than 10°C. The summer season is less hot, the winter is very cold. The westerly wind blows in these places. The main places with this type of climate are east Siberia, North China, Manchuria, Korea and North Japan. In this type of climate, deserts are also formed at some places. The distribution of rains, trees and plants vary from place to place.

High-latitude Climate

This climate is found in places lying between 60° North and South latitudes to the poles. In these places, temperature is very low during the winter and it is cold even during the summer. The Polar regions are covered with snow. The main areas in the polar region are Antarctica, Greenland, North America and Eurasia. During the winter, darkness pervades in these places for a very long time, while during the summer they remain lighted for a very long time.

High-altitude Climate

This climate is generally native to high mountains. In these areas it is very cold and rains are in the form of snowfall. Himalayas and other mountain ranges are example.

We know that Earth revolves round the sun and also rotates on its own axis. Days and nights are caused by the rotation of the Earth on its axis. The axis of the Earth makes an angle of 23½° with the vertical. It is this inclination which causes changes in seasons. With its inclined axis, when the earth revolves around the sun, the sun's rays make different angles at the same place at different times. Due to the variations in angles, the distribution of the solar heat is not the same at the same place. This uneven distribution of solar heat on the Earth leads to the summer or the winter season.

If we look at the above pictures minutely, we will see that sun's rays are falling straight on the Northern Hemisphere which means it would be summer there. The Southern Hemisphere would be having winter at this time. After about six months, the situation is reversed, with the solar rays falling obliquely on the Northern Hemisphere and it is winter there, whereas the sun's rays fall straight on the Southern Hemisphere this time and it has summer season. This is how the seasons are formed. We have to design the building in order to manipulate temperature, lighting and airflow. In hot climate, temperature can be controlled by double wall solution, which provides a thermal seal between the inside and the outside. High latticed brick walls and a pond or swimming pool etc. can be used to draw the surface and thus cool the building—this is a traditional cooling system. Design has to be according to the climate, for e.g. in a hilly area like Himalayas, local building materials available are rock, mud, laterite, cowdung etc., these should be used in construction to overcome the climatic conditions. Now-a-days buildings are constructed without corporate, regional or historic identity. The concern for climate, location, vegetation and living style has been totally ignored. Unless architecture transcends into vernacular and traditional styles, architects will do incalculable damage to the environment.

A peculiar state like Kerala with tropical climate (hot and wet humid climatic conditions) local forms are made of the brick screen wall, the sloping tile-roof and the overhanging eaves should be incorporated into the design elements. Brick *jali* is another solution to overcome the climatic conditions. *Jali* is a perforated screen made of bricks placed with gaps so that small regular openings are formed in the wall. It permits light and air inside and diffuses glare. Breezeways can be set up using brick *jali*. On the other hand, it gives complete privacy and security—combining the functions of a window and a ventilator. A *jali* opening allows good air circulation. Local materials like brick, tiles, lime, palm thatch, stone, granite and laterite etc. should be used appropriate to the climate. If timber is available locally, it can replace steel and glass. Not only these materials are appropriate for hot, humid climate but they also help in conserving the non-renewable resources. An interior courtyard can be designed to generate convective air currents and induce a cool breeze through the interiors.

Design need to be with the organic profile of the site, so architectural elements should be introduced that express the duality of inside and outside i.e. of man-made and natural. The cyclonic wind meets no resistance and can be allowed to pass through the house by the continuous lattice work in the exposed walls, the low sloped roofs and courts can serve as wind-catchers.

Kerala has a hot, wet, humid, tropical climate, so the roof pitch is kept steep and the eaves come down low to protect the walls from heavy rain and, at other times of the year, from hot strong sunlight.

This day's buildings are an expression of anarchy without any thought of harmony, unity or honesty with itself, neither with its neighbors nor with the environment. The contemporary approach seems to be towards an architectural anarchy of ruthless arrogance. Instead of the harmonious, honest and traditional architecture, we now seem to prefer a senseless jumble of high-rise concrete structures; each unit is constructed out of the most unsuitable materials we can think of. The materials more close to nature and environment — 'wonder materials'–like mud thatch, bamboo, seeds, grasses, canes, bark, leaves, stalk or even roots should be used. These materials prove as good insulators too.

Indian Climatology

Climatology refers to the weather at a place at a given time is the sum total of meteorological elements, such as temperature, pressure, wind, humidity, precipitation and the state of the sky. A generalization of the weather conditions at a place over a long period of time (usually over 30 years) is known as the climate. The branch of Meteorology that deals with the climates found on the earth is known as Climatology.

The Seasons of India

India is a typical monsoon land. There are two monsoons in the year, separated by short periods during which there is a transition from the one to the other. There are four seasons in India:

1. North-East Monsoon—Winter season (December, January and February)
2. Pre-Monsoon—Summer season (March, April and May)
3. South-West Monsoon—Rainy season (June, July, August and September)
4. Post-Monsoon—Retreating Monsoon season (October and November)

North-East Monsoon—Winter season (December, January and February)

Temperature and pressure

During this season due to radiation, the land areas loose more heat than the sea does and is colder than the Arabian sea and the Bay of Bengal. A high is therefore set up over North-West India. Air flows out from land to the sea.

Winds

They are westerly to northwesterly over North India and northeasterly over South India. The weather is generally fine and the skies clear.

Rainfall

The rainfall is about 10" in Western Himalayas and in the South Coromandal coast. Elsewhere it is practically negligible in amount.

Special Weather Features

During this season, 4 to 6 depressions enter North India from West and travel Eastwards of North-eastwards. These are called "*Western*

Disturbances." These have extratropical frontal structures. They may not be detected as 'lows' on the surface chart as they are generally occluded by the time they arrive in India across Syria, Northern Iraq and Afghanistan. They sometimes give rise to secondaries further to the South. Such secondaries affect the weather over a large part of North India. These disturbances cause snowfall in the higher Himalayas and light rainfall is maximum in Kashmir, which decreases towards the East, and South.

Easterly Low Pressure Waves

They move across the South coast, especially in the first half of this season, causing moderate rainfall mostly along the coast.

Pre-Monsoon—Summer Season (March, April and May)

Temperature and Pressure

The land gets rapidly heated during this season. The temperature rises and pressure falls towards the interiors over North-West and Central India, the mean temperature increases from 100° F in April to 105°F to 110°F in May. By the end of the May, a well-marked trough of low is established over the Indo-Gangetic Plains.

Winds

At the surface, the sea being colder, local sea winds occur in coastal regions. In north India, the winds are strong westerly during day and week during night. Northerly on the West coast and Southerly over the East coast of the peninsula winds blow where they are weaker.

Rainfall

Rainfall is maximum in Southwest and Northeast India. It increases from 5" over West Mysore to 15" in South Malabar coast and from 10' in West Bengal to 30' in Upper Assam, 2 to 6' of rain occur in Bihar, Orissa, Andhra Pradesh, upper Uttar Pradesh and Punjab hills. In Central and Northwest India, it is scanty.

Special Weather Features

Western disturbances continue to move across North India during this season, the frequency being 5 each in March and April and 3 in may. They cause about 2-5" of rainfall in Kashmir and Punjab hills.

Duststorms and Thunderstorms

Duststorms and dust raising winds are common in this season in the drier tracts of north India. Thunderstorms occur on 8-12 days per month in Assam, West Bengal, West Mysore and South Malabar Coast. These are due to the moist air from the sea meeting the hot and dry continental air over land. The thunderstorms are sometimes accompanied by hail.

Nor' Westers

Some of the thunderstorms which occur in this season in Bengal and Orissa are the most violent types. They are locally known as "Kalbaisakhis." They are of four types. The most important is the type of thunderstorm, which originates in the Chhota-Nagpur plateau and advances Southeastwards with a speed of 30-40 m.p.h. The squalls caused by these thunderstorms are from the Northwesterly direction; hence, the name: "Nor Wester" for these thunderstorm.

South-West Monsoon—Rainy season (June, July, August and September)

Temperature and Pressure

The maximum temperature is the highest in the year and exceeds 120°F in West Rajasthan. The high maximum temperature continues in North-West India in June but fall in the peninsula with the advent of rains. In July and August, the temperature generally falls slightly over the country. In September as the rain ceases in North-West India, the maximum rises there again. A systematic fall of temperature commences by the end of the season all over India.

The low-pressure trough over the Indo-Gangetic plains is most intense in June, July and August. By September, its axis tends to shift southwards and it becomes less marked. The lowest portion of the trough lies over North-West India throughout the season.

Winds

The surface winds are West to South-West over both the land and the sea lying to the South of the axis of the monsoon trough. They are stronger over the open sea. On the average, over land the speeds are less. To the North of the axis of the trough, the winds are light Easterly.

The upper winds are controlled by the monsoon trough, being Westerly to the South of its axis and easterly to its North. Westerlies are strongest over the peninsula.

Rainfall

Under the influence of the Indo-Gangetic trough, the humid South-East trades of the Southern Hemisphere are drawn across the equator into South Bay and South Arabian Sea. During their Northward march, they suffer a deflection to the South-West and become the "South-West monsoon". Monsoon enters India in two branches, one from Arabian Sea and the other from the Bay of Bengal. The Arabian Sea branch strikes the West Coast in the first week of June. After causing copious rains there, it extends across the Peninsula and central India upto axis of the monsoon trough. The Bay of Bengal is deflected first northwards through Burma and Assam where heavy rainfall is caused due to the orographic uplift. It is then deflected westwards into the monsoon trough, where it meets the Arabian Sea current along the axis of the trough causing general rainfall there. As the monsoon is a deep, conditionally unstable airmass, orography and surface heating lead to instability in showers within the airmass itself.

Monsoon is fully established over the whole country by the middle of the July. It weakens steadily and begins to withdraw from Northeast India in the first week of September. Its withdrawal from the peninsula is completed by the end of November. It causes a rainfall over 100" in the West Coast and in the Assam valley; 40" to 50" in North Bengal, Bihar, Orissa, East U.P. and Punjab hills and 20" to 30" in West U.P., East Rajasthan, Punjab, South Bengal and the part of the Peninsula lying to the east of the western ghats, much of this rainfall occurs in June and July.

Character of the Monsoon rainfall

Monsoon may commence later and terminate earlier than the normal dates. The rainfall is not continuous but is punctuated by spells of dry weather caused by a Northward shift of the monsoon trough. When the axis of the trough shifts right upto the Himalayas, the rainfall completely ceases everywhere except in eastern Himalayas. Such a situation is termed as a break in the monsoon. Rains at any given time may occur more in one part of the country than another. The monsoon trough varies in depth and position. It is displaced East or West along its axis; it also oscillates North or South of its seasonal position. The rainfall associated with the trough also migrates with the trough.

Special Weather Features

Monsoon depressions—A fresh advance of monsoon current after a break usually leads to the formation of depressions in the head of the Bay of Bengal. Three to four such depressions are formed per month during the monsoon season. They are mild tropical storms and rarely show a calm center and hurricane winds around. They are nevertheless a source of danger to pilots as they cause torrential and blinding rain with local rainsqualls often of a severe type. Strong winds are experienced only in the South and Southeast quadrants and only at sea. Monsoon depressions concentrate the rainfall in their vicinity. Locally, heavy rain of 3-8" over several districts within 24 hours is usual in depression areas. They move Northwestwards along the axis of the monsoon trough. They weaken on crossing the coast and the rainfall caused by them decreases as they move inland. They carry the rainfall into the remote interior of North-West India before they decay

Post Monsoon—Retreating Monsoon
(October to November)

Temperature and Pressure

With the cessation of rain in North India and Southward migration of the sun, the temperature in North India falls rapidly in October, the mean maximum being below 100° F. Fall of temperature continues over India during this season. The low-pressure area is transferred to the center of the Bay in October and to the South of Bay in November.

Winds

The winds are light and North-Westerly to westerly over North-West India and North to North-Easterly over the rest of the country. North-westerly to westerly over North-West and central India and North to North-easterly over the Peninsula.

Rainfall

The Bay branch of the retreating monsoon curves round the low pressure trough and causes moderate to heavy rainfall on the East Coast of the peninsula. The rainfall is heaviest along the coast and decreases rapidly towards the interior. It is often associated with thunder. In October, about 10" of rainfall is received in the South Coromandal coast. Rainfall rapidly decreases towards the interior and is less than the inch to the West of Mangalore–Dibrugarh line.

The rainfall caused by the retreating South-West monsoon in South India is also sometimes referred to as "Northeast Monsoon" rainfall due to the fact that the winds are mainly North-Easterly in the Peninsula during this period.

Special Weather Features—During this period, the low-pressure area in the bay becomes the seat of development of "Tropical cyclonic storms" which are sometimes severe. On the average 2-3 cyclones develop in the Indian sea during this season. They move initially North-Westwards and often recursive towards North or North-East later and strike the Madras or Arakan coasts usually. The worst weather and strongest winds occur in the dangerous semi-circle of the storm. When crossing the coast, these storms cause storm waves resulting in flooding of low coastal areas.

Western Disturbances—These effect North-West India where they cause light rainfall of less than 1". About two disturbances enter India on the average in November.

Orientation of Building

The placing of the building with respect to the geographical direction (East, West, North and South), the direction of the wind, and the altitude and azimuth of sun is known as the orientation of building. The building should be placed in such a way that it drives maximum benefit from sun, air and nature and at the same time it is protected from their harmful effects. It may not be possible to orient each building in the desired direction to have the maximum benefit of sun, air and nature, as in towns the orientation of individual building is decided on various factors like the position and direction of the streets, position of garden and park, the shape and size of the plot of the land, etc. In such cases, the orientation should be fixed with respect to the frontage of the building only. The proper orientation of each room should be worked out taking into account of its functional requirements, as for example the garage. the stair case and other general service facilities could be grouped on the Western side to protect the living rooms from the more hot afternoon sun.

In cities as the orientation of the buildings to the choice is not possible, the buildings should be planned to have the maximum advantage of nature. The rooms should be arranged suitably to have the maximum possible comfort within limits, and verandahs, doors and windows, chhajjas, sun'shades, sun breakers etc., should be provided in such a way as to get maximum advantage of natural wind and sun. Where sufficient light is required as in operation theatres, in hospitals and science laboratories, the rooms should be placed on the North with large openings to get North light.

The Problem of Orientation of Building vis-a-vis Climatic Factors are:

1. Air Movement
2. Landscaping
3. Openings and Windows
4. Walls
5. Roof
6. Materials
7. Insulation Index 45
8. Required Value in Relation to south is:

    East   -   1:1
    West   -   1:2
    South   -   1:2
    North   -   1:0
    Roof   -   1:6

9. High Heat Capacity Walls for Heat Balance are:

    East   -   0 Hr.
    South   -   10 Hrs.

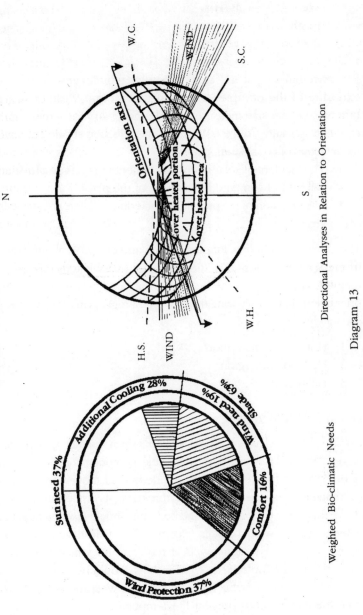

Directional Analyses in Relation to Orientation

Diagram 13

Weighted Bio-climatic Needs

West   -   10 Hrs.
North   -   0 Hr.
Roof   -   12 Hrs.

For office building, it is desirable to orient a building so as to avoid exposure of the occupied rooms to Eastern and Western sun, as otherwise expensive measures may be necessary for screening the sunlight, specially from the West. For the selection of orientation the main factors of consideration are:

- The incident of solar intensities depending on the altitude and azimuth of sun, and the altitude of the place.
- The direction of the prevailing wind during different parts of the year.

The climatic conditions, intensity of sun and direction of wind differ from region to region. It is, therefore, not possible to follow a rigid method with regard to the orientation of buildings. In general, the orientations in the following three different regions may be dealt with separately:

1. Hot and humid region
2. Hot and arid region
3. Hill region

Hot and Humid Region

In this region the climate is humid, temperature in summer is moderately high and rainfall is heavy. The prime object for orientation and design of buildings in this region is to provide free air movement through buildings and to prevent the temperature rise of its inside surface rising above the shade temperature. The buildings should face the direction of the prevailing wind to obtain maximum benefit from air movement. A tilt upto 45° may be allowed, if required, for which the loss in efficiency is only upto 20%. Window-sills should be low to ensure maximum ventilation at the normal living level. Wells should be shaded from the sun so as to prevent the temperature rise. Protection of openings against rain is also necessary.

Buildings should normally have open planning, as far as possible. They should be one room thick so as to ensure through ventilation. In Bengal wind blows generally, North and South and hence facing South is preferable. In Madras, area, the general direction of wind and also the monsoon wind is from the East and hence the building may be oriented East and West, but to avoid afternoon sun the living rooms may be on the East and South-east of the building. Cities falling within hot and humid regions are Ahmedabad, Mumbai, Mangalore, Travancore, Chennai, Coastal, and Andhra Pradesh. Mysore, Kolkata and adjoining team.

Hot and Arid Region

In this region the climate is extreme, the temperature ranges from 45 degrees maximum and 16 degrees minimum or more or less. Cloudless sky, low humidity and high incidence of sun's glare are the main features. The sunny areas are hot and dry in the daytime and cool to cold at night. As far as possible the buildings should be protected from daytime heat and glare during summer, and at the same time the rate of heat loss at night during winter should be reduced. In these regions, the building should be oriented for sun (not for wind as in humid regions). The sun's heat is beneficial during cold season but harmful during the hot season. The sun is in the South during the hottest part of the day and the altitude of sun is high in summer and low in winter. For comfort during over-heated as well as under-heated periods, orientation and construction of building should be such that:

- There is minimum heat gain in the structure during over-heated period.
- Minimum heat flow out of the structure during under-heated period.
- Equal heat gains and heat loss in the period when outside temperature is in the comfort zone.

To minimize the heat gain during summer and to take benefit of solar heat in winter the longer wall should face North and South, and shorter walls East and West, so that least wall area is exposed to the slanting rays of the sun during forenoon and afternoon i.e. the longer axis of building should run East-west, so as to avoid excessive heat from West side. Provision of chhajjas on the Southern walls will give adequate shade to the walls during summer, and provisions of windows and openings on the South will allow sun's ray. Openings in the West should be small and should be properly protected. To save cost of verandah on the West, the afternoon sun may be kept off by providing louvers or tilted vertical sunbreakers. Alternately, a small tilt of the axis of the building may be given away from the West towards the South i.e. facing near about North-east. Attempt should be made to get maximum advantage of breeze during rainy season, autumn and spring to ensure comfort and proper ventilation. Hot and arid regions consist of Central and North India consisting of Delhi, Amritsar, Gwalior, Indore, Nagpur, Agra, Kanpur, Lucknow, and Gaya, Jamshedpur and adjoining areas.

Hill Region

In these regions, temperature is usually much low, and cold prevails according to the altitude. There is a marked drop in temperature during the night. The buildings in these regions should be located in the Southern slope of hill as they receive maximum sunshine for the greatest duration of time. The opening should be placed as to avoid undesirable cold wind in winter. A massive structure with high heat capacity is useful. The heat it stores during the day is welcome except in a very hot day. It is necessary to provide ceilings with good thermal insulation to reduce heat loss. It is necessary to provide ceilings of good thermal insulation to reduce loss of heat by radiation during the night also. Where there is heavy snowfall the roof should be sloping to prevent accumulation of snow.

Ventilation: Ventilation consists an inlet of fresh air and exit of vitiated or stagnant air, and maintaining a movement of air in the rooms and the building. For proper ventilation, windows should have a minimum area of 1/8ᵗʰ of the floor area of the room and the aggregate area of the doors and windows should not be less than 1/4ᵗʰ of the floor area of the room. Windows should be provided 2'-6" above floor level. In addition to the doors and windows, ventilators should be provided having a total area of 4 percent of floor area. Ventilations serve as good exit for inside air and should be located as near the ceiling as possible within 60cm (2 feet) from the ceiling. The area of each ventilator should not be less than .3 sq.m. (3 sq. ft.).

In living room, at least two windows should be provided one in each of the opposite walls and if that is not possible, there should be at least two windows one in each of the adjoining walls. Bath rooms, toilets, kitchens should have at least one window of .9 c.12 m (3'x 4') size.

Environmental Crisis in 21ˢᵗ Century

Throughout the world, government and non-government organizations are straining themselves in organizing and mobilizing intense schedules of action to combat environmental degradation.

First, it should be clearly understood that it is not the planet that is being threatened. The earth with its misty and mysterious history, extending over billions of years, has existed without mankind and it will continue to exist even if the human race vanishes from the earth. Strictly speaking it is the human life that is in peril. And this impending peril has not suddenly emerged from any external factor but through recklessness of man himself.

Our perception of the environmental problems continue to be superficial and time serving—it is related to damage to the land vegetation and or water. Our remedial measures hover around growing more trees, checking grazing and cleansing waterways. Even the syllabus for environmental literacy is primarily focused on the various factors that cause pollution and biospheric damage.

No doubt, environmental degradation directly stems from uncontrolled deforestation, the emission of pollutants, excessive use of toxic products and the destructive exploitation of non-renewal natural resources; but what we fail to underline is that these areas are, one and all, violent acts of aggression of man against nature. The central issue lies in the fact that the present crisis is a crisis of the naive belief in the omnipotence of mankind.

It is, therefore, pertinent that endeavors to reverse the course of mounting danger to life on earth which should be riveted on disarming human beings of their superiority over Nature. This is the core of the problem while degradation of the environment is but its symptom. Hitherto, the focus has been concentrated on curing the symptoms by plans and projects for afforestation, water cleansing, neutralizing toxins etc. In order to resolve the problem, something qualitatively different and quantitatively greater is essential.

Industrial development has generally been equated with ecological degradation and the world today is on the edge of an environmental disaster. Without ecology of spirit and ecology of thought, all our efforts to save mankind would be pointless. When science and rationality cannot help us, there is only one thing that can save us: our conscience and our moral feelings.

Talking about the growing tension between humankind and nature; the technogenic process based on technology and the constant improvement in technologies has not only failed to migrate the conflict between man and Nature, but it has also aggravated that conflict.

Tons of sewerage are dumped into azure blue water bodies. Carbon dioxide is pumped into the atmosphere. Animal and plant species become extinct by the hour as acres of rain forests disappear. It is no more a question of talking about a subject like environment but to press home an issue that means life or death to our planet. The apathy with which we look at our environment despite warning signs (holes in the ozone layer) shows how the earth is moving mindlessly around its own axis uncared for by men and gods.

Man was once in spiritual relationship with his environment. Not only were trees revered and worshipped but this mild form of paganism helped preserve trees. Such villainous by-products of industrial progress as sulphur dioxide, nitric oxide, radioactive microwaves and acid rains, have caused the tragedy of the tree among others. Death of the tree is the death of dignity, beauty and poetry.

Awareness of the landscape in India is reflected in its miniature developed under the Mughals and continued under princely patronage in the Himalayan foothills. In the highly idealized world of the miniature, both wild and tame beasts co-exist with man. Trees and flowers find their own due place in a magical rear arrangement of the familiar. In the 18ᵗʰ century Europe, gardens were to resemble beautiful pictures such as those painted by Claude Lorraine, Poussin and Salvator Rosa.

A pressing question that we all may be afraid to answer is how much longer can human populations go on damaging the world's natural systems before they break down altogether? The earth on its own has the potential of degradation as part of the natural processes that take place within and without. Adding human destructive activity may tend to exceed the earth's carrying capacity. Humanity as we know is making intolerable demands on the world's natural resources. By the time babies born in say 1991 reach the age of 40 they could be sharing resources with as many as 10 billion other people.

The state of our environment today is a matter of grave concern. No doubt, in the last few years awareness about the environment has increased rapidly among the public. More and more people are conscious about the consequences of environmental degradation. Ecology and environment have found a more significant place in school and college curriculum. Environmental awareness campaigns have spread far and wide.

It appears as if we have succeeded in creating great deal of public perception on environmental issues. However, a closer analysis of the public perception on environmental issues might show that much of this awareness is of a negative kind—about all that has gone wrong with the environment—cynical and critical, but seldom action-oriented.

The fact that conservation can begin at home and become a way of life, firmly ingrained in personal habits and ethics needs to be emphasized. In fact, all our actions—the way we utilize natural resources, consume energy, dispose of the waste, build houses, promote developmental activities—are all related to environmental issues. Merely becoming aware of the present day environmental problems without evolving a personal ethics based on environmentally sound lifestyles will be of no use.

The Remedies that Vastu Suggests

Vastu suggests that there are many things that Vastu consultant can do to contribute to the protection of our environment. Here are a few suggestions or advices. Consider them seriously.

- Conserve paper: Sensible use of paper will save immense forests from needless cutting down.
- Save electricity: A great amount of electricity can be saved at no sacrifice in comfort. This will help power generation units to reduce air and water pollution and the nation to conserve energy, by solar passive building design.
- Conserve water: Water is one of our vital natural resources. Use it wisely and without waste. Recycling of water should be done at individual level; at industrial level, harvest things with water.
- Do not litter or scatter paper or waste materials in public places.

- Save wild life: Help save our endangered animals. Do not make hunting your hobby or sport.
- Conserve nature: Do not use plastic bags.
- Don't buy these: Do not buy articles from furs or hides of endangered species of wild life.
- Do not burn paper: Do not burn leaves and paper. Instead, make compost heap that will enrich soil.
- Recycling: Look at anything you are about to discard and ask yourself how it can be re-used.
- Quit smoking: Protect your own life as well as of those who do not smoke.
- Prevent noise pollution: Reduce noise in the home, business places and industries.
- Do not dump waste: Do you have a stream or river in your town? Do you use it as a garbage dump? Stop this and put our rivers and streams to better use.
- Prevent overgrazing: Do not let your livestock overgraze. Overgrazing reduces the water-holding capacity of the land and leads to soil erosion.
- Save gasoline: Ride a bicycle or walk on short trips—for your own health and the health of the environment.
- Grows a garden: Plant native trees and shrubs.
- Keep your eyes open: Report any environmental violation you see to the appropriate authorities. This land belongs to all of us, not to the government alone.
- Limit family size: Population growth is our most frightening problem in 21ˢᵗ century.

Environmental education based on Vastu principle has to be achieved both at the formal and non-formal levels. At the formal level, the responsibility mainly rests with schools, colleges and universities. In school education, in spite of all that has been done so far, environment largely remains in textbooks and is examination oriented with very little attention paid to use the environment itself.

Not enough attention has been paid to train and motivate teachers who teach ecology and environment at the school level. Because of this situation, activities for informal education on environment becomes all the more necessary, important and crucial for creating the right kind of awareness and attitude among people at all levels—children, teenagers, adults, family groups, teachers and decision-makers.

The above are just a few examples. There are many such aspects in our life and behavior that can be made environmentally sound and sustainable. Only then the gap between education and action can be filled and people's participation and support be ensured at the local, national and global level.

All ancient buildings have an identity. By merely looking at them we can tell whether it is a domestic, commercial or industrial building. It had its geographical and cultural characteristics. In India, there is an incredible wealth of regional architectural styles, and there is not the faintest possibility of confusing one with another. Even where the same materials have been used for building, the climatic, cultural and regional variations are so great that different methods of construction have been used to produce unique individual styles. But these distinctions cannot be found anymore. Why?

For one thing—Modern Portland Cement came and suddenly our slow, steady, evolutionary building process came to a devastating and tragic halt. Cement and steel were joined together and universal anonymous expressionless 'Modern Architecture' of reinforced cement concrete came into being, which has been used lavishly and brutally. The saddest thing about it is that it consumes a lot of energy in its manufacture and involves lot of skill and labor for its use in buildings.

Problems of environmental degradation can be sought out only by using non-conventional materials for construction like stone, laterite, mud, lime etc. or recycling them. Random rubble mixed in lime, *surkhi,* mortar can be used in construction of the foundation, load-bearing brick walls can be used. Filter tiles for slabs, and for flooring a mixture of local quarry tiles can be used for in doors and windows, jackwood can be used. Bamboo reinforcement can be used instead of steel reinforcement. Building materials like local wood, bamboo, thatch. stone etc. should be used maximum for construction.

The architect/Vastu consultant has a uncertain, almost unfelt, presence, backed by a conviction that buildings—whatever their function—are secondary to the surroundings and sustained only by their natural harmony with environment. Alternatives to concrete have to be used mainly because both steel and cement have a very high intensive energy consumption in their manufacturing process. So as much brick as possible, should be used.

The old custom of surrounding homes with embracing trees had deeper roots than a desire for the enjoyment of nature's aesthetic variety. Besides satisfying the instinctive need for protection, trees also contribute much to the immediate physical environment. They reduce airborne sounds with great efficiency, if densely planted. The viscous surface of leaves catches dust and filters the air. Vegetation can also secure visual privacy and reduce annoying glare effects.

But a especially beneficial effect of trees is their thermal performance. In summer the surface, of grass and leaves absorbs radiation and their evaporation processes can cool air temperatures. Above all, they provide generous shade at the right season. This trait make deciduous trees especially valuable when placed close to buildings. Vines also constitute another of nature's automatic heat-control devices, cooling by evaporation and providing shade. This combination makes them valuable for sunny walls in hot weather.

In modern world, the use of scientific method based on P.V.C (Polythene plastic) is being used in day-to-day living (plastic, bag, cutlery, packing board etc.) and in building industries, for example roof is covered and sealed with polythene sheets for water proofing, flooring with synthetic marble or tiles, wall to wall synthetic carpet, walls painted with plastic emulsion paints, doors and windows with synthetic wood or PVC, paneling door/windows frame with steel and aluminum. So, in other words we are living in an airtight plastic bag.

This is not the end of our ignorance of what we call a modern comfortable world. After all this, we install a split or window air conditioning which recycles almost 100 percent of inside air. If we check the air quality of the room after two hours, the oxygen content will be reduced and carbon dioxide becomes almost double. This is the condition of our modern comfortable bedroom where we spend a minimum of $1/3^{rd}$ of our life.

In the name of so-called modernization we are inviting problems for our new generation like new diseases which reduce our body resistance and increase tension, stress, fatigue etc. The answer lies with Vastu. Vastu is the bridge between Man and Nature. Only Vastu gyan balances the five elements and nature teaches us how to live.

Chapter 9

Landscaping in 21st Century on Vastu Principles

Introduction

Modern patterns of living level are becoming busy, adopting bureau-cratic values, resulting in tension, worldwide pollution, environmental and ecological problems.

"Green belt with running water gives sense of relaxation." World-wide, population is increasing; green belt and water alongwith other input resources are declining. Landscape engineering design technique requires macro-level study.

Landscaping Engineering Technique

(Input Design)

Built Environment	Natural Environment
• Aesthetic sensitivity	• Topography—Surroundings
• Free Creativity of the Artist	• Geology—Engineering (Scientific study of Earth/Soil)
• Scientific Knowledge	• Climate—Weather and Micro weather
• Intellectual Discipline	• Existing Forest—Soils and Vegetation
• Social Useful Purpose	• Energy Sources—Water and Electricity
• Welfare of Mankind	
• Economical Design	• Weather Hazards?
• Good maintenance in the aim of Engineering	• Pests and Plantation Diseases?

- Selection of Local Material
- Peace and Quality of Life for all
- Energy Saving and Efficient improved design
- To Create Attractive View

- White Ants (Banana tree)?
- Waste Storm Water Disposal?
- Wind Speed?

Climatology

Climatic Parameteres

Climate	Weather	Micro-Weather
Average weather over a period of many years.	Integration variables atmosphere for a brief period of time.	Integration variables atmosphere for a particular place for a brief period of time.
(Forest and Big trees)	(Shrubs and Herbs)	(Seasonal plants, flowers and trees)

These parameters are:

- Solar radiation
- Air Humidity
- Wind Speed and Direction
- Wind Pressure
- Precipitation
- Rainfall (Average)

These are the parameters, which have an effect on build and natural environment.

CLIMATE

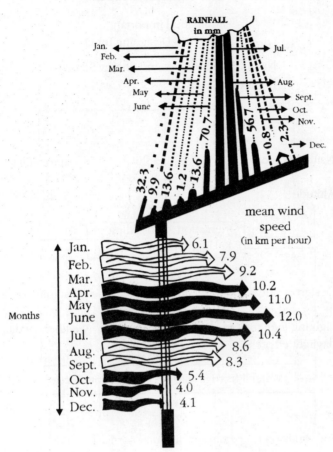

The amount of rainfall is very important in design consideration. Rain water penetrating into the walls and roofs will cause dampness in structure. Water penetrating into the wall through capillaries between the mortar joint weakens the structure. They are liable to crack and their impermeability is likely to record a rapid evaporation of water.

The rainfall data assists at the time of selecting the nature of roof.

The data shows the extreme rainfall and wind speed.

This data shows the northen Indian climate.

Wind speed and Rainfall Data is the guideline for the basic approach to garden design and selection of basic construction materials such as garden furniture, light, tree's, shrub's, and ground coverage, etc.

Diagram 1

Natural Environment in Landscaping

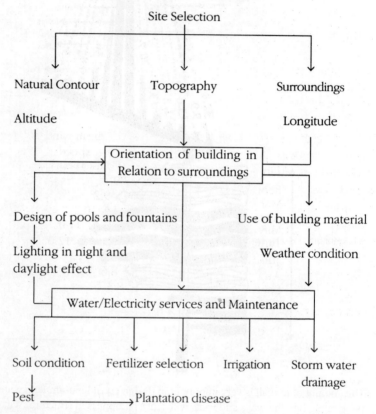

Climatical Important
Planning and Designing Input

Natural Environment and Energy Sources

Site Selection

| Natural Contour | Topography | Surroundings |

Altitude   Longitude

Orientation of building in
Relation to surroundings

Design of pools and fountains   Use of building material

Lighting in night and   Weather condition
daylight effect

Water/Electricity services and Maintenance

Soil condition   Fertilizer selection   Irrigation   Storm water
                                                         drainage

Pest ————————→ Plantation disease

Types of Landscaping

The landscaping is categorized in the following types :

1. Treeless Landscaping.
2. Dry (Waterless) Landscaping.
3. Rock Garden Landscaping.
4. Landscaping with Pattern and Forms.
5. Landscaping with Dry Wood and Artificial Plants.

6. Landscaping with Natural Contour and Slopes.
7. Landscaping with Trees, Plants, Shrubs/Herbs, Flowers, Pool, Waterfalls and Fountains etc.

Landscaping on Vastu Principles

(a) Indian Historical Background

Landscape and garden planning are the most essential features of the town planning of Indo-Aryans. Aryans were worshippers of nature. Water and trees, therefore, had unique importance in the corporate life in ancient India.

A well-laid out garden formed an inseparable aspect of the temple since Hindu gods loved proximity of water and flowery trees. Several trees were held sacred because of their aesthetic and sanitary potentialities; gardens were spread out evenly in the towns, cities and in the palace complexes; gardens were also provided with artificial channels and tanks. So much importance, indeed, was attached to the parks and gardens that the 'Stahapati' or the chief architect of a landscape was always provided with the services of a landscape architect. The poetic descriptions of the spring festival celebrated in ancient India, known as 'Ashokapushpaprachayika', also give us a glimpse of the importance attached to gardens. An Ashoka tree was supposed to flower only when the foot of a charming young girl pressed its roots, by kicking it at the end of a dance with her left foot. Ashokavana—a garden of Ashoka trees was a part of the palace complex.

Apart from 'Ashokapushpaprachayika', or the festival of gathering of Ashoka flowers, many other festivals were celebrated in ancient India, especially during the spring. The 'Salbhanjika' festival was celebrated with great zeal in the city of Sravasti, which was located in the present day district of Gonda. This was the festival of 'Women and Tree'. The Sal tree in full blossom was worshipped for offspring.

The 'Suvasantaka' was one of the merriest spring festivals in ancient India, and was celebrated around Vasant Panchami, during the first week of February. The ceremony of the offering of lamps known as 'Deep Dana', was performed during this festival. The myriad of lighted earthen lamps was set afloat in the sacred waters of the Ganges and Yamuna. Such festivals speak volumes for the love of nature in general and gardens in particular in ancient India.

Vatsyayana enumerates four types of gardens for the princely class. 'Pramododhyan' for the enjoyment of kings and queens; 'Udyan' for kings and their courtiers, 'Vrikshavatika' for ministers and courtiers, and 'Nandanvana' dedicated to Lord Indra. Apart from these, there were parks for public use and sacred groves. Various pavilions were also provided within the gardens.

Since the geometric patterns were followed for the cities and towns according to 'Vastupurushamandala', the gardens also assumed geometric forms, with the pavilions placed either at the center or at the ends to suit the design requirements. "Gardens, as a part of the total city could not follow any unplanned form on its own." The present belief that the Hindu and the Buddhist gardens did not follow planned geometric growth is unfounded. If the geometric pattern was essential because of the chessboard system of General City planning, the rectangular or square form of the interior courts inside the palace complexes also necessitated it. Thus, the so-called Mughal gardens in India do not owe their origin to the gardens in Persia; they are truly Indian in the design concept. The historians of medieval garden art are so carried away by the accounts of Muslim chronicles that even though the so-called Mughal gardens in India show Hindu influence, these historians tend to classify these gardens as belonging to Persian origin. This is clear when Andreas Volwahsen writes, "Of all the possible sub-divisions it was the 'Charbagh' (Four gardens) which characteristically enough predominated in India. Its two axes oriented towards the four cardinal points and its basic square fitted in exactly with Hindu cosmology. If we did not know that Babur had already laid out a charbagh at Kabul before he conquered Hindustan, we would be tempted to see this as the invention of Hindu rather than Islamic architects.

"Already in the design of ancient Indian cities we find the same quadripartite divisions, with each caste being allotted its specific quarter. As early as the second millenium BC Aryan villages were already built in the form of a St. Andrews Cross, at the center of which stood the tree under which the elders met. This management of the cosmic axis reappears in Buddhist architecture, as a period 'honorary umbrella', as well as in the Hindu temples of Southern India, as a cella standing on a small island in a square lake. From this it was but a modest step to the classical Indo-Islamic charbagh complex. The axial streets had water ways: in the middle of the lake stood the 'Baradari', an open water pavilion modeled on the Persian prototype: the garden was enclosed by a high wall such as surrounds all large Hindu temples. A mausoleum may take the place of the pavilion. The first such monumental garden containing a tomb is the one surrounding Humayun's mausoleum in Delhi. Each hedge and each tree serves to accentuate the square network of waterways." Andreas Volwahsen, like most other European scholars is quite confused about the origin of the Indian garden art. Though he admits that the so-called charbagh pattern can be exactly fitted in the square form of the vastupurushamandala, he still believes that these garden patterns are Persian. Even the so-called Baradari finds its origin in the Shilpa-Shastra in the form of pillard pavilions. Such garden pavilions were a part of ancient Indian gardens also. The garden surrounding 'Humayun's tomb, the Taj Mahal garden and the old Indian garden planning tradition which is followed in the gardens inside the Rajput palaces at Amber and elsewhere.

(b) Water Reservoirs and Channels

Climatic conditions made it essential to provide a continuous supply of water for the gardens through a network of water channels. The rigid geometric division of the gardens was carried out by means of irrigation system. Some European scholars while tracing the fancied Persian influence in the planning of so-called charbagh gardens in India exhibit a 16th or 17th Century Persian 'garden carpet' as a proof of its origin. The same scholars fail to take stock of the advancement of knowledge achieved by Indo-Aryans not only in garden planning but irrigation systems also.

Indo-Aryans exhibited considerable knowhow in the field of hydraulic engineering. This is evident from the extent of ancient Indian engineering expounded in Brigu Samhita. The consummate engineering skill of ancient India is testified by a world famous irrigation specialist, Sir Williams Willcox in the following words: "Following the genius of your country, your ancient writers described the physical facts that they were writing about in the Puranas in spiritual language, but facts were there all the same. Every canal, which went Southwards, whether it has become a river like Bhagirathi, or remained a canal like the Mathabhanga, was originally a canal. They were lined out and dug fairly parallel to each other, they were spaced apart and placed just about the distance apart that canals should be placed. I remember quiet well when I begun to line out a system of canals for the irrigation of the country. I was astonished to find everywhere that so called 'Dead River' on the map was just where a canal should be placed."

Wells, like canals, were also used for irrigation purpose in ancient India. While commenting on the mastery of Indo-Aryans in this field, in the chapter titled 'Early Forms of Storage and Irrigation', a longmans Green publications states, "The classic method of using natural storage is that of tapping the sub-soil water by means of wells. In India, the use of deep wells, the volume of water used restricted, and in the Indo-Gangetic alluvial plain use of the sub-soil water found nearer the ground surface helps. The early inhabitants of India were masters in the art of sinking wells of brick masonry in sandy soil. Many of these originally sunk to a great depth near the banks of rivers have survived subsequent river embankments and have inspired engineers centuries later to employ wells as foundations for constructions built on shifting sand foundations in river beds. Contemporary with this early form of irrigation was the practice of cultivating the margins of rivers exposed annually on the recession of flood". This is an eye opener for those who believed that the irrigation systems were not known in India prior to the Mohammedan invasion. All types of canals, lakes, cisterns, wells and stepped wells were effectively used for the irrigation systems in ancient India. The same expertise and knowledge was used for irrigating gardens in ancient and medieval period with great skill.

The sensed quality of a place is an interaction between its form and its perceiver. It is irrelevant in a sewer layout or in an automated warehouse. But wherever people are, it is a crucial quality. Sensuous requirements may concede or conflict with other demands but cannot be separated from them in judging a place. They are not "impractical", or merely decorative, or even nobler than other concerns. Sending is being alive. Perception includes aesthetic experience, where the dialogue between perceiver and object is immediate, tense and profound, seemingly detached from other consequences. But it is also an indispensable component of everyday life.

What we look for in a landscape is a technically organized subject so that its parts work together, but which is also perceptually coherent one whose visual image is congruent with its life and action. In nature an integrated landscape is shaped by the consistent impact of well-balanced forces of five elements. In art it is the result of comprehensive purpose spillfully applied.

The designer shapes his form so that it will be willing partner in that sensed interaction, helping the perceiver to create a coherent, meaningful and moving image.

(c) How to Give Natural Shape to Landscape by Applying the Law of Five Elements

The designer works to enhance the expression of place: to communicate its nature as a system of living things residing in a particular habitat. To this end, he will open up woodland, put a meeting house on the dominant point, accentuate the topography, or create an oasis in an arid climate. Using his knowledge of perception, he sharpens the rooted, indigenous character by means of simplification and contrast, by the principle of five elements.

(1) Air

The sensuous experience of a place is first a spatial one, a perception of the volume of air that surrounds the observer, read through the eyes, the ears, and the skin. Outdoor space, like architectural space, is made palpable by light and sound and defined by enclosure. But it has characteristics that have implications for site planning. Site space is more extended than architectural space and loose in its form. Horizontal dimensions are normally much greater than the vertical ones. Structures are less geometric, connections less precise, shapes more irregular. A deviance in plan that would be intolerable in a room may even be desirable in a city square. The site plan uses different materials—notably earth, rock, water and plants—and is subject to constant change: the rhythm of human cycles, the cumulative effects of growth, decay and alteration. The light that gives it forms shifts with the hour, day and season. The place is seen in sequence, and over an extended period of time.

These differences call for corresponding variations of technique. The looseness of outdoor space, combined with the difficulty that any but a trained eye has in estimating distance, plan, form, or gradient allows

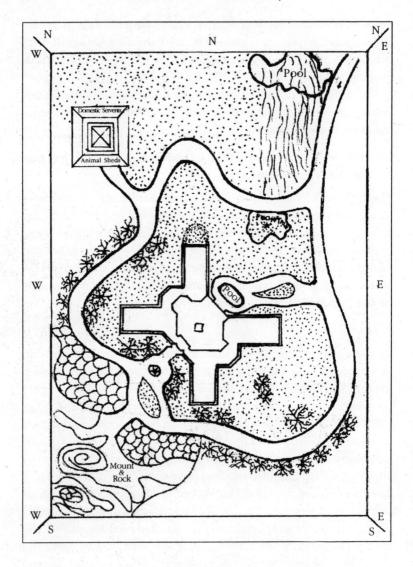

Land Scaping of Pedestrian, Road Side Lawn's and Car Parking

Diagram 2

AIR MOVEMENT AND SPEED

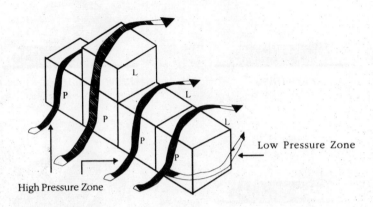

Low Pressure Zone

High Pressure Zone

FIG. I AIR MOVEMENT AND CALM ZONE

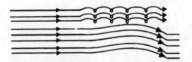

FIG. II (a) WITHOUT WIND BREAK

(b) WITH THICK TREE'S

FIG. III PLANTED WIND BREAK
(a) Sparse Planting
(b) Thick Planting

Landscaping to Modify Micro-climate

Diagram 3

AIR-FLOW PATTERN

AT BUILDING   5 FEET FROM BUILDING AT CENTER

10 FEET FROM BUILDING

10 FEET FROM BUILDING AT CENTER

20 FEET FROM BUILDING

WITHOUT LANDSCAPING

30 FEET FROM BUILDING

Air Flow Pattern Modification with Landscaping

Diagram 4

a certain freedom of layout. Flaws can be masked and illusions created: two water bodies coalesce because their outlines seem to match; a large object disappears because it is blocked out by a small thing nearby; an axis appears straight, although in reality it is bent. Level areas tilt by contrast with adjacent counterslopes. The apparent relative elevations of two objects may be reversed by the treatment of the grades adjacent to them.

(2) Space

Trees, hedges, buildings define outdoor spaces and hills but are rarely completely enclosed. They are partially bounded, their form completed by the shape of the floor and by small elements that mark-off imaginary aerial definitions. Since horizontal things dominate, the out-of-doors, vertical features take on an exaggerated importance. We are surprised to find that our photographs of awesome mountain landscape record a minor disturbance of the horizon. Level changes can define spaces and create effects of dynamic movement. A regularly organized space will be tilted easily if it contains a steep slope. Thus, it is safer to make up vertical differences in the approach or in the transitions between important openings. The general shape of a site plan may have less bearing on its success than its levels, or the small projections or focal objects that make up the real visual space on the ground. But once a readable space is established, it has a strong emotional impact. The intimacy of a small enclosure and the exhilaration of a great opening are universal sensations. The transition between the two is even stronger: the powerful sense of contraction or release.

Spaces are enclosed by opaque barriers, but also by walls that are semi-transparent or broken. Space definers may be visual suggestions rather than visual stops: colonnades, bollards, even changes in ground pattern or the imaginary extensions of things. Buildings have been the traditional enclosures of urban space, but the demand for open areas around the buildings has grown. Overlaps and staggered openings may mask such breaks, by bridging the street, by screen walls and colonnades, or even by a continuous line of low fencing. More often now, enclosure is achieved with trees and hedges, supported by the shaping of the ground. Trees may form great walls, or columnar lines, or canopies overhead. Shrubs, on the other hand, are of human height length, and so are more decisive obstacles to our vision and our movement.

Other effects are due to our angle of vision and to the way in which we scan a scene. An object whose major dimension equals its distance from the eye is difficult to see as a whole but can be scanned in detail.

When it is twice as far, it appears as a unit; when it is three times as far, it is still dominant in the visual field but tends to be seen in relation to other objects. As the distance increases beyond four times the major dimension, the object becomes one element of the general scene, unless it has other qualities that focus our attention. Thus, an external enclosure is most comfortable when its walls are one-half to one-third as high as the width of the space enclosed, while, if that ratio falls below one-fourth, the space begins to lack a sense of enclosure. If the height of the walls is greater than the width, then one ceases to notice the sky. The space becomes a pit or trench or outdoor room—secure or stifling depending on its scale with respect to the body and how the light falls into it. Another example of a visual rule based on the human anatomy is our sensitivity to an ambiguity at eye level as might be caused by a narrow barrier at that level or by a vertical surface terminating there. Vision should be kept clear at that touchy elevation or decisively blocked. Walls should either be low or over six feet high; railings at eye-level are to be avoided.

The appearance of a space is modified by the activity that goes on within it, by the way one passes through it by the color and texture of walls and floor, by the way it is lighted and the objects with which it is furnish. An empty room is notoriously smaller than the same room when furnished; distances are shortened over open water. A few an-sized objects can establish a scale relation between a person and a big space, and a tall object can relate a small space to a larger world. Blue and grey surfaces seem farther away, while hot, strong colors advance toward us.

(3) Light and Sun

The light that bathes a space is a determinant of its character. Light will sharpen or blur definitions, emphasize silhouette or texture, conceal or reveal, contract or expand dimensions. An object frontally lit is flattened, while sidelights bring out its surfaces. This is the effect produced by the grazing rays of morning and evening sun or the vertical illumination of a tropical sun. Light reflected from below brings out unsuspected qualities, which may be dramatic or disturbing. Backlight makes silhouettes and polarizes tones to black and white.

Silhouetted objects are prominent visual features, and the designer is always careful about things that appear against the sky. Shadow patterns can be attractive features—large masses or delicate traceries, dark and opaque or scintillating with light. Shadows may explain the modeling of a surface. A lighted opening seen beyond a shadowed wood is a dramatic vision.

Most sites are now used at night as well as in the daytime, and some even more intensively after dark. Artificial light can modify a space even create it after the sun has set, transform textures, pick out entrances, indicate the structure of paths or the presence of activity, confer a special character. Fine trees or monuments can be dramatized, moving water can be made to glow and sparkle; changing light can be an intriguing display in itself. This resource is rarely used effectively. The fear of crime, our obsession with the moving vehicle, the false standards' of the lighting industry, and the costs of energy and of maintenance have all conspired to impose a harsh, even, yellow glare on us. The varied requirements of pedestrians and driver, the need to differentiate and structure the night time scene, the pleasure of modulation and visual drama, the qualities of moonlight and starlight, indeed the wonder of darkness itself, are all banished. Utilitarian standards, mechanically applied, flatten out the visual landscape, except in an occasional extravaganza of signs or shop windows.

The sense of hearing also conveys the shape of space. Nocturnal animals and blind human beings use echo-location to move through the world. We interpret an absence of echo, for example, as extended openness. Similarly, if to a lesser extent, the feel of a surface (or how it looks as if it should feel) affects us and by the presence of a wall is reinforced if it reflects sound, or looks rough to touch, or radiates heat. Places have particular smells that are part of their identity, even if it is undignified in our culture to say so. The micro-climate is a marked feature of a place: it will be remembered as cool and moist, hot, bright and windy, or warm and sheltered. All these sensations of light, sound, smell and the designer can exploit through touch, although he is not accustomed to do so.

Forms have common symbolic connotations: the awesomeness of great size and the pleasurable interest of diminutive scale; the aspirations of tall, slender verticals, and the passivity and permanence of the horizontal line; the closed, static appearance of circular forms and the dynamism of projecting jagged shapes. Strong feelings are evoked by fundamental elements of human shelter, such as the roof and the door, and by basic natural materials, such as earth, rock, water and trees.

Sight lines are manipulated in the design by slight shifts in ground level or path direction or by the position of opaque barriers. The eye may be directed by framing or sub-dividing the view or be drawn along a path or rank of repeated forms. The visual attraction of some focal object can blot out the surrounding detail. A distant view is enhanced by a foreground with which it is contrasted. Indeed, it is often the middle ground that is most difficult to manage, and a design may mask it out by planting or by a drop in level so that some carefully chosen foreground detail can stand against the distant landscape. The distant view itself can be organized by what is permitted to be seen. Seats and shelters are located at key points for some special contemplation: to watch the dawn, see the moon on the water, enjoy the autumn foliage or the wind blowing through the bamboo. The garden is a set of carefully prepared sensations, linked but distinct.

Since a moving observer usually experiences the landscape, especially in our day, the single view is not as important as the cumulative effect of a sequence than the balance over time. Coming out of a narrow slot into a wide expanse is a strong effect. The dancing of the landscape as one moves by it can be a pleasure. Potential motion takes on importance: a road suggests direction and the eye follows as a connecting thread. Broad, flat steps invite one; a narrow, curving street leads to some hidden promise. Orientation is significant—the direction to some goal, the marking of the distance traversed, the clarity of entrance and exit, the location of the observer in the structure of the whole. A major view may be hinted at, that hint can be succeeded by an intimate scene, the view then can reappear behind a dominant foreground, to be replaced by a tightly confined space and at last open fully before one. A succession of arrivals, like the runs and landings of a stair will be more interesting than a protracted approach. Each new event prepared for the next: an ever new but coherent development. A number of graphic languages have been invented to make the design of sequence possible.

The form of motion itself has meaning: direct or indirect, fluid or formal, smooth or erratic, purposeful or whimsical. Objects can be disposed to heighten this sense of motion. The observer's speed is significant since vision is restricted to a narrow forward quadrant as speed increases, and spatial effects that are pleasant at a walking pace may be imperceptible at 60 miles per hour. The spatial form, seen as a sequence, is a fundamental component of the site plan. So, it is often useful to outline the spaces lying between the opaque objects in order to study this primary visual sensation. These spaces must not be thought of flatware, however, but as a progression through which one moves. Sequence is the radial difference between landscape and pictorial composition, along with our perception of space by scanning and peripheral vision. That why it is often impossible to take good photographs of fine environments.

Spaces are primarily defined by vertical surfaces, but the only continuous surface is underfoot. The configuration of this floor is determined by the existing topography, although modern machinery now allows rapid, cheap (and risky) reshaping of land, such as the point at which the gradient changes abruptly or from which a commanding view may be enjoyed. The land may be divisible into small regions, each of homogenous character, linked to one another along certain strategic lines. Most sites have their own special character or come pivotal features to which the plan can respond. Sites of strong character will dictate the basic organization of the plan and call for a simple arrangement that clarifies the terrain. Flat ground and sites of more neutral character allow a freer, more intricate patterning.

There is an easy visual relation between a manmade structures and rolling topography when the long dimension of the structure, whether a road or a building, lies along the contour lines. The base level of the structure meets the ground happily, its alignment accentuates the landform, and the natural contours are left relatively undisturbed. This is often the cheapest solution. On the other hand, if contour following is used on steep ground, then the land falls sharply toward or away from the structure on either side, and this may cause difficulties of drainage or harmonious appearance. Here the best solution is to let the road or access of the building plunge directly across the contours. Road gradients will then be steep, and the cross-fall across the face of the building may have to be handled by step-like forms, but the topographic structure is dramatized just as the streets of San Francisco, which seem to ignore the contours, or in fact are very expressive of them. When the axes are diagonal to the contours, however, a more awkward relation occurs.

(4) Earth

Rock and earth are the friendly site materials; our environmental base. Cut and fills, pits and outcrops, cliffs, caves, and hills communicate sense of mass, a sense of endurance, and intuition of the planet whose surface we inhabit. Rock is a handsome material. We hide it with topsoil or use it in rock gardens. It expresses strength and permanence, the working of powerful forces over long span of time. It displays a great range of color, grain and surface texture, especially when it is long weathered. It appears as pebbles cobbles, boulders, beds and massive outcrops; men fashion it into sets, blocks, slates, slabs and crushed fragments. Stone is expensive but can be the ideal material for wall, steps and pavings. Weathered stones are stunning objects in the landscapes, then the manner in which the local rock is exposed must be carefully observed, whether as ledge or talus, or scattered boulders. On the other hand, the bold artificial cut through rock strata seen along our highway is often their most striking feature.

(5) Water

Water is equally elemental but extremely varied in its effects. The number of its names in the common language marks its richness; ocean, pool, sheet, jet, torment, rill, drop, spray, cascade, film, stream, rivulet, mist, wave, pond, lake—to which add the words for liquid motion; trickle, splash, foam, flood, pour, spout, spurt, ripple, surge, run, seep. The form, the changeableness and yet the unity, the intricate repetitive fluid movement, the suggestion of coolness and delight, the play and sound, as well as its intimate connection with life and its attraction for birds and animals, all make water a superb material for outdoor use. It affects sound, smell, and touch, as well as sight.

Moving water gives a sense of life; still water conveys unity and rest. But water must appear to lie naturally within the land: it appears tilted and unstable unless the ground slopes down to it. Water plays with light, and if still can act as a mirror. Unruffled, brimful, and with open borders, it reflects the changing sky. If dark and low, it catches the images of sunlight and things nearby. If shallow, a dark button improves reflectivity. Water running in the shade is a grateful thing in a hot and arid climate. In a grey, humid one, it will seem damp and gloomy and so is better disposed where it will be open to the sky.

(d) The Sound and the Movement

The form of its container enhances the sound and the movement of the running water. A well-crafted channel will throw water into the air, strike it against obstacles, and make it swirl and gurgle. If the lip of a fall is undercut, then all its volume will be visible, its force heard and seen, as it drops into a pool below. A small amount of water can perform repeatedly, to make a surprisingly large effect. The Moorish gardeners were masters of this. Even a tiny drip will strike a musical note. The Japanese may use only a slow-dripping source in the shade, or even a symbolic stream of rock and sand.

So magnetic is the attraction of water that observers look inward towards it, and so it can be the centerpiece of a design. Its edge is the important feature and requires careful thought. That edge can be abrupt and definite, or low, shelving and obscure. A simple form conveys clarity and stability. If complex and partly hidden, it evokes expectancy and extended space. Stones just below the water surface make its depth legible. Objects at the water's edge are sharply seen; the Japanese place their waterside stones with great care. To make a natural shore, one must attend to the ways of water in that region. But if there will be many people about, it will be wiser to pave the water's edge, since it is sure to attract hard wear.

For all its quality, water can be expensive to introduce and to maintain especially in an urban setting. It may raise safety problems. It catches trash and dust, and exhibits them proudly. It breeds insects and weeds; it floods, erodes its banks, and fills it with silt. It is a dynamic, transitory element of the echo system. The designer must decide whether to provide clean water, free of plants and other living

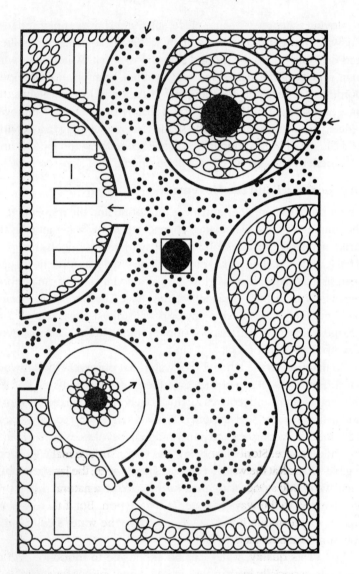

Treeless Landscape
- Dry
- Rock Garden
- Pattern and Forms

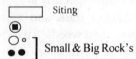

Diagram 5

ELEVATION

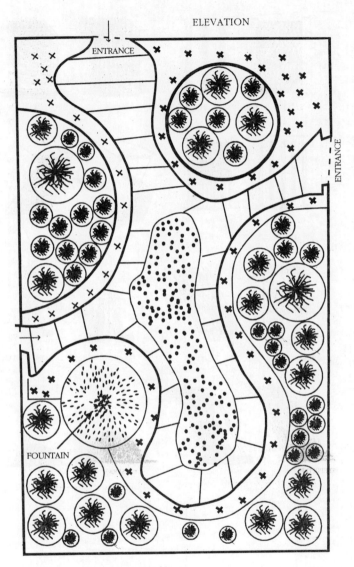

PLAN

- Pattern and Forms
- With Dry Wood and Artificial Plants

Diagram 6

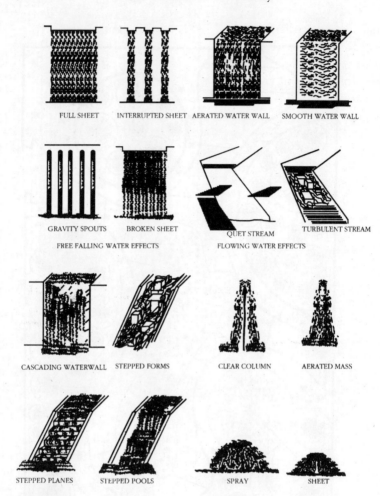

FULL SHEET   INTERRUPTED SHEET   AERATED WATER WALL   SMOOTH WATER WALL

GRAVITY SPOUTS   BROKEN SHEET

FREE FALLING WATER EFFECTS

QUIET STREAM   TURBULENT STREAM

FLOWING WATER EFFECTS

CASCADING WATERWALL   STEPPED FORMS   CLEAR COLUMN   AERATED MASS

STEPPED PLANES   STEPPED POOLS   SPRAY   SHEET

Pools and Fountains, Free-Falling Water Effects

Diagram 7

things, or to make a balanced ecological system. If the former, he uses filtered and recycled water in artificial basins and provides for frequent cleaning. In the winter and during shutdowns for repairs or scrubbing, these containers will be dry and must be handsome in that guise. If the latter, he introduces the bottom soil, plants and fish which will compose a complete nutrient cycle. Along with them, of course, come the algae, mud and insect life which are part of that cycle, just as down timber and brush are part of a neutral woodland. A "clean" pond can be extremely shallow and can be located anywhere. A balanced pond needs sunlight, and of at least a foot and a half of depth, if small fish are to survive the winter. Either pond requires a watertight lining of masonry, puddle clay, or plastic sheeting.

Living Plants

Next in importance is the living plant material, the trees, shrubs, and herbs, the material popularly associated with landscape work, which is usually thought to be concerned with the spotting of trees on a plan after buildings and roads have been located. More correctly, the plant cover is one element in the organization of outdoor space. Some great landscapes are treeless and there are handsome squares that do not include a plant of any description. Nevertheless, plants are one of the fundamental materials. If in public, we worship the tree, in practice we destroy it. Planting is the 'extra' in-site development, the first item to be cut when the budget pinches.

Site planning is concerned with groups of plants and the general character of planted areas rather than with individual specimens. Trees, shrubs, and ground covers are the basic materials. Trees are the backbone; they form the structure of the plan, while the occasional specimen tree may be used for particular effect. Simple in essence, intricate in form, fluttering and swaying in the wind, leafless or deep with foliage, they are enduring and yet alive. The shrubs, man-height, are the effective space formers. They are privacy screens and barriers to movement.

Plants take on a bewildering variety of forms under the influence of their environment, and those forms change as the plant grows and ages. But each species has its own habit of growth, its own way in which leaves, stems and buds are connected and succeed each other. This

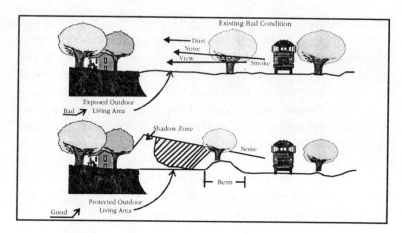

A: Landscaping for Noise Control and Wind Control near Main Road

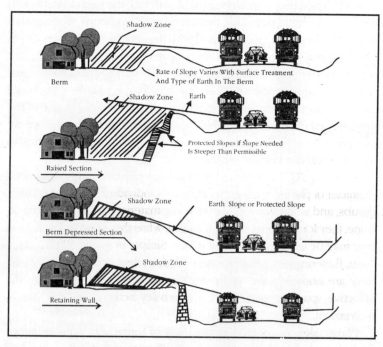

B: Alternative Method under Different Conditions

Diagram 8

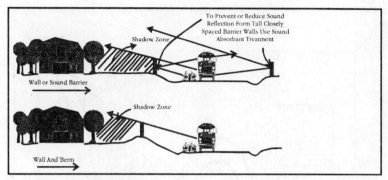

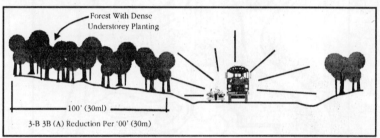

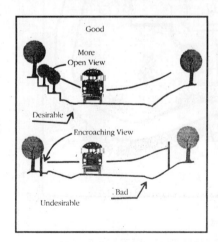

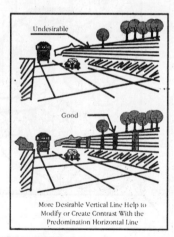

Landscaping for Highway and Roadway Design for
Control of Noise, Sound, Dust and Smoke

Diagram 9

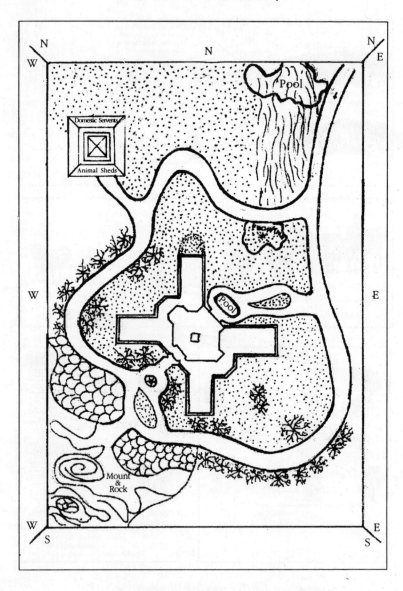

Land Scaping of Pedestrian, Road Side Lawn's and
Car Parking

Diagram 10

pattern, distorted by any one individual by the accidents of age and exposure, produces the characteristics mass, structure, and texture of that species. When working at the site planning scale, dispose plants according to their habit texture and mass as a group, rather than by their individual form, since the former are the features that can be predicted and are less likely to vary from different points of view. The surface of a plant may have texture that is fine or coarse, shiny or dull, closed or open, stiff or trembling, clustered or even, smooth or modeled in depth. The habit may be prostrate, upright, vasiform, fastigiate, main-stemmed, crookedly branching, or high canopied.

Other characteristics, such as growth rate, eventual size, color, life span, scent and seasonal effect are the next considerations. Species must be chosen which are hard for a given micro-climate and soil condition. They must stand up to the expected traffic, be resistant to disease and insect attack, and demand no more care than can be furnished at the expected level of maintenance. Desert urban areas are particularly difficult for plants because of lack of water, light and humidity, as well as air pollution, the reflected sound, and the presence of poisonous chemicals. Trees must be specially chosen for this harsh habitat. Impervious paved surfaces must be kept at least three feet from their trunk.

Landscaping to Modify Micro-climate

This freedom to deceive imposes a corresponding responsibility to make a clearly connected whole. A simple, readable, well-proportioned outdoor space is a powerful event. Structure is explained in a way that purely natural forces rarely accomplish. Connections are established that defy time and distance. Dimensions difficult to grasp are made legible by visual measuring devices. One part is connected with the whole by echoes of shapes or material. The designer uses every resource to confirm the form he seeks with an air of mystery and doubt, he makes sure that spaces are well defined and clearly joined. Changes in plan are co-ordinated with changes in section.

Light, color, texture and details reinforce spatial dimensions. The eye judges distance by many features, and some of them can be manipulated to exaggerate or to diminish apparent depth, such as the overlapping of distant objects by closer ones; the paratactic movement of objects disposed in-depth when seen by the moving eyes; the way in which distant things "rise" toward the far horizon; the smaller size and finer texture of things far away, and their bluish color; or the apparent convergence of parallel lines. Used with restraint, the manipulation of such features heightens the spatial effect, whether by making real depth legible, as by planting a line of trees whose intersectings overlap and convergence in perspective mark off an otherwise "empty" distance, or by creating an illusion of depth, as by using smaller, blue-green, fine-textured trees in the background. In any illusion, there is always the danger that from some other viewpoint the trick will be exposed. An illusion of some characteristic that is indirectly perceived (such as level, or geometric plan) is easier to maintain. An illusion of direct perception, such as an imitation of the color and texture of some other material in a substitute, is far more difficult to carry out.

Some Vastu Tips on Landscaping

1. Rock and earth high mount must be on the West or Southwest side of the garden.
2. Moving water/waterfall should be from West to East or South-West to North-East flow.
3. The sound and running water must flow towards North or East or North-East slope.
4. Water pool, water body, lotus plant flower is recorded on the North or North-East Side of the garden.
5. Tall or shaded trees must be planted on Southwest to West Side.
6. Seasonal plants, shrubs, flower plants with green grass be put on eastern side of the garden.
7. Tulsi be put either at Brahm Sthan i.e. center courtyard or eastern northern part of the house on a higher platform/pedestal.
8. Neem tree is planted on Westnorth corner.
9. Peepal or bard tree on Westsouth corner with maximum distance from building.
10. Eucalyptus on West or Westnorth and or where the sub-soil level of the ground much above the ground level.

11. No family of Cactus plant particularly those having sharp thorns, should be put near buildings or inside house, their right place being the desert and are thus associated with barren influences.

12. Ashok trees are planted near where females spend their maximum time.

13. Banana trees are planted where white-ants give problems and to keep the white ants away plant banana tree.

14. Many Vastu consultants were not allowing Bonsai plants in most homes. Suppressing the growth of a tree capable of achieving its full form imparts it with negative vibration though there are cases where vastudoshas are corrected using particular Bonsai plants.

15. In general, Vastu Shastra prohibits thorny trees like *ber, babool* as well as trees from which white milky extracts exude, like the mahua and vata.

16. Trees with a big spread like that of banyan, peepal, mango and tall trees like coconut should not be planted in the east and North-East as they block out the early morning beneficial sun. Also peepal, tamarind and banyan tree is not meant for homes.

17. Shaded trees especially the larger ones should be planted on the southern and western borders and care should be taken that their shadow does not fall on the main building till the afternoon.

18. The fruit trees like jamun, plantain, mango and jackfruit are considered very auspicious in the southern part of the garden.

19. Palm, amla, vat, tamarind, silk-cotton trees are normally grown in a house as they are said to destroy wealth. Coconut, betel, *neem,* margosa, bilva, sandal, tulsi, marigold (red), roses (all except black), *raat ki rani, champa,* jasmine, are also auspicious. Other plants considered good by Vastu pradeep are the Ashok, *naagkeshar, shami, palash, arisht, maulsree* etc. Out of these the Ashok tree is said to banish all vastudoshas when planted at the periphery.

Chapter 10

Positive and Negative Energies

We usually talk about the Positive and Negative Energies, in our daily life in houses, work places, travelling or even when we are not doing any job or resting.

But what are these energies? Is it generated within ourselves, from the human body? Or from the surrounding environments? Or from the Nature? These are the big questions generally our minds put up.

Before we find answers to these questions, let us discuss and try to find out the type of energies and from where they come?

As well we all know human body generates energy and produces current and voltage to keep the body active and healthy, but after a day-long work the body exhaust major portion of the energy and to regain the energy, body the needs food. This is inner energy.

Similarly, we need outer energy, which we get from our surroundings and environment in which we are living and working. These are two basic forms of energy. A day energy which we call positive energy. The solar energy we get during the day.

All human beings work during the positive energy. The second part is during night when we do not get solar radiation it is negative energy and we do not work and take rest. From the nature also we can learn that all animals, birds etc., start their job right from sunrise and go to there nests at sunset. They are healthy and do not require any medical attention. *Refer Diagram Number 1 and 2.*

In both parts of energy, our body is surrounded by two major energy forms. One is gifted by Nature and the second form of energy is created by man. Both of these energies human eyes cannot see with their naked eyes. Only about 10 percent can be seen or visualized, but these energies can be measured by the help of instruments *Refer Diagram 3.* These are Direct and Indirect Energies or Positive and Negative Energies. *Refer Diagram 4.*

POSITIVE AND NEGATIVE ENERGIES

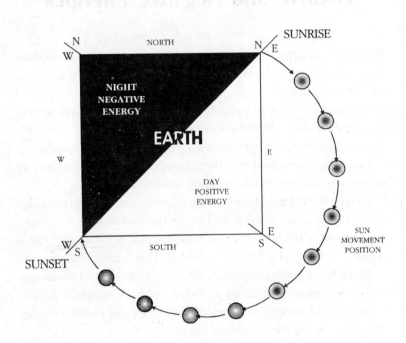

Diagram 1

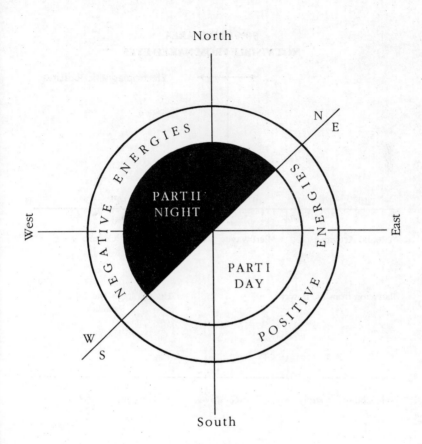

North

West

East

South

N
E

W
S

NEGATIVE ENERGIES

POSITIVE ENERGIES

PART II
NIGHT

PART I
DAY

**NATURAL ENERGY
THE GIFT OF NATURE**

Diagram 2

Energies Created by Modern Science for 21ˢᵗ Century

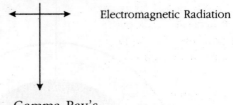

90% BLIND AREA
NOT VISIBLE FROM NAKED EYES

Electromagnetic Radiation

Gamma Ray's

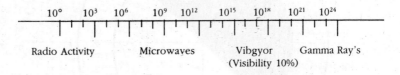

10^0 10^3 10^6 10^9 10^{12} 10^{15} 10^{18} 10^{21} 10^{24}

Radio Activity   Microwaves   Vibgyor   Gamma Ray's
                                (Visibility 10%)

Radiation from AC Power   High Voltage Transmission
                                        Radiation

FM   TV   X-Rays

Tele Communication   Radio Waves   Ultraviolet   Rays

Light

Satellite   Cell Phone   Infra-red Radiation

10^9 10^6 10^3 10^0 10^{-3} 10^{-6} 10^{-9} 10^{-12} 10^{-15}

◄——————— Wavelength in Frequency HZ ———————►

Diagram 3

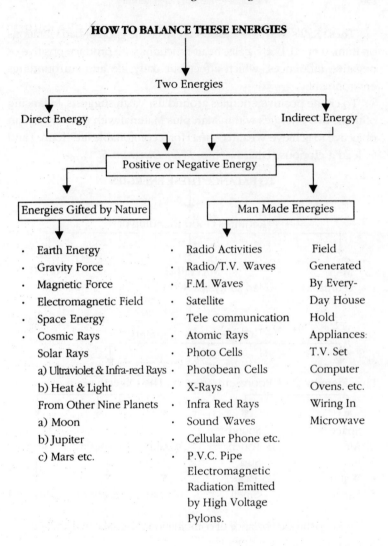

HOW TO BALANCE THESE ENERGIES

Two Energies

Direct Energy   Indirect Energy

Positive or Negative Energy

Energies Gifted by Nature   Man Made Energies

- Earth Energy
- Gravity Force
- Magnetic Force
- Electromagnetic Field
- Space Energy
- Cosmic Rays
  Solar Rays
  a) Ultraviolet & Infra-red Rays
  b) Heat & Light
  From Other Nine Planets
  a) Moon
  b) Jupiter
  c) Mars etc.

- Radio Activities
- Radio/T.V. Waves
- F.M. Waves
- Satellite
- Tele communication
- Atomic Rays
- Photo Cells
- Photobean Cells
- X-Rays
- Infra Red Rays
- Sound Waves
- Cellular Phone etc.
- P.V.C. Pipe
  Electromagnetic
  Radiation Emitted
  by High Voltage
  Pylons.

Field
Generated
By Every-
Day House
Hold
Appliances:
T.V. Set
Computer
Ovens. etc.
Wiring In
Microwave

These Rays and Waves create good/bad vibration and produce
Positive or Negative Energies, which effect our daily life and
surrounding. To create Positive Energies Vastu suggests

To Balance the Man+Material+Nature.

Diagram 4

These Ray's, waves or radiations can create good or bad vibrations on human mind, body, cells, heart functions with produce positive or negative influences, which affect our daily life and surroundings environment.

To create positive energies around us, Vastu suggests, balancing of these two energies within Man plus Material with nature, with an objective to achieve Wealth (Artha) for a comfortable life (Kama) and to lead a glorious (Dharma) life. *Refer Diagram 5.*

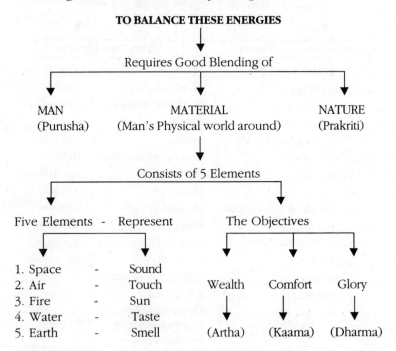

To Keep the total balance of combination "Man, Material and Nature" in relation with five elements.

Diagram 5

Sloka

> *shastrenanen Servasya Lokasya Param Sukham |*
> *chaturvaerga Phalprapti Shlokash Bhavedyuvam ||*
> *shilp Shastra Parigyana Mrityoapi Sujatham Vrajet |*
> *parmanand Janakasya Devanamidimiritam ||*
> *shilpvinah Nahi Jagtishu Lokeshu Vidyate |*
> *jagadVina Na Shilpanch Vertatae Vasav Prabho ||*

Meaning: Because of Vastu Shastra the whole Universe gets good health, happiness and all round prosperity. Human Beings attain divinity with this knowledge. Followers of Vastu Shastra get not only worldly pleasures but also experience heavenly bliss.

Sloka

> *sukham Dhanani Budhimsch Santati Servadanrinam |*
> *priyanesham ch Sansidhim Servasyat Shubhlaxanam ||*
> *yatra Nindit laxmatra tahitesham vidhakrit |*
> *athservamupadeyam Yabhdavet Shubhlaxanam ||*
> *deshah purniwashch Sabhavisam Sanani Ch |*
> *yadyadidrisamanyashch Tathashreyaskaram Matam ||*
> *vastusahstradritetasya Na Syallaxannirnayah |*
> *tasmat Lokasya Kripya satmetbhaduriyate ||*

Meaning: Properly designed and pleasing house will be an abode of good health, wealth, family, peace and happiness. Negligence of canons of Architecture will result in bad name, sorrows and disappointments. So Vastu Shastra has brought works for the betterment of all and overall peace and welfare in the Universe.

How to balance these energies in relationship with human comfort level. I have tried to explain the five basic elements, with Vastu architecture transformation is related to materials very close to the Nature.

The 21st Century is going to be one of Super specialization in every field. Technologies are based on scientific search and research. Energy from the Space Refer *diagram 6,* Energy from Air *Refer diagram 7,* Energy from Sun (Fire) Refer *diagram 8,* Energy from Water *Refer diagram 9,* Energy from Earth *Refer diagram 10,* Earth has been scientifically explained with logic. A Vedic Tradition Graphic has been shown in *Diagram 11.*

To Balance the Energies in Relationship with Human Comfort Level

From the Space

1.	Basic Elements	Sound
2.	Technological Field	Vibration
3.	Instrument of Perception: a) To acquire Inward b) To acquire Outward	 Ear Speech
4.	Work Organs	Communication
5.	Controlling Central Force: a) Flow of Thoughts b) Emotions or Joy	Mind
6.	The Presiding Force	Cosmos Rays
7.	Supreme energy	Soul (Prana)

Vastu Architecture Transformation Related to Material and Technology

    (a) Silence
    (b) Acoustics
    (c) Reflection
    (d) Vibrations
    (e) Texture Surfaces
    (f) Texture Forms
    (g) Design Language System
    (h) Non-measurable Dimensions Depicting Mental Comforts.

From the Air

1.	Basic Elements	Touch
2.	Technological Field	Climate
3.	Instrumental of Perception a) To Acquire Inward b) To Acquire Outward	Skin finger
4.	Work Organs	Hands
5.	Controlling Central Force	Weather Conditioning
6.	Presiding force	Circulation System

Vastu Architecture Transformation Related to Material and Technology

(a)   Climatology: To Study and Apply in Design

From Sun (Fire)

1.	Basic Elements	Sun
2.	Technological Field	Light
3.	Instrumental of Perception a) To acquire Inward b) To acquire Outward	Eyes Heat
4.	Work Organs	Light and Heat
5.	Controlling Central Force	Color
6.	Presiding force	Texture (Visual)

Vastu Architecture Transformation Related to Materials and Technology

(a) Light
(b) Color
(c) Solar System (Gain or Loss)

From Water

1.	Basic Elements	Taste
2.	Technological Field	Life Source
3.	Instrumental of Perception a) To acquire Inward b) To acquire Outward	Tongue Sweating
4.	Work Organs	ANUS (Lower Part of the Canal)
5.	Controlling Central Force a) River b) Well c) Tube well	River
6.	Presiding Force	Sea

Vastu Architecture Transformation related to Material and Technology

    (a) Plumbing
    (b) Heating and Cooling
    (c) Water Supply System Net Work and Disposal
    (d) Sewerage System
    (e) Drainage System
    (f) Flora, Water Fall, Fountain, Pool
    (g) Water Management
    (h) Water Engineering

From Earth

1.	Basic Elements	Smell
2.	Technological Field	Basic Raw Material
3.	Instrumental of Perception a) To acquire Inward b) To acquire Outward	Nose Nose
4.	Work Organs	Genitals Procreates
5.	Controlling Central Force	Formation
6.	Presiding force	Mud (Earth)

Vastu Architecture Transformation related to Materials and Technology

   (a) Basic Building Raw Materials
   (b) Mud Architecture are famous internationally
   (c) Landscape
   (d) Insulation
   (e) Recycling

Chapter 11

Proportion and Measurement for Vastu Shilpa and Vastu Kala

The text of the Vastu Shastra has been waiting for hundreds of years to be unearthed from manuscripts which are quite inaccessible without the guidance of a special dictionary that would also be instrumental in bringing to light many new things hitherto left unexplained in inscriptions and general literature.

All architectural terms used in Manasara, with explanations in English and illustrative quotations from cognate literature were available for the purpose in Manasara series.

In Vastu Shastra, architecture is taken in its broadest sense and implies what is built or constructed. Thus, in the first place, it denotes all sorts of buildings, religious, residential and military and their auxiliary members and component mouldings. Secondly, it implies town planning; laying out gardens; constructing market places; making roads, bridges, gates; digging wells, tanks, trenches, drains, sewers, moats; building enclosure walls, embankments, dams, railings, ghats; flights of steps for hills, ladders etc. Thirdly, it denotes articles of house furniture, such as bedsteads, couches, tables, chairs, thrones, fans, wardrobes, clocks, baskets, conveyances, cages, nests, mills etc.

Vastu architecture also implies sculpture and deals with the making of phallic, idols of deities, statues of sages, images of animals and birds. It includes the making of garments and ornaments etc.

Vastu architecture is also concerned with such preliminary matters, as the selection of site, testing of soil, planning, designing, finding out cardinal points by means of gnomon, dialing; and astronomical and astrological calculations.

In this chapter, we discuss in brief about Pattern and Formation, Creation, Proportion and Measurement in regard to Vastu Shilpa and Vastu Kala.

In Vastu Shilpa there are two main branches:

- Deva Shilpa
- Manava Shilpa

They call it Shilpa Shastra.

The Deva Shilpa

The Deva Shilpa is mainly used for the designing and construction of temples, Garbha-Griha, *Pavillions* and the detailing of ornamental design such as decoration pillars, beams, walls, *jali* etc. Also, images of different Gods and Goddesses, deities and their ornaments.

The Manava Shilpa

The Manava Shilpa is mainly used for designing and construction of buildings, used for public utility such as Public Places, Public Buildings, Houses, Resting House (Dharamshala or Hotels) stables for horses, birds and their detailing of carvings in stone and in wood, on pillars beams, walls and furnishings. *Refer Diagram No. 1a & 1b.*

Proportion and Measurement in Vastu Shilpa and Vastu Kala

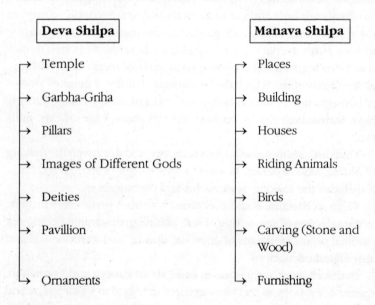

Deva Shilpa	Manava Shilpa
→ Temple	→ Places
→ Garbha-Griha	→ Building
→ Pillars	→ Houses
→ Images of Different Gods	→ Riding Animals
→ Deities	→ Birds
→ Pavillion	→ Carving (Stone and Wood)
→ Ornaments	→ Furnishing

VASTUPURUSHA MANDALA (YOGINI)

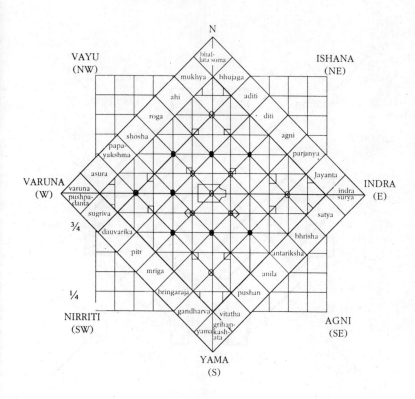

For Manava Shilpa and other Buildings

Diagram 1a

BRIHAT SAMHITA

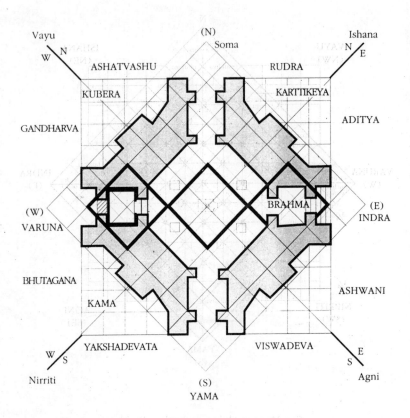

For Deva Shilpa
(Temple Design)

Diagram 1b

In Shilpa Shastra, the artist who is responsible for design and carving the design has to be very accurate in measurements and has to be particular about proportion in relation to height, breadth and length and their carvings have to be perfect to the scale.

The system of measurement was so perfect that the smaller unit of scale was 1/8 the human hair and was called *Paramanu* or the Atom as, explained below:

The System of Smallest Unit of Measurement in Shilpa Shastra was Paramanu or Atom

8 PARAMANU (ATOM)	=	1 HAIR END
8 HAIR END	=	1 NIT
8 NIT	=	1 LOUSE
8 LOUSE	=	1 BARLEY CORN
8 BARLEY CORN	=	1 ANGULA (FINGER)
ANGULA THE FINGER BREADTH = 3/4 INCHES)		
12 ANGULA	=	1 SPAN
2 SPAN OR 24 ANGULAS	=	1 HASTA
4 HASTAS	=	1 DHANUSH (BOW) OR DANDA (ROD)

Tala : A Principle Unit of Sculptural Measure Equal to the Length of the Force or (Storey)

Proportion and Measurements of Temple Building and Structure

The height of an image or structure or temple was determined and compared with its length and breadth. The same mainly of five proportions systems are highly technical and extremely minute in detail and are found in *Manasara II page 124 and vol. IV page 100 are:*

* Santika   (Height) = (breadth)

* Paushtika   (Height) = 1/4 of (breadth)

* Jayada   (Height) = 1, 1/2 (breadth)

* Dhanada   (Height) = 1, 3/4 (breadth)

* Adbhuta   (Height) = twice (breadth)

That is breadth - 12, 14, 16, 18, 20

Length - 13, 15, 17, 19, 21

Height - 22, 23, 24, 25, 26

In the case of large type building four-storeyed or more the dimension proportion are:

* *Breadth - 11, 13, 15, 17 or 19*

* *Length - 12, 14, 16, 18 or 20*

* *Height - 21, 22, 23, 24 & 25*

and so on.

They have two different scales, as system of measurement was for Deva Shilpa particularly for Deities where they have larger scales, a bigger measurement than for the Manava Shilpa. Similarly, they reduce their scales for Goddesses than to ordinary human then to animals and to birds etc., as shown and explained in

---

* (Manasara IV ch. XI Page No. 102)

VASTU KALA

Largest Type of Dasa Tala
with Comparative illustrations
of the other Nine Tala

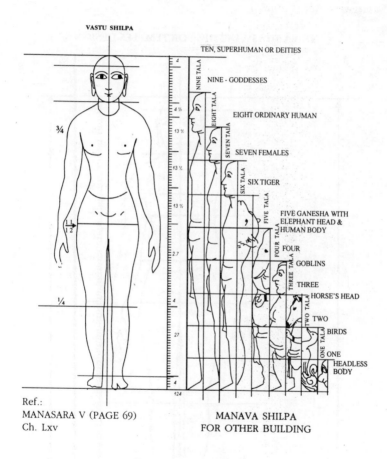

VASTU SHILPA

TEN, SUPERHUMAN OR DEITIES

NINE - GODDESSES

EIGHT ORDINARY HUMAN

SEVEN FEMALES

SIX TIGER

FIVE GANESHA WITH
ELEPHANT HEAD &
HUMAN BODY

FOUR

GOBLINS

THREE

HORSE'S HEAD

TWO

BIRDS

ONE

HEADLESS
BODY

Ref.:
MANASARA V (PAGE 69)
Ch. Lxv

MANAVA SHILPA
FOR OTHER BUILDING

Vastu Shilpa and Manava Shilpa

Diagram 2

Diagram Number No. 2.

The most interesting thing to know is that they were also more particular about the size, shape, proportion of the body line particularly for the Superhuman, The Deities. They used Plumb Lines to draw out perpendicular and horizontal proportion of the Body Line as shown in *Diagram No. 3 and 4.*

DEVA SHILPA DEITIES FOR TEMPLES DESIGN

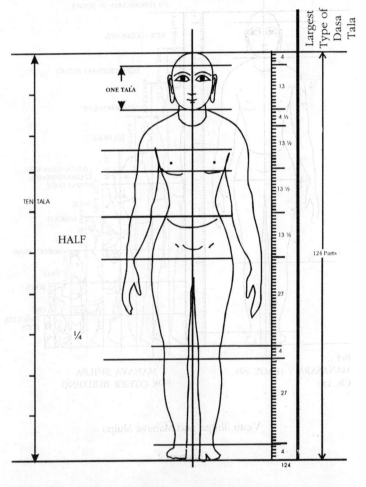

Largest Type of Dasa (Ten) Tala in this Measures of 124 Parts (Limbs) of the Body. It is used for Measuring Superhuman and Deities

Diagram 3

PLUMB LINES ELEVEN TO
FIND OUT PERPENDICULAR
AND
HORIZONTAL MEASUREMENTS

VASTU SHIPLA

Distance Measurement between Different Parts of the
Body of an Image

Diagram 4

In Vastu Kala also a particular attention has been given for the proportion of body line as shown in *Diagram No. 5.*

VASTU KALA

Diagram 5

Temple Buildings

In Temple Buildings they used stone and timber of different types and quality for structure, column and beams. Similarly, they give much attention to the proportion in respect to the height, breadth and length as shown in *Diagram No. 6*.

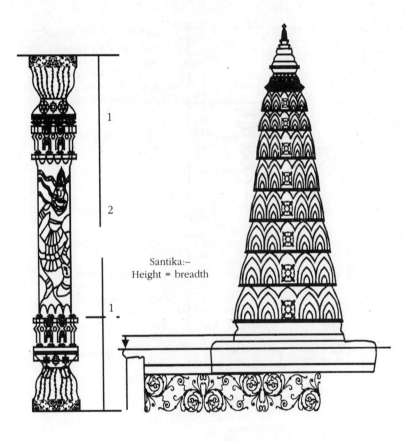

Santika:–
Height = breadth

Proportion Measurement

Diagram 6

Structure and Column (Stambha)

The roof rest on the load bearing column called (Stambha or Kumbha) of different shape from Square or Circular to Octagonal, Pentagonal and Hexagonal divided in four parts. The bottom part called Pedestal, then Base, then Shaft and upper part. *Refer Diagram 7.*

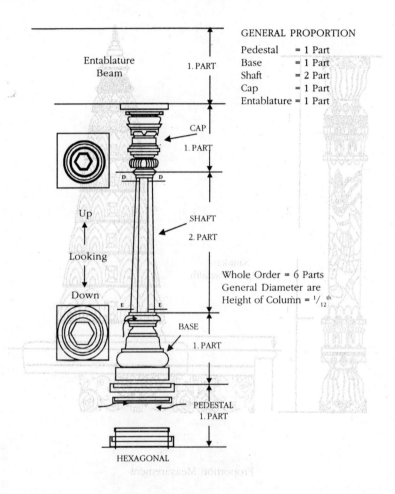

GENERAL PROPORTION

Pedestal　　= 1 Part
Base　　　 = 1 Part
Shaft　　　 = 2 Part
Cap　　　　= 1 Part
Entablature = 1 Part

Entablature
Beam　　　　　1. PART

CAP
1. PART

SHAFT
2. PART

Whole Order = 6 Parts
General Diameter are
Height of Column = $\frac{1}{12}^{th}$

BASE
1. PART

PEDESTAL
1. PART

Up

Looking

Down

HEXAGONAL

Column Kumbha-Stambha

Diagram 7

The detailed drawing of circular, square, Hexagon and Pentagonal Columns with beam (Entablature) and the supporting brackets are as shown in *Diagram 8 and 9*.

THE COLUMNS

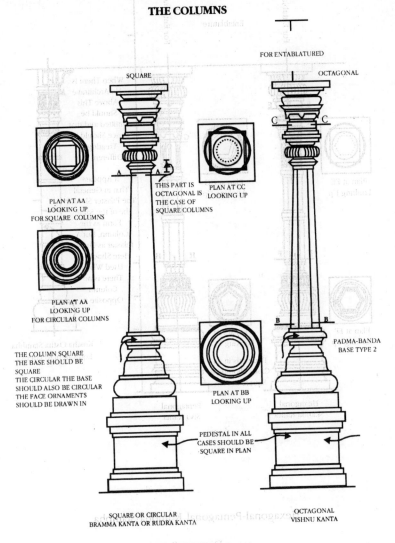

FOR ENTABLATURED

OCTAGONAL

SQUARE

PLAN AT AA
LOOKING UP
FOR SQUARE COLUMNS

THIS PART IS
OCTAGONAL IS
THE CASE OF
SQUARE COLUMNS

PLAN AT CC
LOOKING UP

PLAN AT AA
LOOKING UP
FOR CIRCULAR COLUMNS

THE COLUMN SQUARE
THE BASE SHOULD BE
SQUARE
THE CIRCULAR THE BASE
SHOULD ALSO BE CIRCULAR
THE FACE ORNAMENTS
SHOULD BE DRAWN IN

PLAN AT BB
LOOKING UP

PADMA-BANDA
BASE TYPE 2

PEDESTAL IN ALL
CASES SHOULD BE
SQUARE IN PLAN

SQUARE OR CIRCULAR
BRAMMA KANTA OR RUDRA KANTA

OCTAGONAL
VISHNU KANTA

The Palika Stambha Class

Diagram 8

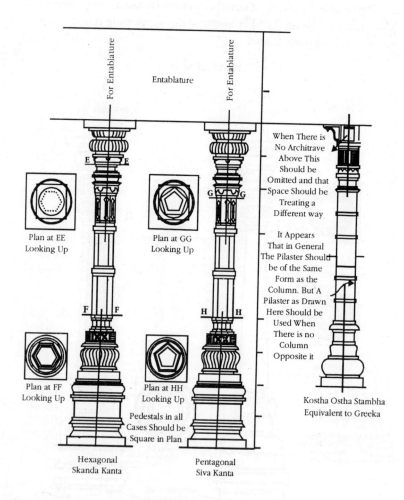

Hexagonal-Pentagonal Kumbha-Stambha

Diagram 9

Gates and Windows

They gave special attention in Vastu Shilpa and Vastu Kala Shastra for the position of Main Gate, its size and decoration according to the status of the owners *Refer Diagram No. 10*

The Gate-House and Windows–Ch. xxxiii
Windows for Temples, Kings, Brahmins, Vaishyas and Sudras.

Note:

The Windows openings have been divided into 4 Rectangular units and the *Jalis* have mainly been designed on those units.

The Window Walls for Temples and Palaced may be of an elaborate creepers pattern also.

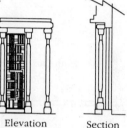

Elevation   Section

Windows for Vaishyas and Sudras

Plan

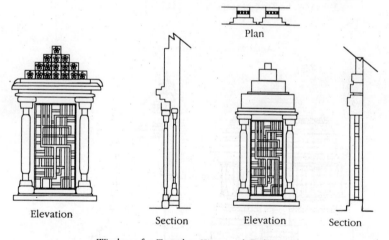

Elevation   Section   Elevation   Section

Windows for Temples, Kings and Brahmins

Plan   Plan

For Temples of King 'Kshatriyas' and Brahmins

Diagram 10

The other gates and window opening depend on the orientation of the building, the size of inner courtyard and numbers of storeys as described in *Diagram No. 11* for single storey building where windows and doors are on all the four sides.

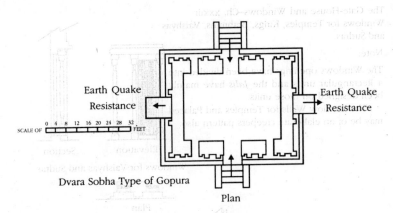

Earth Quake Resistance

Earth Quake Resistance

SCALE OF ⎓ 0 4 8 12 16 20 24 28 32 ⎓ FEET

Dvara Sobha Type of Gopura

Plan

Antar Mandala (Inner Court)

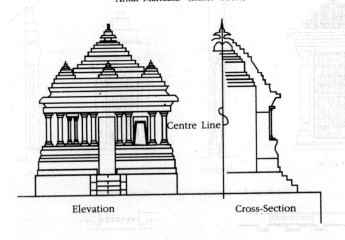

Centre Line

Elevation

Cross-Section

Dvara-Shobha (Beauty of the Gate) Single Storey for Temples & Residential

Diagram 11

In two-storey buildings, the first floor structure and load of structure have been taken on the extra column, taken from the inner courtyard *Refer Diagram No. 12* and open from all sides.

WINDOW AND GATE FOR TWO-STOREYS

The Gate Houses and Windows—

Dvar-Shala Type for the second Court
Length (In plan)=1 Width
Height in Elevation=Width

Note:

All these gate houses are both for Temples and Residential Buildings.
In residential building the Gopuras should always be less in number of storey's than the main edifice, but not so in Temples

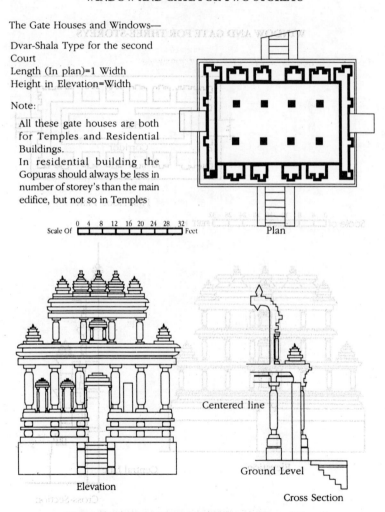

Scale Of   0 4 8 12 16 20 24 28 32   Feet

Plan

Centered line

Ground Level

Elevation

Cross Section

Dvara-Shala (Gate House) Antanihara (Second Court)
Earth Quake Resistance

Diagram 12

Similarly, in three-storey buildings, the first and second-storey are equal in size but smaller from ground floor. The load has been equally distributed in all four sides to balance the structure. Equal opening of windows has been provided *Refer Diagram No. 13.*

WINDOW AND GATE FOR THREE-STOREYS

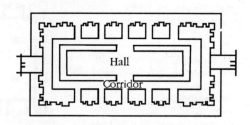

First Floor Plan

Scale of [0 4 8 12 16 20 24 28 32] FEET ▶

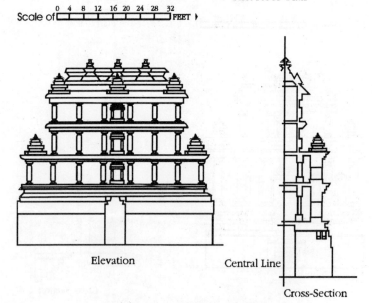

Elevation   Central Line

Cross-Section

Dvara-Prasada (Gate-Palace) (Third Court)
Earth Quake Resistance

Diagram 13

Four-storey buildings for temples or residence, the ground and first floor are equal in size as well as second floor and third floor are also equal but smaller than ground and first floor, windows and doors are all equal in size *Refer Diagram No. 14.*

FOR FOUR-STOREYS

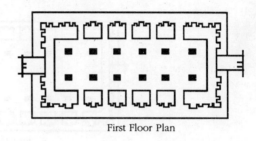

First Floor Plan

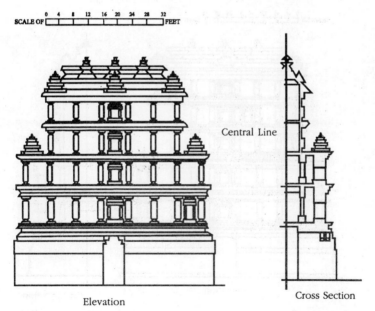

Elevation

Central Line

Cross Section

Dvara-Harmy (Gate-Edifice) Fourth Court for Temples & Residential Earthquake Resistence

Diagram 14

Five-Storey buildings had also been divided in equal proportion as shown in *Diagram No. 15.* In all the structures we observe that the plinth height is equal to ground floor to make the structure more safe and long lasting.

FOR FIVE-STOREYS

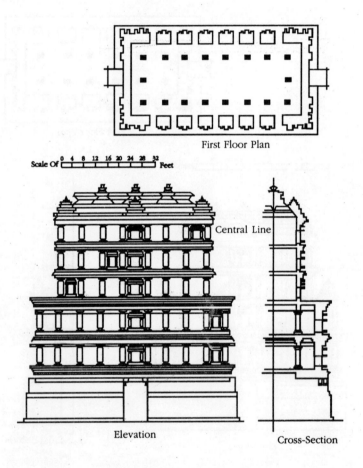

First Floor Plan

Scale Of ⊢ 0 4 8 12 16 20 24 28 32 ⊣ Feet

Central Line

Elevation   Cross-Section

Mahagopura (Grest Gate House) Extreme Boundary

Diagram 15

Timber Work of Temple

A very special and seasoned wood was after used for timber work of temples. All joints were wooden. Their tradition was not to use nail or screw for the jointary job. As per the principle of Vastu it was said that the positive energy comes from the main entry gate, door frame (chokhat) must be good seasoned wood with four members frame that too without using any nail or screw. *Refer Diagram No. 16 and 17.*

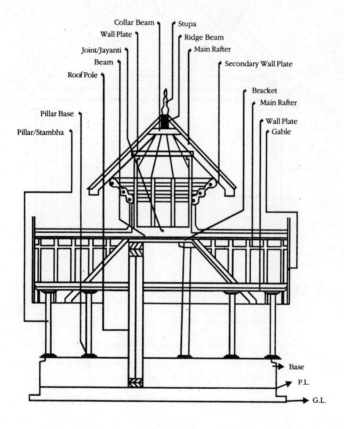

Timber Work of a Temple Gateway in Kerala Earthquake Resistance

(Ref: Mayamatam-Vol. 1, Pg. 16, Fig. 14)

Diagram 16

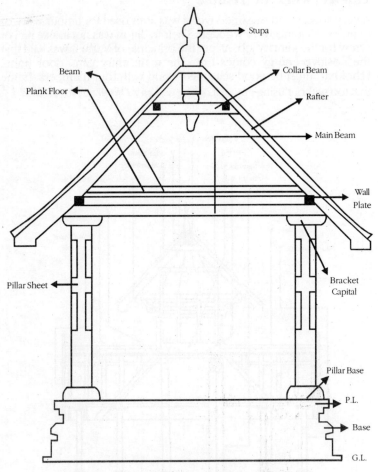

Timber Work of a Pavilion with a Pyramidal Roof in Kerala
Earthquake Resistance

(Ref.: Mayamatam: Vol. 1, Pg. Lxv, Fig. 13)

Diagram 17

Learning from the past and requirement of present, we can combine
the present and past and create a new design for 21st Century for a
peaceful prayer hall *Refer Diagram No. 18, 19* and *20*.

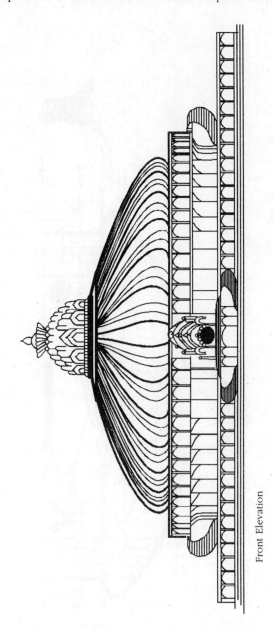

Front Elevation

Proposed Prayerhall for 21st Century

Diagram 18

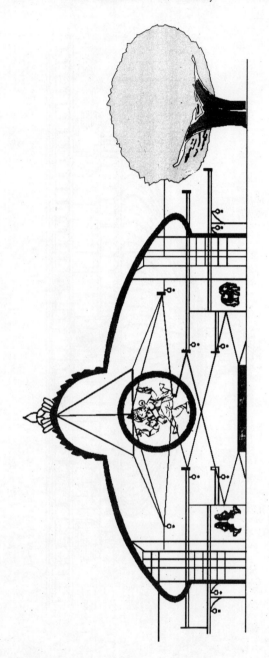

COMPLEX

Diagram 19

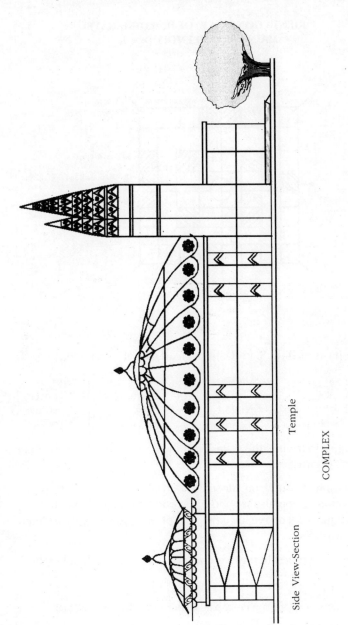

COMPLEX

Temple

Side View-Section

Diagram 20

ORIENTATION (FACE) OF BUILDING GATE/
MAIN GATE OR ENTRY DOOR

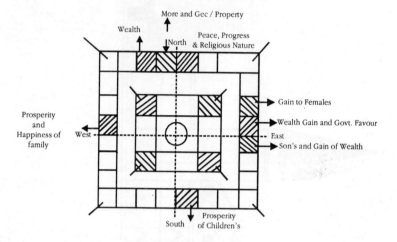

On the Basis of Birth Sign-Rashi of Head owner of the House.

→ North	→ South	→ West	→ East
* Aries	* Gemini	* Taurus	* Cancer
* Leo	* Virgo	* Libra	* Scorpio
* Sagittarius	* Capricorn	* Aquarius	* Pisces

NOTE : Just in front of the Gate/Door there should not be any of the following obstructions:

- Temple, Gurudwara, Mosq, Church etc.
- Corner of neighbour building, septic tank, main Sewerage.
- A lane or road, tree, electric pole, pillar, ladders are considered inauspicious.

If/or keep more than twice distance from the building height.

The position of main entry gate as per Vastu and Zodiac Sign.

Diagram 21

Chapter 12

Cosmic Energy from Air, Light and Color

Exposure to Sunlight

Sunlight and fresh air is the basic element from which all life originates, develops, heals and evolves. The body is a living cell which is stimulated and regulated by light. It has a profound effect on the regulation of human physiological and emotional functioning and the development of our consciousness. Light effectively enhances learning abilities, strengthens the immunizing properties and plays a role in the extension of life. Energies developed by Sun, Light and Air play a vital role in formation of principles of Vastu Shastra.

Sunlight is composed of a variety of energies that are transmitted to Earth in the form of electromagnetic waves. Only a small portion of these waves actually reach the Earth's surface and only about one percent of the total electromagnetic spectrum is perceived by the eyes. This visible portion of the electromagnetic spectrum, containing all the colors of the rainbow from violet (with the largest wavelength) to red (with the shortest wavelength) is a most important key to human functioning and evolution. Our lives, health and well being are truly dependent on the sun.

Sunlight is a holistic approach for the development of physiological, emotional and spiritual bodies. The profound human evolution in some deep way is related to our ability to take in and utilize light on physical and spiritual level. The vision of our sages of the past is not different from the scientific discoveries of the present. Sunlight, our source of light, warmth and energy, not only sustains all life on Earth, but it sustains the Earth itself. It provides plants with the energy of photosynthesis, which in turn sustains life on Earth.

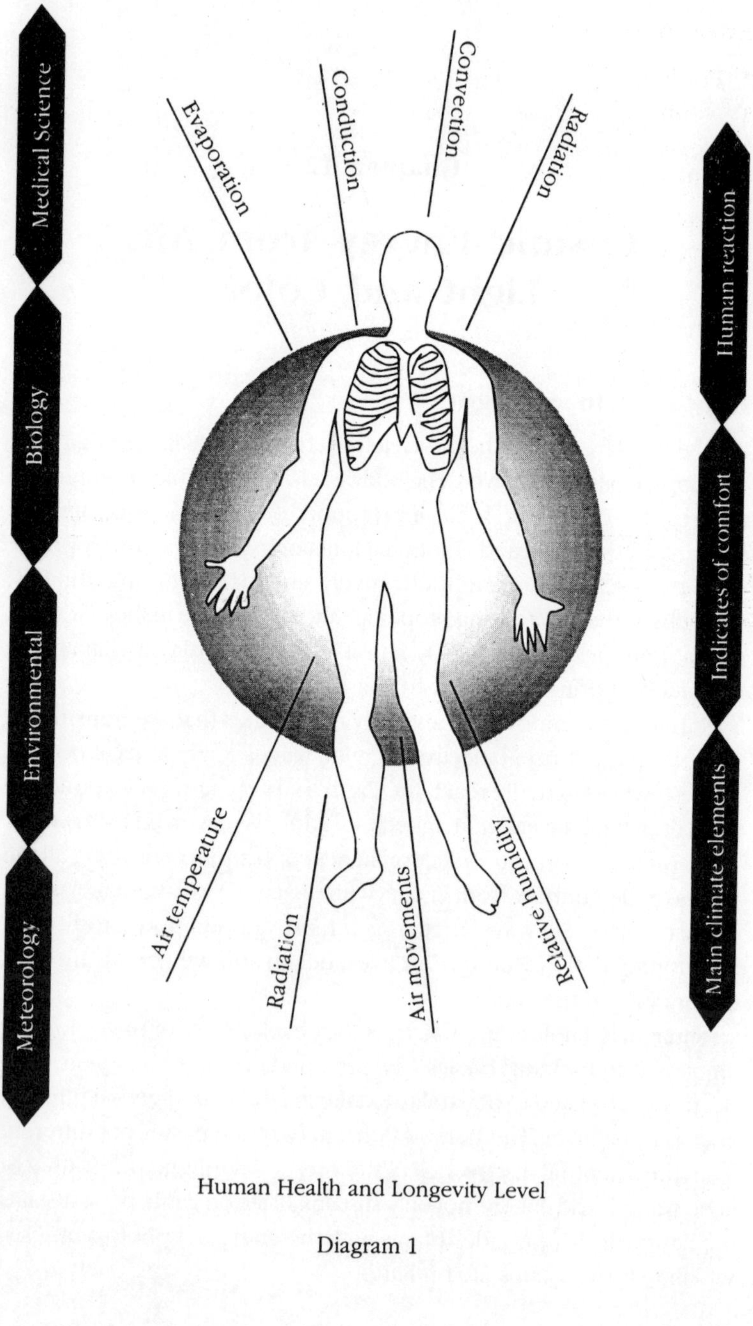

Human Health and Longevity Level

Diagram 1

Exposure to Sunlight

- Producing Vitamin D in the body.
- Normal growth and development of bones.
- Decrease Blood Sugar.
- Balance Blood Pressure.
- Decrease resting heart rate.
- Decrease respiratory rate.
- Decrease Lactic Acid in blood.
- Increases resistance to Arthritis.

Yoga and Meditation

- Increase energy and strength in the body.
- Increase tolerance to stress.
- Balance the breathing rhythm.
- Increase ability of blood to absorb and carry oxygen.
- Increase storage of oxygen.

Rhythm of Life with Changing Color

From sunrise to sunset environmental color changes and correspondingly effect all living things. The very first sunrise to the sunset of the present, we continued to be awed by the beauty, power, life-creating and life sustaining properties emanating from light. It would appear, then that our physiological and emotional centres are synchronized with nature by way of light and that we truly seem to be the offspring of nature. Based on the awareness that daily color variations in the environment are intimately connected to the body's daily rhythmic changes, humans have recognized that the seasonal color changes also reflect biological alterations within all living things. Harmony within our life processes is related to the level of communication between our body and the environment. Unbalanced responses to specific rhythms, seasons and their associated cycles are related to specific kinds of physical and emotional problems. Longevity may be related to our ability to integrate and synchronize ourselves with the planetary and solar-stellar energies that surround us. In humans, exposure to sunlight significantly influences physiological and psychological functions. Among these, fertility and mood are two most profoundly affected. Light has played a consistent role in the development of all living things. More recently, Albert Szent Gyorgyi, Nobel prize winner and the discoverer of Vitamin C, has recognized how profoundly color and light affect us. From his work he concluded that "all the energy which we take into our bodies is derived from the sun." He saw that, through the process of photosynthesis, the sun's energy is stored in plant which are in turn eaten by animals and oxygen released is taken in by humans. Sun is a source of mental energy and the best minds evolved in a natural process where the sun was temperate. Not very hot, not very cold, just the right temperature (+ or –3) of 24° c. The hot sun has glare, sharp light and dark shadows. Cool sun has colors and cold sun rarely rises above horizon or often geographically couples with heavy clouds in the sky and snow on earth. Generally, gloomy but beautiful, silvery and long hours of twilight. Hot humid zones with heavy cloudy sky for a longer periods of the year also have distinctive culture and architecture. Sun has played an important role in development of visual qualities of architecture in terms of textures, color, roof forms and above in all expressions of vitality.

Scientific Discovery

The human body is nourished directly by the stimulation of the sunlight or nourished directly by eating foods, drinking fluids or breathing air that has been vitalized by the sun's light energy. Dr. Zame Kime, in his book "Sunlight", states that a series of exposure to sunlight will decrease resting heart rate, blood pressure, respiratory rate, blood sugar and lactic acid in the blood following exercise; and help increase in energy, strength, endurance, tolerance to stress and ability of the blood to absorb and carry oxygen. The human body is truly a living photocell that is energized by the sun's light, the nutrient of humankind. Szent Gyorgyi discovered that many enzymes and hormones involved in processing this energy are color responsive and very sensitive to light. He added that light striking the body can literally alter the basic biological functions involved in processing the body's fuel, which powers our lives. Martinek and Brezin in 1979 found that (a) colors of light can stimulate certain bodily enzymes to be 500 percent more effective and (b) some colors can increase the rate of enzymatic reactions, activate or deactivate certain enzymes. Light not only affects us but our state of consciousness determines how we use light.

Use Sunlight for Our Health

Sunlight has been used by all the major historical cultures and it has touched the hearts and creative minds of those who have learned to appreciate its potential. It wasn't until the 1800s that physicians throughout the world became fully aware of the healing properties of sunlight. At this point in time, cures using light were being claimed for conditions ranging from simple inflammation and paralysis to tuberculosis. It was later discovered that sunlight striking the skin initiated a series of reactions in the body leading to the production of Vitamin D, a necessary ingredient for the absorption of calcium and other minerals from the diet. If Vitamin D is absent, the body will not absorb the amount of calcium required for normal growth and development of bones. In 1903 Niels Finsen of Denmark was awarded the Nobel Prize for being the first person to successfully treat skin tuberculosis with ultraviolet light. During his many years of work with both sunlight and ultraviolet light, Finsen reported miraculous cures on thousands of patients.

The cosmic cycles affect our universe, which then affects the Solar system, which then affects the Earth and so on down through Earth's climate, seasons, inhabitants, right down to the smallest particle within an atom.

Since all things are integrally connected in this way, everything affects each other. Nothing escapes this process. Universally occurring variation affects all living things. Nature has a master plan for us to spend part of our lives exploring our external environments and part of our lives exploring our internal environments.

What Veda Says?

Since most of the modern population spends its working hours indoors eliminating the morning sunlight and fresh air from their daily intake, it is very important to discuss and discover the indoor environment particularly in 21st Century, where the environment throughout the world is becoming more and more polluted, in relation to our health, productivity and in general universal peace and well-being. If the absence or imbalance of certain naturally present spectral light components cause a reduction in our physiological, emotional and intellectual functioning, light must play an integral role in the proper biological functioning of all living organism.

In this regard Vastu plays a very important role in helping clean environment for the building, free from pollution of any kind, full of light and color needed by balancing the Five Elements of Nature.

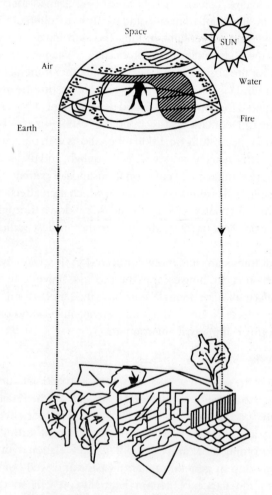

Theoretical Approach to Balanced Shelter in
Line with Five Elements

Diagram 2

Sloka

> *na Pranena Na Apranena Matyo Jivati Kaschana |*
> *itarena Tu Jivanti Yasmin Etavapsritau ||*

Meaning: Our life doesn't depend merely on the breathing process. The intake of diet is indeed important for health, but health does not rest on food alone, because everything can be thrown out of order if the mind is upset. A turbulence injected into the mind is enough to disturb the entire balance of personality. Your strength is in you. Religion begins where science ends; the beginning of the higher wisdom.

Sloka

> *shastrenanena Sarvasya Lokasya Param Sukham |*
> *chaturvarga Phalaprapti ssallokashch Bhaveddhruvam ||*
> *shilp shastra Parigyanmartyoapi Suratam Vrajet |*
> *paramanand Janakasya Devanamidmiritam ||*
> *shilpam Vina Na hi Jagattrishu Lokeshu Vidyate |*
> *jagad Vina Na Shilpam ch Vertate Vasav ! Prabho ! ||*

Meaning: Because of Vastu Shastra, the whole Universe gets good health, happiness and all-round prosperity. Human beings attain divinity with this knowledge. Followers of Vastu Shastra get not only worldly pleasures but also experience heavenly bliss.

Radiant Energy

Ancient civilizations apparently knew about light, namely its route of entry into the body and some of its major effects on the body's regulatory centres and their functions. Major control centres of the body are directly stimulated and regulated by light, to an extent far beyond what modern science, until recently, has been willing to accept. Though the body's balance is regulated by autonomic nervous system which is regulated by an important part of the brain, the hypothalamus, which receives light energy through eyes, co-ordinates and regulates most of our life sustaining functions and also initiates and direct our reactions and adaptation to stress.

Many of us spend our lifetime chasing mental images rather than observing the realities of life. The general lack of awareness has already

MONOLITHIC STATUE OF GOMATESHWAR IN
SITU GRANITE AND FIVE SENSES

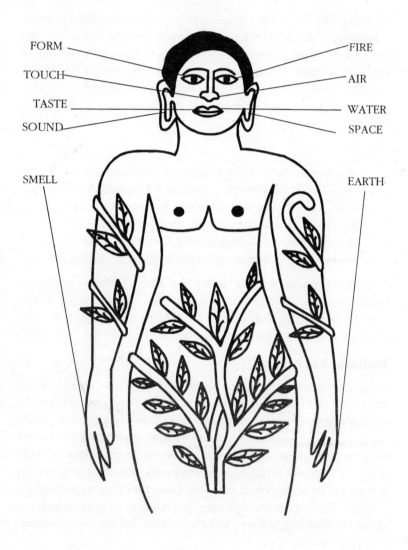

Diagram 3

led to the toxification of life's most important basic elements : light, air, food and water. Light is the major nutrient sustaining all life and it follows that poor and/or incomplete lighting will significantly affect every aspect of human existence. It is important to initially look at the constituents of sunlight as well as the kinds of artificial light to which we are exposed in our daily lives.

Light is composed of waves of radiant energy. Sunlight, which contains all the different wavelengths, provides the total electromagnetic spectrum under which all life on this planet has evolved. Until 1879, when Edison perfected the light bulb, people spent most of their time outdoors and received adequate daily doses of natural full spectrum sunlight. The light bulb became largely an "indoor event", which drastically reduced the amount of time to which people exposed themselves to full spectrum sunlight.

Since most of us spend our working hours indoors, eliminating sunlight from our daily diets, it is important to find this indoor environment in relation to our health, and productivity in general.

Seven Stages of Human Awareness

chanchalam hi manah krishna pramathi balavaddridham ||

Means, Oh! Lord the man is chanchal. It cannot stay firm. 'Mann' (thought) travels at the speed much more than sound or light and takes you thousands of miles away. This can be controlled by meditation. Our heart (mann) always misguides you. The above five senses do their duties regularly without knowing what is good or bad. The eye will see any type of scene, ears will listen any type of sound without knowing whether it is good sound or bad sound, a horror sound etc., nose breath good or bad smell, similarly touch and taste do their job. Our brain *(buddhi)* controls all the senses and tell whether our experience is good or bad. For the above education *(gyan)* one has to train the brain to judge between good and bad. Above all is Atma (Soul). All the above five stages are within your control, you can train them, control them the way you want by doing regular practice. Whatever training you give, you get the consequential result.

But, above this is *Atma* (the Soul), which is beyond your control. It is independent, it does not die with you. So, if you make friendship with the soul by understanding it, you become a Rishi. Away from this materialistic world, you become very close to him. And above all, comes the seventh stage where Atma is lean (blended) with Maha Atma i.e. (Param Atma, Paramatma) in this stage I and You become He, there is no difference between I and you, all are one and this triangle becomes circle. We are the bindu, a point of start. When I and You become one, we become love, we are not in love, but we are love. You always say you are my life, I give my heart to you, you are my breadth, in this stage of awareness all ego goes , you are without ego. So, I , You and He become one, neither you are attached nor detached with this materialistic world and enjoy all stages of awareness.

To be in discipline always sounds difficult. Everyone says that to be in discipline is very difficult but I always say that it is very easy to be in discipline. What is Discipline ? Formation of Human Habits ?

1. Good Habit which is as per environment and liked by every-one is being in discipline.
2. Bad Habits are not liked by others and according to the environment means that you are not in Discipline.

Everyone has certain habits and if you develop with practice and add some more good habits. Everybody says you are a very disciplined person and you will be successful in all fields and liked by everyone.

Chapter 13

Sunlight for Efficient Building Design

Energy from Sunlight

1. The Sun has abundant energy to make life comfortable and prosper on this planet Earth.
2. Energy from the nature is the base of Vastu Science. The whole Universe is a dynamic Web of energy pattern. Duration of time for exhausting of Earth Energy resources is as shown in *Diagram 1*.

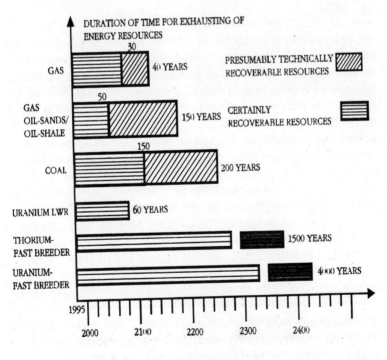

Diagram 1

3. Human beings get 99 percent energy from Sun which is the rhythm of daily life in the form of warmth and light for all actions/ reactions for all the life forms of Universe. Vastu consultant and architecture therefore, has to conserve energy with climatological response for the overall growth of the inmates living/working in the built space. We have to learn to handle the delicate balance and sensitivities of natural energy, especially the Sun in design process so as to produce an environment full of energy.

Life on Earth is under the constant influence of natural sunlight. The world have always recognized connection with sunlight. It was profoundly recognized by the ancient cultures that they revered the Sun as God for its blessing.

Sustainer of Healthy Life

Sunlight containing Ultraviolet Rays (Invisible form of light) is beneficial to humans, and there are certain adverse effects too. Let us not say that the God may have made mistake in giving harmful Ultraviolet Light and Rays.

It is a misconception that 'nature' is hostile to man. If approached in true harmony, its secrets can be revealed and its energies harnessed for the benefit of the living. Nature, man and product are within evolutionary network guided by performance standards. Architectural beauty is to be seen, felt, perceived, conceived and experienced, the so-called 'moderns' are looking to the orient for the desired peace of mind. India is the source; the fountainhead of the vast ancient Vedic knowledge available on the planet. This open secret is relatively unknown: When the Vedic concept is presented through modern high-tech and technological advances, the sublime information becomes available and can be easily understood. This would give a new outlook in the world of architecture, art and sciences in 21ˢᵗ Century.

In the Vedic period, people built homes, temples, and hermitages, applying Vastu principles by balancing the five elements with a view to having a peaceful living, offering prayers and to live in common harmony. But in the modern world people built concrete clusters, mainly for a high rate of return. After the Second World War, the architectural practice has turned into a race towards the so-called modernization. Adopting bureaucratic values that have resulted in worldwide pollution, environmental and ecological problems; with no peace of mind whatsoever under any kind of shelter.

SPECTRUM OF THE SUN

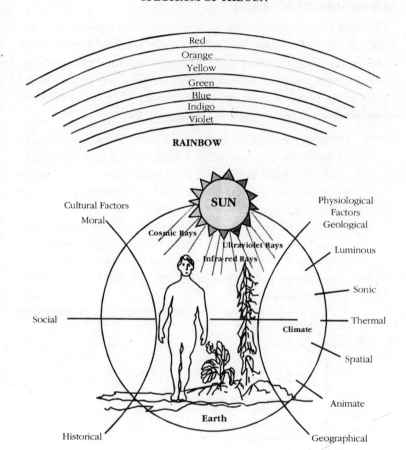

Red
Orange
Yellow
Green
Blue
Indigo
Violet

RAINBOW

SUN

Cultural Factors
Moral

Cosmic Rays

Ultraviolet Rays

Infra-red Rays

Social

Climate

Earth

Historical

Physiological
Factors
Geological

Luminous

Sonic

Thermal

Spatial

Animate

Geographical

Human Comfort Level

Diagram 2

Ultraviolet (UV) Light

Ultraviolet light is an effective treatment for many diseases. The Sun Therapy is very commonly used as Naturopathy which includes treatment of anaemia, gouts, colites, cystities, arteriosclerosis, rheumatoid arthritis, eczema, acne, herpes, lupus, sciatica, asthma, kidney problems and even burns. People will have to understand that there are lot of health benefits from ultraviolet light as enumerated below:

1. UV Light increases the efficiency of heart. At the Tulane School of Medicine, Dr. Raymond Johnson exposed 20 people to Ultraviolet light. In 18 of out of 20 people their cardiac output increased an average of 39 percent ! In other words, their hearts became stronger and pumped more blood.

2. UV Light reduces cholesterol. In one experiment, patients with hypertension and related circulatory problems were exposed to UV Light. Two hours after the first exposure, 97 percent of the patients had almost a 13 percent decrease in serum Cholesterol levels.

3. UV Light is an effective treatment for psoriasis. Reports from

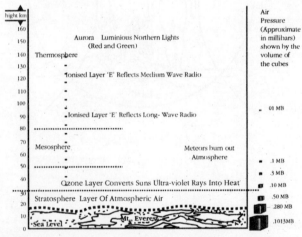

Ozone Layer is a form of oxygen which protects us from most of the sun's ultra-violet radiation.

Solar energy that reaches our planet is effected in many ways by the atmosphere, that envelopes the land and water surface.

Diagram 3

the National Psoriasis Foundation indicate that 80 percent of those suffering from this skin disease improve when they are exposed to UV Light.

4. UV Light activates the synthesis of Vitamin D, which is a prerequisite for the absorption of calcium and other minerals from the diet. Robert Neer and Associates conducted a study on a group of elderly persons to determine if extra sunlight would increase their ability to absorb calcium from their diets. The group which did not receive UV rays had 25 percent decrease in Calcium absorption while the other group receiving UV Rays had a 15 percent increase in absorption.

5. UV Light increases the level of sex hormones. In a study at Boston State Hospital, Dr. Abraham Myerson found that ultra-violet light increased male hormones level by 120 percent. UV Light activates an important skin hormone.

6. UV Light is an effective treatment for many diseases indicated above. UV Light has been found very effective in killing infectious bacteria, including several forms of tuberculosis bacteria.

Today, practically all sources of ultraviolet exposure are seen as detrimental to humans. It is well-known that tuberculosis was one of the main disease that was treated by sunshine and many patients were completely cured.

It is very important to know and study in deep the UV Light and Infra-red rays, which we have discussed in next chapters , but first we must know that too much UV light is bad, "we need a basic amount to support life and maintain a healthy immune system." If someone says that oxygen is hazardous to our health we will say he does not understand gift of nature. Similar is conclusion for Ultraviolet light. People are spending most of their lives under artificial lighting and suffering. They have to understand about benefit of Ultraviolet light.

Since sunlight (containing UV) is beneficial to humans and that there are certain adverse effects on persons living and working in artificial lighting. The light in most houses looks yellowish and dingy. The wavelengths of light in the orange-pink-red range caused laboratory animals to lose their hair, show excessive calcium deposits in their hearts and develop large fast growing tumors. It was also found that when animals cells were exposed to red and infra-red portions of the spectrum, their cell walls ruptured and cell division process (mitosis) stopped. Sunlight consists of a fairly balanced spectrum of color. Interestingly enough, blue is the wavelength most lacking in incandescent light bulbs. It has been established that ultraviolet light is a nutrient, just like a vitamin or a mineral. Daily allowance for UV light has, therefore, recommended just as in case of vitamin C.

In fact, overexposure to the sun, in conjunction with certain skin types, is a major factor in the development of skin cancer. The solution is quite simple, mild, sensible exposure to sunlight is not only safe, it is desirable. One of the constituent of sunlight is "ultravoilet" (UV) rays for which modern science has made us to think that it causes cancer, cataracts, aging and wrinkles. This blocking of ultraviolet rays may severely weaken the body's defenses.

What does nature say about solar light? The researchers have to understand the fact that humans have evolved under nature sunlight. Are we supposed to dismiss five million years of evolution because science doesn't understand the supreme wisdom of nature?

According to photo biologist Dr. John Ott, there are strong indications that UV light through eyes stimulates the immune system. UV light in large amount is harmful; however in trace amounts, UV rays in nature sunlight, it acts, as a "life-supporting nutrient" which is highly beneficial.

Sunlight contains different ultraviolet (UV) radiation. UV light is classified as UV-A , UV-B , or UV-C depending on its wavelength. UV-A (320-380 NM), directly adjoining the violet end of the visible-light spectrum is responsible for the tanning response in humans. UV-B (290-320 NM) activates the synthesis of vitamin D and the absorption of calcium and other minerals. UV-C (100-290 NM).

What are Ultraviolet Rays?

Ultraviolet rays are an invisible form of light. They lie just beyond the violet end of the visible spectrum . The sun is the major nature source of ultraviolet rays. Lightning, or any other electrical spark in the air, also emits ultraviolet rays. The rays can be produced artificially by passing an electric current through a gas or vapor, such as mercury vapor. Ultraviolet rays can cause sunburn. Overexposure to these rays can cause skin cancer. Ultraviolet rays also destroy harmful organisms and have other useful effects.

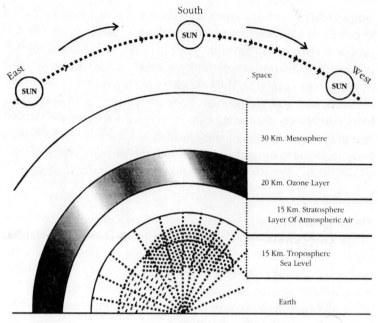

Diagram 4

Ultraviolet rays (UV) have shorter wavelengths (WL) than visible light. A wavelength is the distance between the crests of two waves, is often measured in units called nanometers. One nanometers (NM) equals 0.000001 millimeter (0.000000039 inch.) wavelength of visible light range from about 400 to 700 nm. Ultraviolet wavelength range from about 1 to 400 nm. The wavelength of Ultraviolet rays determines whether a material they shine on absorbs the rays or transmits them. For example, only ultraviolet rays with shorter wavelengths can pass through ordinary window glass. The glass absorbs rays with shorter wavelength, though they can pass through other materials.

Uses of Ultraviolet Rays

Ultraviolet rays (UV) with wavelength (WL) shorter than 300 nm. are effective in killing bacteria and viruses. Hospitals use germicidal lamps that produce these short rays to sterilize surgical instruments, water and the air in operating rooms. Many food and drug companies use germicidal lamps to disinfect various types of products and their containers. Direct exposure to ultraviolet rays with wavelengths shorter than 320 nm. produces vitamin D in the body. Physicians once used sun lamps that produced these rays to prevent and treat rickets, a bone diseases caused by the lack of Vitamin D. The lamps are used today to treat some skin disorders, such acne and psoriasis. Some instruments use ultraviolet rays to identify the chemical composition of unknown materials. Medical researchers use such instruments to analyze substances in the human body, including amino acids, enzymes, and other proteins. The electronics industry uses ultraviolet rays in manufacturing integrated circuits.

Harmful Effects

The sun's shortest ultraviolet rays those with wavelength below about 320 nm. are particularly harmful to living things. Too much exposure to these rays can cause painful eye irritation or eye inflammation. High quality sun glasses protect the eyes from these rays. Overexposure to ultraviolet rays also can cause a painful burn. Melanin, a brown pigment in the skin, provides some protection against sunburn. Sunscreen lotion absorbs the sun's burning rays.

Exposure to the sun ultraviolet rays over a long period can cause skin cancer and other changes in human cells. Such exposure can also damage or kill plants. Ozone, a form of oxygen in earth's upper atmosphere, absorbs most of the sun's ultraviolet radiation. Without the ozone layer, ultraviolet rays would probably destroy most plant and animal life.

Scientific Research

Ultraviolet rays originate within the atoms of the elements. Scientists learn about the make up and energy levels of atoms by studying the rays. Experts also learn about distant stars and galaxies by analyzing the ultraviolet rays that they give off.

Much research has focused on the role of ultraviolet rays in chemical reactions that break down the earth's protective ozone layer. As the ozone layer breaks down it becomes less effective as a barrier against harmful ultraviolet rays.

Example, only ultraviolet rays with shorter wavelengths can pass through ordinary window glass. The glass absorbs rays with shorter wavelength, though they can pass through other materials.

Experiments indicate that bees, butterflies, and other insects can see ultraviolet light. The reflection of ultraviolet rays of wings reveals patterns that help insects identify mates.

What is Ozone?

Ozone, OH zohn, is a form of oxygen that is present in the earth's atmosphere in small amounts. Ozone in the upper atmosphere is a major factor in making life on the earth possible. But ozone in the lower atmosphere contributes to air pollution. Ozone is used commercially in water purification processes and as a bleaching agent.

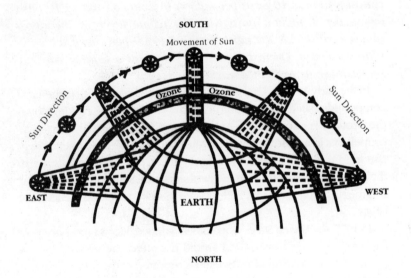

Diagram 5

Ordinary oxygen molecules have two oxygen atoms. Ozone molecules contain three oxygen atoms. Ozone is produced naturally through photochemical and electric discharge reactions. Photochemical production occurs when high energy radiation from the sun strikes ordinary oxygen in the earth's upper atmosphere and converts some of it to ozone. Electric discharge reactions, including lightning and electric sparks from motors, also converts some oxygen to ozone. Ozone is produced commercially by electric discharge in a machine called ozonizer.

Most ozone is found in the upper atmosphere. The highest concentration is reached, depending on the latitude, between 14 and 19 miles (23 and 30 Km.) above the earth's surface. This concentration is 10 parts per million by volume—that is 10 parts ozone per 1 million parts air. The ozone layer in the upper atmosphere shields the earth from 95 to 99 percent of the sun's ultraviolet rays. Overexposure to these rays is a leading cause of skin cancer as explained earlier.

In the early 1970's, some scientists expressed concern that chemical compounds called chloro-fluoro-carbons (CFCs) were breaking down the protective ozone layer. At that time, CFCs were widely used as propellants in aerosol spray cans. After CFCs are released, they slowly rise in to the atmosphere. When they reach the upper atmosphere, the sun's ultraviolet radiation breaks them apart. Some of the molecular fragments that result react with ozone, thereby reducing the amount of it.

In 1978, the United States Government banned fluorocarbon aerosols for most uses. However, the ban did not affect the use of CFCs as refrigerants or in insulation. Scientists reported early in 1988 that the ozone layer above Antarctica was disappearing at a faster rate than expected. In 1989, an international treaty limited the production of CFC by several major producers of these chemicals.

Most ozone in the lower atmosphere is considered an air pollutant. It is formed by chemical reactions between sunlight and pollutants already in the atmosphere. Ozone produced in this manner is a component of photochemical smog. Such ozone can directly damage rubber, plastic, and plant and animal tissue. It may undergo further chemical reactions that produce other damaging chemicals.

Exposure to certain concentrations causes headaches , burning eyes, and irritation of the respiratory tract in many individuals.

Ozone has the chemical formula O_3 and a molecular weight of 47.998. Pure ozone is a pale blue gas. It was first detected by means of its sharp, irritating odor, which is often noticed near electrical switches and machinery. The German chemist Christian Friedrich Schonbein discovered ozone in 1840.

What are Infra-red Rays?

1. The Sun's ultraviolet rays striking or falling on any object or human beings etc. on the Earth, produce Infra-red rays in relation to its temperature with surrounding temperature.

2. INFRA-RED RAYS : Infra-red rays are often called heat rays, resemble light rays, but they cannot be seen by the human eye. They behave similarly to light rays in both Reflection and Refraction. Any object such as building material, metal furniture and much more made out of conductor and less in insulation etc. gives off infra-red rays in relation to its temperature. As an object gets hotter, it gives off more and more infra-red rays. Such devices as the sniperscope, which was invented during World War II (1939-1945), can pick up infra-red rays from object that are warmer than their surroundings. In this way, these devices can "see" such objects in the dark or through fog.

3. Photographers use film that is sensitive to infra-red rays to take pictures in places where there is no visible light. Doctors use infrared lamps to treat skin diseases and sore muscles. In these treatments, the infra-red rays pass through the patient's skin and produce heat when they strike the affected area.

4. Infra-red waves lie just beyond the red end of the visible light spectrum. Sir William Herschel, a British astronomer, discovered infra-red rays in 1800 by observing the effect of the heat they produced.

How to Use Ultraviolet Light for Perfect Health?

With the previous explanation we come to a conclusion that UV rays with WL 1 to 300 n. m. is harmful for human consumption and WL of 320 n.m. produces Vitamin D in our body and about 320 to 400 is good for human consumption. *Refer Diagram No. 6.*

Now the early morning sun-rays reaches the Earth Surface, passes through Ozone with more area, though reaches the earth surface with lesser radiation and cover more earth surface. Though the W/L during sun rise up to 2 hours is 320 to 400 nm. is good for human consumption and if it mixes with cold water it multiplies the vitamin capacity and is very good for human skin and eye as well as produces positive energy.

As sun rises it comes closer to the earth and distance of WL between the crust comes closer much below 300 nm. and between 10:00 a.m. to 4:00 p.m. becomes Infra-red rays. This scientific theory has been discovered much earlier by authors of Vastu and they suggested the placement of five elements and to balance this they recommended as below:

1. Spend at least one hour outdoors everyday without worrying of the weather. However, whatever is required to be done outdoors should not be done indoors. Taking a walk outdoors, breathe in nature and see its beauty. Avoid exposure between the hours of 8:00 a.m. to 5:00 p.m. and avoid directly looking into the sun as it will damage your eyes. While indoors, sit by an open window. This will provide you with the full visible spectrum of light including the UV and the view of the outdoors will be relaxing to both the eyes and mind like green garden etc.

2. Wear neutral gray color sunglasses.

3. For those who wear glasses ask the specialist about UV—transmitting lenses.

4. Don't use colored contact lenses, as it can cause many problems as sunglasses. As such use clear white contacts.

5. UV-Transmitting Plastic Windows should be considered instead of regular glass, on the southside of the building.

6. Avoid use of Suntan Lotions having PABA. The U.S. Food Drug Administration has concluded that fourteen out of seventeen Suntan Lotions containing PABA can be carcinogenic when used in the sun and can cause genetic damage to the DNA in the skin.

Exposure to Electromagnetic Waves and Electric Radiation

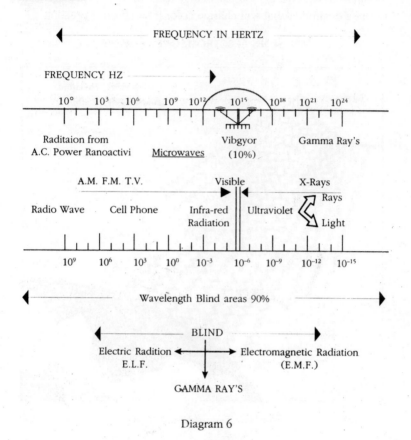

Diagram 6

Many people who work in areas where radiation may be present use an electroscope as a dosimeter. A Dosimeter is a device that measures the amount of radiation to which a person has been exposed. An electroscope must be charged before it can be used as a dosimeter. It gradually discharges when exposed to gamma rays, X-rays, or other forms of radiation. The amount of charge lost shows the level of exposure.

The first electroscope was made by William Gilbert, the physician of Queen Elizabeth I of England. He described it in a book published in 1600.

A dosimeter is a type of electroscope that measures the amount of radiation to which a person has been exposed. An X-rays technician wears a dosimeter that will change color if radiation is present.

THE SUN'S ELECTROMAGNETIC WAVES

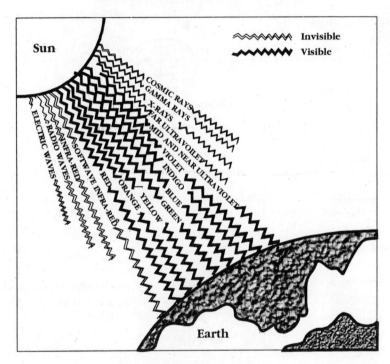

The Sun's Electromagnetic Waves

Diagram 7

Electromagnetic Waves

These are related patterns of electric and magnetic force. They are generated by the Oscillation (movement back and forth) of electric charges. Electromagnetic Waves travel through space at the speed of light—186, 282 miles (299, 792 Kilometers) per second. The simplest electromagnetic waves are plane waves. They move through space in straight lines. The strength of the wave varies in space and time with alternating crests and troughs. The distance from crest-to-crest is called the wavelength.

The Electromagnetic Spectrum

It consists of bands of different wavelengths. The chief kinds of electromagnetic waves are in order of increasing wavelength— gamma rays, X-rays, ultraviolet light, visible light, infra-red rays, microwaves and radio waves. Gamma rays are less than 10 trillionths of a meter in length, and some long radio waves measure more than 10,000 km.

All types of electromagnetic waves have the properties of visible light. They can be reflected, diffracted (spread), and refracted (bent). The direction of magnetic force in all electromagnetic waves is perpendicular to the direction in which the wave is moving. The direction of electric force is perpendicular to both the direction of magnetic force and the direction of wave motion. The strength of magnetic force always equals the strength of electric force.

The electromagnetic spectrum extends from short gamma rays through light waves to long radio waves. Thus, spectrum diagrammed below gives the frequency and wavelength for the various waves. Frequencies are given in hertz and wavelengths in meters. The raised figures with the 10's are a way of abbreviating numbers. For example 10^{15} hertz equals 1 followed by 15 zeros, or 1, 000, 000,000,000,000 hertz. The number with a minus sign tell how many places the decimal point must be moved in front of the number. For example, 10^7 meters equals 0.0000001 meter.

Uses of Electromagnetic Waves

Doctors use gamma rays, which are given off by radium, to treat cancer. They also use X-rays to treat cancer and, in addition, to help, locate and diagnose internal disorders. Ultraviolet rays are used in Sun lamps and fluorescent light and as a disinfectant. Infra-red rays, which are given off by hot objects, are used in infra-red lamps to treat skin disease and to bake enamel. Micro waves are used to cook food. Radio waves are used in radio and T.V. broadcasting.

The technological use of electromagnetic waves depends on the ease with which the various wavelength can be dictated and produced. Wavelength is related to the vibration rate of electrons in the energy source. The slower the vibration, the longer the wavelength. Long waves are the easiest to produce, and the use of radio waves in communication begun soon after 1900.

Shorter waves were not effectively utilized until the development of such devices as the Klystron, a type of microwave tube. Development of the laser during the 1960 provided new uses for short waves. For example, the laser enables ultraviolet and infra-red rays to transmit voice messages and television signals.

Electromagnetism

Electromagnetism is the branch of physics that studies the relationship between electricity and magnetism. Electromagnetism is based on the fact that (1) an electric current produces a magnetic field, and (2) a changing magnetic field produces an electric field.

In 1820s, the Danish scientist Hans Oersted discovered that a conductor carrying an electric current is surrounded by a magnetic field. When he brought a magnetized needle near a wire in which an electric current was following, the needle moved. Because a magnetized needle is moved by magnetic forces, the experiment demonstrated that an electric current produces magnetism.

During the 1820s the French physicist Andre Marie Ampere declared that electric current produces all magnetism. He concluded that a permanent bar magnet has tiny currents flowing in it. The work of Oersted and Ampere led to the development of the electromagnet, which is used in such devices as the telegraph and the electric bell. Most electromagnets consist of a coil of wire wound around an iron core. The electromagnet becomes temporarily magnetized when an electric current flows through the wire. If the direction of the current changes, the poles of the electromagnet switch places.

Magnetism produces an electric current by means of electromagnetic induction. The English scientist Michael Faraday and the American physicist Joseph Henry discovered electromagnetic induction independently in 1831. In electromagnetic induction, a changing magnetic fields set up an electric field and within the conductor. For example, a magnet moving through a coil of wire causes the voltage to vary from point-to-point along the wire. An electric current flows along the wire as long as the amount of magnetism passing through the wire is changing. Electromagnetic induction is the basis of electric generator. An electric motor reverses the process. A current sent through the wire sets up a magnetic field, which causes the wire to move.

In 1864, James Clerk Maxwell, a British scientist, used the earlier experiment to show that electric and magnetic fields act together to produce radiant energy in the form of electromagnetic waves.

How to Use Ultraviolet Light and Infra-red Rays for Efficient Building Design Based on Vastu Principles

Solar Energy

Sun is the greatest source of energy. But its distribution on earth is unequal. Certain places get more of its heat and certain places comparatively less. Why is it so?

We know that our earth is spherical in shape and flat at the poles. The Sun's rays fall on different places of the earth's surface at different angles. On the Equator, they fall straight but on the North and the South of the equator they fall obliquely. Because of the straightness of the falling rays, it is very hot at the equator, but as we go away it becomes progressively colder towards the poles.

Naturally, the question arises, why does the obliqueness of the rays reduces the heating effects. This is so because the rays falling obliquely have to travel longer distances in the atmosphere. The dust particles, vapor and other materials present in the atmosphere absorb much of the heat contained in these rays. Hence, the longer the distance travelled by the sun's rays, the larger is the absorption of the heat by the atmosphere. Therefore, areas receiving the sun's rays obliquely receive less heat.

Thus, the places on or around the equator are very hot because they receive the sun's rays straight. On the other hand, places to the North and the South of the Equator are cold because they receive Sun's rays obliquely. The hotness or coldness of a place also depends on the distribution of water, its height above the sea level and distance from the sea-shore.

Methods of Heat Transfer

There are three ways in which heat is transferred namely:
 (a) Conduction, (b) Convection, and (c) Radiation

 (a) Conduction : Conduction is the process by which heat is transferred
     through matter from place of high temperature to that of low
     temperature, without transfer of matter itself. If one end of an
     iron rod is placed in fire, the other end gets heated by conduction.
 (b) Convection: In Convection, heat is carried from one place to
     another place by the bodily transfer of the matter contained in
     it. Fluids, whether liquids or gaseous, are generally heated by
     this process. Water in a cane placed on a stove gets heated by
     convection.
 (c) Radiation: Radiation is the process by which heat is transferred
     from one body to another without heating the intervening
     medium.

Out of these methods of heat transfer, radiation plays the most
important part in the transfer of heat in the atmosphere. The sun is
intensely hot, the temperature of its surface being estimated as 6000°C.
About a half of the solar radiation heating the earth is reflected back
to space. The atmosphere does not absorb any appreciable amount
of the sun's radiation. It is only when the energy penetrates to the
earth's surface that it is absorbed and tends to raise the temperature
of the ground, in turn, warms the air-layers in contact. Thus, the air
in the atmosphere is heated, not directly by the sun but indirectly by
the earth.

Solar power can be harnessed only if sun's rays are concentrated
by using a series of mirrors. Solar energy has been tapped to generate
electricity, heating homes, providing hot water and hot air for industries.
Satellites and space stations tap solar energy. Solar energy can be
tapped only during periods of sunshine. Widespread use of solar energy
will depend on technological developments so as to reduce costs and
enable storage of power for use during cloudy periods or night. The
solar energy would then provide continuous supply of abundant power.

Radiation and Insulation

Radiation means movement of rays. The quantity of solar heat transmitted in one minute to one square cm. of the earth's surface normal

to the sun's rays beyond the earth's atmosphere are defined as solar constant which is approximately 2 cal. per sq. cm. per minute. One square meter of the sun's surface radiates energy presumably equal to 100,000 hp. at the velocity of light. This energy is transmitted as ultraviolet radiation (short waves) and infra-red radiation (long waves). Most of these radiations are perceived as heat and only an insignificant part as visible light.

As is known, every in 24 hours the earth completes a radiation around its axis at a speed of 27 kilometers per minute. At the same time, the earth revolves around the sun on a slightly elliptical orbit at a speed of 28.7 kilometers per second the period of revolution is equal to 365 days.

The movement of the earth around the sun together with the inclination of its axis of rotation results in an uneven distribution of light and heat in the various regions of the earth for any given year.

The position of the earth during its revolution around the sun is measured by the angle of the sun's rays in relation to the equatorial plan of the earth. This angle is called the solar declination and varies between 23.5° North latitude and 23.5° South latitude. The days of the year when the solar declination reaches these values are called the solstices. The days when the declination is equal to 0° are called the equinoxes. In the period of solstices the perpendicular rays of the sun areas of the earth that are at the maximum distance to the North and South of the Equator. The boundaries of these areas are indicated by imaginary lines on the surface of the earth designating the Tropic of Cancer as the northern limit and the Tropic of Capricorn as the southern limit.

Passing through the atmosphere, the solar energy is dispersed and absorbed, thus greatly depleting the solar radiation of the earth. The thermal conditions of an urban environment are made up of direct solar irradiation (Insulation) and its derivatives, scattered and reflected radiation and ambient air temperature. In regions with hot climates, direct radiation is a factor exerting the greatest influence on urban environments. The action of direct radiation can be greatly moderated by urban planning methods such as water impounding, shading, special landscaping, etc.

With an increase in the elevation above sea level, the intensity of radiation increases on an average by 10 percent for each 300 meter above sea level.

In large towns and deserts where there is a high dust content in the air, depletion of the intensity of scattered radiation is as much as 30-45 percent of the total amount of solar energy reaching the earth, the atmosphere absorbs 15 percent, consequently the depletion of solar radiation by dispersion and absorption for different latitudes of the earth varies greatly. It is primarily determined by the incident angle of the sun's rays. When the sun is at the zenith, the rays, falling vertically, intersect the atmosphere by the shortest path. With a decrease in the incident angle the path of the sun's rays becomes longer and depletion of solar radiation becomes greater.

On the other hand, the surface of the earth has the property of reflecting heat in to space. Temperature conditions of sea and land are by no means identical, moreover the surface of the land is not heated uniformly since some places are steppe land, meadow and plough land, other places—forests and swamp lands, still other places — deserts which do not have a soil covering. Vegetative covering darkens the earth's surface thereby decreasing the flow of heat into the soil. At night, on the contrary, the vegetative covering protects the soil from heat loss. Besides, part of thermal energy is also expended on the transpiration of plants. As a result, soils covered with greenery receive less heat in the daytime. During the daytime, especially in summer, the surface of the ground becomes heated and at night is cooled. The difference between maximum and minimum temperatures is called the daily fluctuation amplitude.

As is known, the heat capacity of water is two times greater than the heat capacity of land which means that under the same conditions for a definite period of time the surface of the land receives twice as much heat, as the surface of water. Besides, when water is heated it evaporates thus, expending a considerable part of thermal energy. However, having a greater heat capacity, the sea accumulates more heat then land with the result that the surface of the sea is warmer than the surface of land. The mean temperature of the surface of seas and ocean exceeds the average air temperature of the planet by 3^0C.

The annual air temperature cycle for various parts of the world varies greatly, and is largely determined by the latitude of the localities.

Depending on latitude, there are four basic types of annual temperature cycles: equatorial, tropical, temperature and arctic.

Insulation is the direct solar irradiation on the earth's surface which exerts a thermal, light and biophysical effect on man's organism.

In this connection, an interesting proposal was made by architect K. Gutchov recommending a "solar hour" (direct solar radiation per hour) as a convenient unit of measurement in calculating insulation, which takes into account the varying intensity of solar illumination for various times of the day and year. However, only those hours are of value when the sun is at an altitude of not less than 6 degree above the horizon and the angle of its rays to the surface of wall and window is not less than 15 degree.

In the planning and construction of a town, its territory is divided so that buildings will alternate with open spaces (lawns, greenery and water basins). This stimulates the exchange of air and retards overheating. Temperature fluctuations are also caused by varying building densities and the character of the topography of the site.

With the aim of lowering the heat load, the building pattern should take into account the closely related problems of orientation, insulation, ventilation, building heights and building density. When buildings are placed on the perimeter of super blocks, it is advisable that the orientation of the street network be agreed with the position of the sun. In that case, the necessary insulation of building will depend on the accepted width of streets, building heights and their location along the street line.

Spacing between the buildings should ensure required insulation. Spacing between buildings depends on how the buildings are placed with their main facades parallel to the street or perpendicular to it. In hot climates the spaces between the buildings should provide sufficient area for green spaces as a means of protection against reflected radiation. With these conditions in mind, it is inadvisable to place buildings directly on the street line.

Building density also affects the microclimate in hot-humid and dry zones. In the humid pattern, in which groups of buildings shade each other, it improves the micro-climate. Thus, in the first instance, an open layout of buildings on the site is advisable. A latitudinal position of the larger axis of a building with a deviation of up to 15 degree on both sides (for better insulation) is believed to be the best orientation for many hot countries. With minimum spacing, buildings will receive maximum mutual shading.

Playing an effective role in the depletion of solar radiation are green spaces. Depending on their density, radiation is decreased by as much as 86 percent compared with an open area.

In a tropical climate, it is advisable to provide covered passageways for pedestrian traffic for protection against sun and rain.

Solar Architecture and Energy Conservation through Building Design

Today, the world finds itself in the grip of an energy crisis more particularly in the 21st century. The known sources of conventional energy are dwindling very fast. The demand for energy especially in the third world, is growing. And their efforts for development are constantly being threatened by environmental issues. The developed nations which are the largest consumers and producers of energy face biggest the crunch.

This has aroused an interest in the development of energy resources as well as conservation of the available sources. And a lot of research and thinking is being generated in this new field. Solar energy, bio-technology and superconductivity have the highest priorities in research fields.

We, in India , have very low energy consumption levels as compared to consumption in developed countries. However, much we may be wise to increase the production of conventional energy, our efforts are going to face resistance. The Narmada project is a very good example of this. Hence, before achieving any increase in the consumption of energy, we have to start thinking of conserving the same.

This situation forces upon us the issues of conservation of energy techniques. We can learn from the developed nation's efforts in this sphere. It gives us a chance to reallocate our resources in better ways even before the energy situation becomes acute.

Building construction, building design and architecture are such fields where the studies and research in energy conservation and renewable energy can be applied innovatively and creatively.

Passive solar energy system collects transported heat by natural means. Passive systems are simple in concept and use. The most striking difference between passive and active system is that the former operates on the energy available in its immediate environment and the latter imports energy to make the system work.

Architecture in the twentieth century has been characterized by an emphasis on technology to the exclusion of other values. There is an increasing dependence on mechanical control of the indoor environment rather than exploitation of climatic and other nature processes to satisfy our comfort requirements. Little attention is paid to the unique character and variation of local climate, building materials as well as the result is the monotonous character of our buildings. Since the passive solar system uses its energy and material from local environment, this can result into an ambient architectural character. Since solar energy is conveniently distributed to all parts of the globe, expensive transportation and distribution networks of energy are also eliminated.

Application of passive solar energy has to be included in every step of building design whereas conventional cooling and heating system can be independent of the conceptual organization of a building. It is extremely difficult to add passive solar system to a building once it is constructed.

Building Location, Shape and Orientation

Building shapes without regard for the sun's impact require large amounts of energy to cool in summer or heat in winter in cold climates.

A building elongated along the East-West axis will expose more surface area to the south during the summer and collect solar radiation and heat. This elongated shapes is the most efficient shape in all climates for minimizing cooling requirements in summer and heating requirements in winter. In hot climates, buildings oriented along the North-South axis pay a severe price in energy consumption for cooling.

Besides orientation and shape, each façade of building needs careful treatment so as to gain maximum advantages to heat, light and wind.

India is broadly divided into two climatic zones. One zone below 28° NL and one above the same. The first has hot climate while the northern zone is in cooler zone. Hence, treatment of South and North facades depends on the locations.

North Side Kuber: The North side of a building is the coolest and darkest side. In severe summer conditions, room on North side provides cool atmosphere while in severe cold they are very cold and uncomfortable and should be avoided at any cost. However, north side gives very comfortable day-light in the interiors as provided in the north light roof in factory buildings.

South Side Yama: A room on the south side with large openings and glass areas will convert the room in a hot case which is comfortable in cold region while the same is to be completely avoided in hot and arid zones. A cavity wall on South side will help in keeping heat away from indoors while a heat storage wall with glass panel in the front can provide the necessary heat on the inside in cold climates. In both cases, careful treatment of south façade is important in reducing the mechanical cost of heating or cooling.

Inner Courtyard Brahma: It is our common experience that old, traditional houses in hot regions in India provide very comfortable, cool atmosphere inside the buildings. A great interest has been aroused in studying this phenomenon and careful location and proportion of inner courtyards help provide comfortable light and ventilation and have great significance in passive solar architecture.

Heat Strong Wall: In cold climates, as they are found in northern part of our country, heating of room is necessary. The southern side specially treated with "TROMBE WALL" construction or addition of a green house can naturally provide heating not only in daytime but also at night. While the same wall can help sun radiation and heat reaching on inside in summer.

Roof Shading: The roof receives maximum radiation and heat from the sun in the daytime in the hot regions and make the interior very hot. The various methods of providing shading devices can be used to protect roof while in cold climates, the roof radiates heat from inside to the atmosphere, rendering the interiors very cold. Hence, insulation of roofs is also very important. Water ponds over the roof have advantage in both the climates.

Earth Sheltered and Earth Bermed Structures: The Earth bermed structures are suitable for areas where solar heating and cooling are designed. In such structures, the reduced infiltration of air from outside and the thermal resistance of surrounding earth considerably reduces the average thermal load.

Ventilation and Cooling: Air vents and wind towers operate in various ways. They are useful in hot arid climates. Air in the upper part of the wind tower is cooled. Water is introduced in the system and evaporative cooling takes place. This involves a change in water-vapor content and air temperature. And this air is admitted at the lower level of the room which creates a comfortable atmosphere inside. Air vents are employed in areas where dusty winds make wind towers impractical.

East-West orientation, with courtyards in the main building, bermed earth construction, south facing solar panels for generating energy, north light and well-protected main entrance on North with shading devices, solar water distillation plants on roof etc. can be given.

The houses are designed around a courtyard with all the main activity areas facing the same. While the outer walls are earth bermed, the houses are taken below the ground level, the courtyard has platform for solar cookers. Solar water heaters are provided on the rooftops for hot water requirements of housing.

Sol-Air Approach: The "sol-air" approach to orientation recognized that air temperature and solar radiation act together to produce one sensation of heat in the human body. Thus, to utilize the sun's rays fully, their thermal impacts must be considered in conjunction with heat convection , and the total effect measured by its ability to maintain temperature levels near the "comfort zone."

The importance of the sun's heat will, then, vary according to regions and seasons. Under cold conditions its additional radiation will be welcome and a building should be positioned to receive as much radiation as possible, while under conditions of excessive heat, the orientation of the same building should decrease undesirable solar impacts. By means of the bio-climatic chart these two conditions can be defined as the underheated and overheated periods of the year. An optimum orientation for a given site would give maximum radiation in the underheated period. Simultaneously, reducing insulation to a minimum in the overheated period.

The variation in orientation produced by regional requirements is diagrammatically presented in the accompanying illustration. In northern latitudes, the air is generally cool and there is a great need for the sun's heat. Consequently, buildings should be oriented so as to receive the maximum amount of radiation throughout the year. However, the same building in the South, where the air is heavy with heat, should turn its axis to avoid the sun's unwanted radiation and pick up cooling breezes instead.

The effects of solar radiation upon various orientations are illustrated here by rotating a vertical surface around the compass at 30 degree intervals and calculating the resultant thermal impacts.

Solar Control

The age-old problems of controlling the reception of solar radiation in buildings have been sharply enlarged by the modern developments in architectural planning and construction. Traditional massive bearing-walls, which combined the function of support with protection from light and heat, have been supplanted by clear structural members devoted to load-bearing (the skeleton) and covered with curtain walls (the skin) made of many materials.

The skin of a building performs the role of a filter between indoor and outdoor conditions, to control the intake of air, heat, cold, light, sounds, and odors. It is generally agreed that air, temperature, wind, and sound are best controlled within the wall itself, while light is easier to control inside the building shell, and heat radiation is most efficiently halted before it reaches the building envelope proper.

The materials of a building skin play a decisive part in the utilization and control of solar rays. The first example is a full glass window wall. With its straight approach, appealing as it is, the wall has to absorb all the penalties of the environmental variations, since the bare glass pane offers very little (around 12 percent) protection from radiation.

A diametrically opposite example, is the fully opaque curtain wall.

In some cases this envelops a building totally, leaving the entirely independent interior free for manmade conditioning. No doubt this solution has its rightful place in specific and peculiar situations, but a fully engineered atmosphere divorced from nature leaves known psychological deficiencies and most probably has still undiscovered drawbacks.

The use of heat—intercepting glass permits the use of large window walls with less heat penetration than allowed by ordinary glass. A relatively light—colored heat—absorbing glass intercepts over 40 percent of the radiant energy. This is a considerable aid in summer cooling, but unfortunately it also represents a loss of useful heat in winter.

The last example illustrates a radiation control solution with shading device. The method is fundamentally sound. Interception of the energy happens at the right place—before it attacks the building. In this way the obstructed heat is reflected and can dissipate into the outside air. Shading device gives by far the most efficient performance, since by shaping them according to the changing seasonal sun-path, both summer shading and winter heat gain can be achieved.

Location, latitude, and orientation all contribute the formulation of an effective device. In addition, the sun breaker can express a strong spatial character, add new elements to the architectural vocabulary, and phrase a truly regional consciousness.

The material which provides a screen between man and the natural environment offer rich possibilities for visual expression. Many materials only elaborate the surface others invite a play of light and shadow or add to the spatial composition, while some constitute their own architectural entities. To their plastic appearance they add visual ties or rhythm, light, color, and texture.

To control heat entry—The first line of heat control lies at the surface. Since the surface temperature of a sunlit material will be higher than that of the air, air movement over an exposed surface will reduce the external heat impact and be particularly beneficial under hot conditions. The exchange effect can be increased by diluting the radiation over a larger area by means of curved surfaces (such as vaults and domes), or corrugated uneven surfaces (such as alternating recessed brick layers), which will also simultaneously increases the rate of convection transfer.

The selective absorptivity and emissivity characteristics of materials are another very effective defense against radiation impacts and especially important in overheated conditions. Materials which reflect rather than absorb radiation and which more readily release the absorbed quantity as thermal radiation, will cause lower temperatures with in the structure.

The sun's energy, by the time it falls upon a building, has been cut down by the atmosphere and arrives through several different channels. The solar radiation consists of visible wavelengths (0.3 to 0.7 microns). Since this energy is concentrated near the visible part of the spectrum, the criterion of reflectivity is an approximate relation to color values. White materials may reflect 90 percent or more, black materials 15 percent or less, of the radiation received.

On the other hand, the thermal exchange with the surroundings consists of longer infra-red wavelengths (over 2.5 usually from 5 to 20 microns. This range can also be classified as 9 microns. The characteristics of materials in regards to reflectivity of long-wave infra-red heat depend more on the density of surface and on molecular composition than on color.

The summer rays of high elevation may be intercepted by building elements of high reflectivity. In zones where hot conditions prevail, the net effect of reflectivity combined with the emissive thermal radiation characteristic of the material has to be considered.

If surfaces exposed to the irradiation of the sun and to a clear sky are whitewashed, painted white or built of light-colored material such as marble, they will remain cooler than surface of polished metal such as aluminum. Despite the fact that aluminum has a higher reflectivity to solar radiation, the effect is outbalanced by the emissive capability of the white surface which loses heat by thermal radiation towards the sky. This principle accounts for the white exteriors of tropical buildings. However, if the same materials are exposed not only to the sun but to hot ground where the white surface is not capable of losing heat by emissivity, the polished aluminum will be the cooler of the two materials. The application of both processes is utilized by aeroplanes, where the upper part exposed to solar radiation is painted white, while the lower portion remains metallic.

By converting solar energy into heat, heating can be provided locally.
The selection of color and materials can reduce the effect of solar
heating to some extent. The greatest source of heat gain can be the
solar radiation entering through a window. This could, in fact, increase
the indoor temperature far above the door temperature, even in
moderate climates. Because once the radiant heat has entered through
a window it is trapped inside the building.

The four methods to control solar heat gain through windows are
explained here.

1. *Orientation and Size of the Window:* In the equatorial location
    to avoid solar heat gain the main windows should face north or
    south. Minor opening of unimportant room should be placed on
    the East and West side. Solar heat gain on the West side can be
    particularly troublesome as its maximum intensity coincides with
    the hottest part of the day.

2. *Internal Blinds and Curtains:* They are not very effective ways
    to solar control but they do stop the passage of radiation, and
    they themselves absorb the solar heat and can reach a very high
    temperature.

3. *Special Glasses*

    (a) *Heat absorbing glasses:* Achieve a selection transmittance
         by selectonity in absorption they reduce substantially the
         infra-red transmission.

    (b) *Heat reflecting glasses:* Achieves a similar selective
         transmittance by selectinity in reflection. The glass is coated
         by a thin film of metal (nickle or gold) applied by vacuum
         evaporation. Such glasses absorb very little heat, therefore,
         the improvement in reducing the total solar gain is far
         greater.

    (c) *Light sensitive glasses:* (Photocromatic glasses) These contain
         submicroscopic halide crystals which turns dark when
         exposed to strong light and regain their transpirancy when
         the light source is removed.

4. *Shading Devices:* Three Different Types:

    (a) *Vertical devices:* Course blades or projecting fins in a vertical position. This type of device is most effective when the sun is to one side of the elevations, such as an eastern or western elevation. A vertical device to be effective when the sun is opposite to the wall considered, would have to give almost complete cover of the whole windows.

        (Vertical and Horizontal Suitable For South and West Angle Facing Sun.)

    (b) *Horizontal devices:* May be canopies, horizontal louvre blades or externally applied venetian blinds. These will be most effective when the sun is opposite to the building face considered and at a high angle such as for North and South facing walls.

    (c) *Egg-crate devices:* They are combination of horizontal and vertical elements the many types of grille-blocks and decorative screens may fall into this category. These can be effective for any orientation depending on detail dimensions. Construction of a shading mask also comes under this category.

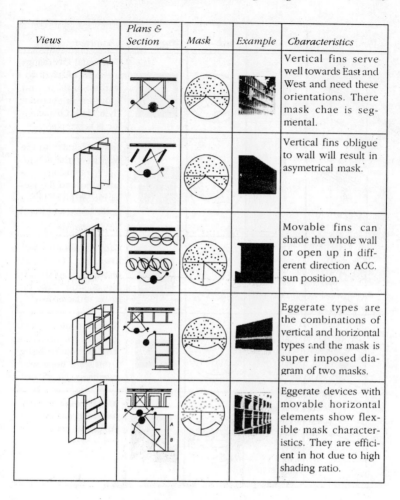

Views	Plans & Section	Mask	Example	Characteristics
				Vertical fins serve well towards East and West and need these orientations. There mask chae is segmental.
				Vertical fins obligue to wall will result in asymetrical mask.
				Movable fins can shade the whole wall or open up in different direction ACC. sun position.
				Eggerate types are the combinations of vertical and horizontal types and the mask is super imposed diagram of two masks.
				Eggerate devices with movable horizontal elements show flexible mask characteristics. They are efficient in hot due to high shading ratio.

Vertical and Eggerate types of Shading devices

Diagram 8

View	Section	Mask	Example	Characteristics
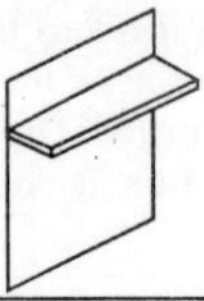		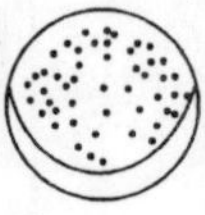		Horizontal Overhangs are most efficient towards South around Southern orientation. Their Mask Characteristic is segmental.
	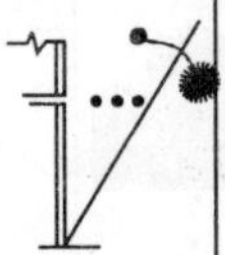	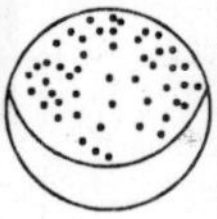		Louvre parallel to the wall have the advantage to permit air circulation near to the elevation. It gives better protection than vertical ones.
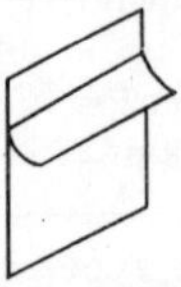	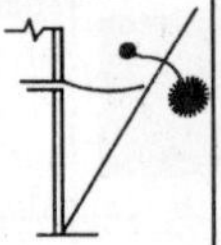	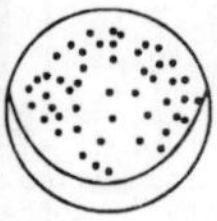		Canvas canopies will have the same characteristic as solid overhangs and can be made retractable.
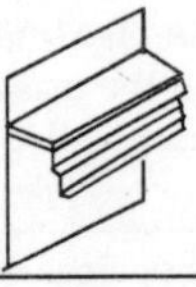		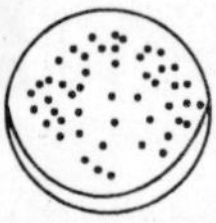		Where protection is needed for low sun angles, louvre hung from soild horizontal overhangs are efficient.
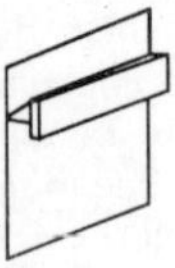		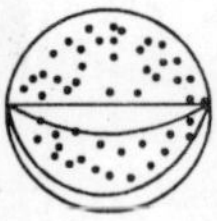		A solid screen strip parallel to wall cuts out the lower rays of the sun.

Example of various types of shading devices in horizontal type

Diagram 9

Chapter 14

How Dangerous are Electric and Electromagnetic Radiations?

Radiation Generated by Modern and Ultra-modern Equipment

Electric currents emit electric and electromagnetic radiation, which may be linked to health problems such as cancer, blood circulation, pregnancy, brain cells etc.

Electric and electronic equipment, particularly in kitchen and office, electric blanket, a power line and a broadcast tower all these emit electric and electromagnetic radiation. These invisible electromagnetic fields (EMFs), and electric radiation (ELF) generated by low voltage currents running through electric wires, are not powerful and destructive like unclear or X-ray radiation. Radio therapy studies have suggested that people exposed to EMFs run a higher risk of certain health problems, including miscarriages, learning disabilities and cancer.

No clear cause-and-effect relationship has been established between EMFs and illnesses, but the mounting evidence makes EMFs appear extremely suspicious. And because EMFs are generated by many sources—including cell phone, microwave ovens, television, radio, radar system and ironically, nuclear treatment, radio therapy etc. Studies over the last 15 years have hinted at a connection between EMFs and ELFs and health problems.

EMFs and ELFs have been implicated in behavioral changes, birth defects, memory loss and Alzheimer's disease. In 1976, two doctors at the Veterans Administration Hospital in Syracuse, N.Y., showed that the offspring of mice exposed to extremely low frequency EMFs from power lines were born stunted. Other studies have focused specifically on the suspected connection between EMF exposure and cancer. In 1979, two University of Colorado researchers, pored through childhood mortality records in the Denver area and correlated long-term exposure to weak EMFs with a higher incidence of cancer.

Seven years later, Dr. Lennart Tomenius, a Swedish researcher, found the same relationship between EMF exposure and cancer rates among children in Stockholm. And in 1982 Samuel Milham, an occupational health physician in the Washington State Department of Social and Health Services, noted that he found more leukemia-related deaths in men whose work brought them in contact with electrical and magnetic fields, such as employees of utility companies.

Furthermore, EMFs have been implicated in pregnancy problems. In 1986, Wertheimer reported that women who used heated waterbeds or electric blankets, both of which emit EMFs had longer pregnancies and a higher miscarriage rate, and in 1987, Kurt Slazinger, a psychology professor at the Brooklyn polytechnic institute N.Y. found that rats exposed to EMFs for 30 days had more problems than unexposed rats in learning to press a bar on commend. Their offspring, exposed in the womb and for nine days after birth developed permanent learning disabilities.

In their attempts to establish a cause-and-effect connection between EMF exposure and health problems, scientists have been trying to uncover just what effect EMFs have on the body. One theory says that EMFs of certain frequencies disrupt the normal role of calcium in the brain. Another theory says that EMFs affect how cells grow and reproduce. A third belief holds that EMFs make cells manufacture proteins they normally would not reproduce.

Indeed studies on diseases occasionally have the difficulty of trying to prove a casual link when researchers must rely on past records and events instead of controlled experiments. However, this lack of proof has not stopped lawyers from introducing available studies as evidence in EMF related lawsuits. The judgements in several such suits were based on research showing a possible connection and not a definite link. In late 1985, a Texas jury ordered the Houston Lighting and Power company to pay a local school district $25 million punitive damages after the utility built a transmission line through school property without the district's permission. In Florida, juries have awarded more than $1 million to owners of land next to high voltage lines. Another suit illustrates the potential effects of transmission lines and the EMFs they create on home-owners trying to sell their homes. About 60 land-owners in N.Y. state filed a 60-million suit against the New York power line from Canada into the state charging it could produce a 'cancer-phobia corridor' where property values would tumble.

How to deduct/identify excess radiation

At present, the interest remains stronger in Europe than America. Scientists have developed precise scientific instrumentation to actually quantify subtle magnetic field fluctuations in bedrooms, and even in the U.S. medical researchers are acknowledging the role of very weak magnetic fields in physical health. New York in America is gradually edging the importance of "earth rays" and geopathic stress into conventional diagnostic medical procedures. But this is not to say geopathology is being readily endorsed across the board. If you are convinced of danger, you can take remedial steps after consulting the specialists.

Remedies and safety precautions via Vastu

This fear of diminished property values brings up the question of what the general public can do to protect itself from this potential threat EMFs and or ELFs are not like other harmful agents. They have not been proven dangerous, as has the outlawed, cancer-causing food coloring dye etc. EMFs are almost unavoidable. The magnetic fields easily penetrate brick wall, R.C.C. slab, C.C.floor, stonewall or roof and human bodies and as of now, no protective shield is available with such a pervasive yet mysterious force around us, there's not much we can do to totally eliminate EMF exposure. There are ways, though, of minimizing the potential risks.

Vastu suggestions on how to reduce the risk of EMF and ELF radiation:

(a) Unplug after use the electric gadgets or and do not use electric blankets.

(b) Don't sit less than six feet from television.

(c) Don't allow children to peer through the doors of microwave ovens when they are on.

(d) Pregnant women should cut down on if not avoid using video-display terminals (VDTs).

(e) Avoid living in areas where EMF exposure could be high.

(f) People at greatest risk are utility workers and those near transmission lines (study has established a 'safe minimum distance' from power lines depends on the high voltage the conductor is carrying, always wear hard rubber sole shoes without nail.

(g) Use M.S. conduct pipe 16 gage for building wiring and earth both end properly.

(h) All your electric, electronic items must be properly earthed.

(i) Switch off your bedroom wiring from the main in the night.

(j) Keep minimum 2 meter distance from T.V. sets.

(k) Use ear phone and mike for your cell phone and keep cell phone with your waist belt.

(l) After use immediately switch off from the mains all your electric and electronic gadgets.

(m) Use your table lamp made of metal and earth the body properly.

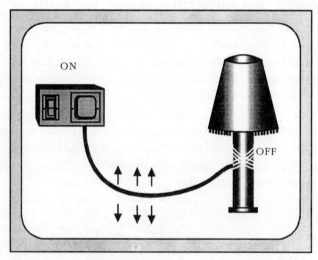

Electric Fields
Produced by Voltage
Measured in Volt per meter (V/m)

Electric Fields

Diagram 1 (a)

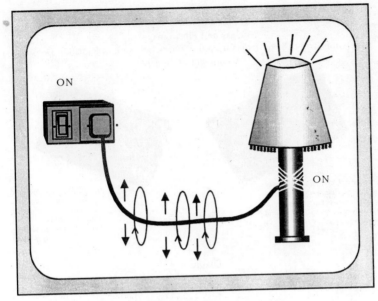

Magnetic Fields
Measured in Gauss (G) on Tesla (T)
1 millgauss = 0.1 microtesla
             = 100 manotesla

Diagram 1 (b): Magnetic Fields

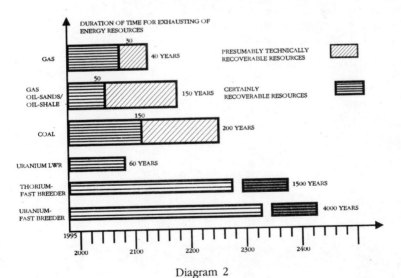

Diagram 2

A New Perspective on Radiation

Nuclear and Electromagnetic
Two handy Top Selling Models from the Widest selection of Radiation Detection
Equipment in the UK

The GEM II checks and measures your
background *radiation*. It is calibrated
for *gamma rays* and will detect the
presence of x-rays and of *alpha and
beta contamination*.

The ELF Monitor *detects and
measures electromagnetic
radiation from electrical
appliances and equipment,
electricity pylons, power lines
and transformers*.

Diagram 3

Chapter 15

Navagraha Mandalas—The Useful Effects of Planetary Yantras as per Vastu

Many of us dream of travelling in space and viewing the wonders of the universe. In reality all of us are space travelers. Our spaceship is the planet Earth, which is hurtling through space at the dizzying speed of 1,08,000 kilometre an hour.

EARTH CO-ORDINATE SYSTEM

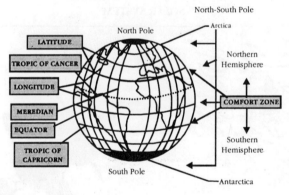

SEASONS OF A YEAR

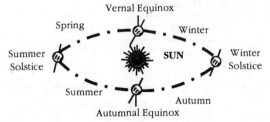

Diagram 1

CELESTIAL BODIES

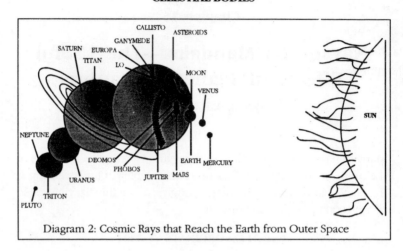

Diagram 2: Cosmic Rays that Reach the Earth from Outer Space

SOLAR SYSTEM

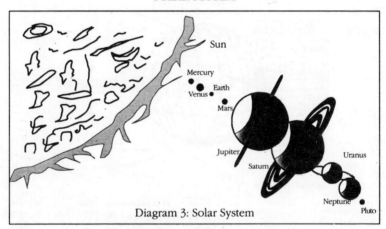

Diagram 3: Solar System

PLANETARY DATA (Nine Planets)

	Mercury	Venus	Earth	Mars	Jupiter	Saturn	Uranus	Neptune	Pluto
Diameter in (km.)	4878	12100	12714	6752	133540	106900	50300	47500	3000
Distance from Sun Crore (km.)	5.8	10.8	15.0	22.8	77.8	142.6	287.9	449.7	591.3
Rotation Period Around Sun	88 days	224.7 days	365.25 days	687 days	11.86 years	29.46 years	85 years	165 years	248 years

The Planets (Graha)

The four innermost planets in the solar system, Mercury, Venus, Earth and Mars are called terrestrial planets. This is because they have a compact, rocky surface like the Earth's.

Jupiter, Saturn, Uranus and Neptune are known as the Jovian (Jupiter-like) planets, because they are all gigantic compared with Earth and they are mostly made of gases, like Jupiter. The Jovian planets are also referred to as the gas giants, although some or all of them might have solid cores.

Galaxies are the basic building blocks of the Universe, just as atoms make up matter. The Milky Way is giant galaxy, far larger, brighter and more massive than most other galaxies in the universe. The Milky Way contains the Solar System and 200 billion other stars and star systems. The Solar System is where our Earth and our immediate neighbors live. The moon, eight other planets and their many satellites, assorted flying objects such as comets, asteroids and meteoroids, and the Sun.

Bright and impressive as the Sun might seem to us, when compared with other stars, it is only considered of average stature. All the same, all the heat and light that bathes the Earth and the other heavenly bodies come from the Sun.

Every star visible to the unaided eye is part of the Milky galaxy. But for every star you see, there are 50 million others which also belong to the Milky Way. The Sun is about 27,000 light years from the Galaxy's Centre, or about 40 percent of the way from the centre to the edge. The galaxy components are spread out in a plane which is called the Galactic Plane.

The distances between bodies in the Solar System is so large that nearly all of it by volume appears to be empty. While it might seem like a lot of nothing, this vacuum of "space" is made of the interplanetary medium, the interstellar gas and dust. This medium is buzzing with energy. Interplanetary gas is a thin flow of a gas and charged particles, mostly protons and electrons—plasma which streams from the Sun, called the Solar wind.

Earth : Prithvi

For us, Earth appears to be big and sturdy with an endless ocean of air. From space, astronauts often get the impression that the Earth is small with a thin, fragile layer of atmosphere. For a space traveler, the Earth features that stand out are the blue waters, brown and green land masses and white clouds set against a black background.

Sun : Surya

In Earth terms, the Sun is quite simply gigantic. 109 Earths could fit quite comfortably across the Sun's face, and it could hold over 1.3 million Earth's inside. The Sun contains 99.85% of all the matter in the Solar system but its not just the Sun's size that is impressive, the amount of energy it produces is equally dazzling. The Sun's outer visible layer is called the photosphere and has a temperature of 6000°C. which is about 125 times hotter than the hottest day in Delhi.

Solar energy is created deep within the core of the sun. The temperature (15,000,000°C) and pressure (340 billion times Earth air pressure at Sea level) here is so intense that nuclear reaction takes place. Energy is expelled as a result.

Energy generated in the Sun's core takes a million years to reach its surface. Every second 700 million tonnes of hydrogen are converted into helium ash. So, five million tonnes of pure energy is released . This means, as time goes on, the sun is becoming lighter every second.

Mercury : Budh

Mercury was named by the Romans after the fleet-footed messenger of the gods because it seemed to move more quickly than any other planet. It is the closest planet to the Sun and the second smallest planet in the Solar System.

If an explorer were to step into the surface of mercury, he would discover a world resembling the moon. Mercury's rolling, dust-covered hills have been eroded by the constant bombardment of meteorites, craters dot the surface. The explorer would notice that the Sun appears 2.5 times larger than on Earth however, the sky is always black because mercury has virtually no atmosphere to cause scattering of light.

Venus : Shukra

The jewel of the sky is named after the Roman goddess of love and beauty and is veiled by a thick swirling cloud cover. Astronomers refer to Venus as earth's sister planet. Both are similar in size, mass, density and volume. Both were formed about the same time. However, the similarity ends here. Venus has no oceans and is surrounded by a heavy atmosphere composed mainly of carbon dioxide with virtually no water vapour. Its clouds are composed of sulphuric acid droplets. Venus is scorching with a surface temperature of about 482°C, making it hotter than mercury, as its atmosphere traps the heat.

Mars : Mangal

Mars, the fourth planet from the sun, is commonly referred to as the red planet. The rocks, soil and sky have a red or pink color. The ancient Egyptians named the planet *herr Descher* meaning the red one. Before space exploration, Mars was considered the best candidate for harboring extraterrestrial life. Astronomers thought they saw straight lines criss-crossing its surface. This led to the popular belief that irrigation canals on the planet had been constructed by intelligent beings. However, according to biologists who have examined Martian soil, Mars is self-sterilizing which prevents the formation of living organisms in the Martian soil.

Jupiter : The Guru

Jupiter is the fifth planet from the sun, the largest one in the solar system and the first of the four gas giants. If Jupiter were hollow, more than 1000 Earths could fit inside. It is the most massive planet with a diameter about 11 times that of the Earth and a mass of about 2.5 times the combined mass of the eight other planets. There are 16 known Jovian moons. The four largest moons were observed by Galileo as long ago as 1610 and are called the Galileans. Jupiter does have rings around it, but these are very faint and are totally invisible from the earth.

Saturn : Shani

Saturn is the second largest planet in the solar system. It rotates planets in the Solar System. It rotates so fast on its axis that the planet is flat at the poles. Saturn is the only planet less dense than water (about 30 percent less). So if you could find an ocean that is large enough, Saturn would float in it.

The origin of Saturn's rings is not known. It is thought that the rings may have been formed from larger moons that were shattered by impacts of comets and meteoroids. No one is certain of the composition of the rings but they do show a large amount of water. Which means the rings might be icebergs and snowballs revolving around Saturn. Saturn has 18 confirmed moons, the largest number of satellites of any planet in the Solar System. As if that weren't enough, in 1995, scientists using the Hubble Space Telescope sighted four objects that might be new moons.

Uranus

Uranus was discovered by William Herschel in 1781. It orbits the Sun once every 84.01 Earth years system and the length of a day on Uranus is 17 hours. Uranus has at least 15 moons. Methane in Uranus, upper atmosphere absorbs red light, giving its planet its blue green color. Uranus stands out from other planets by the fact that it is tipped on its side.

Neptune

The first two-thirds of Neptune is composed of a mixture of molten rock, water, liquid ammonia and methane. The outer third is a mixture of heated gases comprised of hydrogen, helium, water and methane. It is the methane that gives Neptune its blue cloud color.

Neptune is a dynamic planet with several large, dark spots reminiscent of Jupiter's hurricane-like storms. The largest spot, known as the Great Dark Spot, is about the size of the Earth. The strongest winds on any planet were measured on Neptune. Near the Great Dark Spot, winds blow upto 2,000 kilometers an hour.

Pluto

Pluto was discovered on February 18, 1930, making it the last planet found in the Solar System. Pluto is usually farther from the Sun than any of the nine planets; however, due to the shape of its orbit, its path crosses Neptune's and it is closer than Neptune for 20 years out of its 249 years orbit. Pluto made its closest approach during 1989 and remained within the orbit of Neptune till March 14, 1999.

Pluto's surface is covered with methane ice and there is a thin atmosphere that might freeze and fall to the surface as the planet moves away from the Sun. The American Space Agency, NASA plans to launch a spacecraft, the Pluto Express, in 2001 that will allow scientists to study the planet before its atmosphere freezes.

Other Heavenly Bodies

Comets

Comets are small, fragile, irregularly shaped bodies composed of a mixture of non-volatile grains and frozen gases. Their orbits bring them very close to the Sun and swing them deeply into space, often beyond the orbit of Pluto.

Asteroids

Asteroids are planets that didn't quite make it to the right size category. They are little (and sometimes not so little) bits of rock that orbit the Sun but are too small to be considered planets. Only 30 asteroids are larger than Belgium. Asteroids range in size from Ceres, which has a diameter of about 1000 km, down to the size of pebbles. They have been found inside Earth's orbit to beyond Saturn's orbit, but most asteroids tend to hang out within a main belt that exists between the orbits of Mars and Jupiter.

Meteoroids and Meteorites

Asteroids that are on a collision course with Earth are called meteoroids. When a meteoroid strikes our atmosphere at high velocity, friction that causes this chunk of space matter to incinerate in a streak of light is known as a meteor. If the meteoroid does not burn up completely, what's left strikes Earth's surface and is called a meteorite. One of the best preserved examples is Barringer Meteor Crater near Winslow, Arizona.

Keeping an Eye on the Sky

The American Space Agency NASA is to establish a new office to co-ordinate worldwide efforts to keep track of threatening objects in space. The Near Earth Object Program Office will concentrate on finding at least 90 percent of the estimated 2,000 asteroids and comets that are larger than 1 km that can come close to the Earth. These are difficult to detect because of their relatively small size but they are large enough to cause global effect if one hits the Earth. Finding the threatening objects will require an International effort by space agencies, universities and observatories.

The threat to the Earth from a collision with an asteroid or a small comet is remote but real. All over our planet can be found craters and other scars from cosmic impacts. A small object, just 100 meters across could wipe out a city with the force of a nuclear detonation. Anything much larger could cause more widespread damage.

The most famous impact is the one that occurred 65 million years ago in the Gulf of Mexico. It is believed to have led to the extinction of the dinosaurs which had flourished on earth for over 150 million years.

SUN AND PLANETS

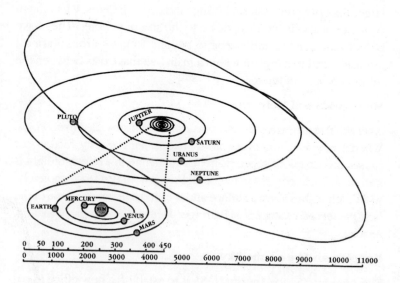

Diagram 4

SOLAR SYSTEM

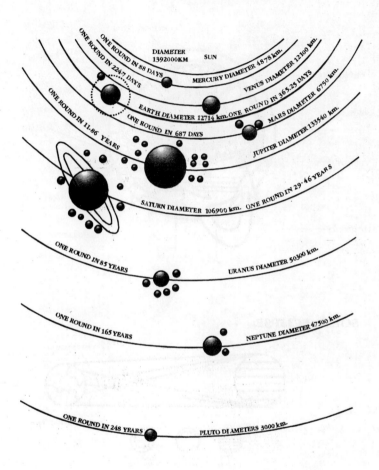

Diagram 5

STRUCTURE OF SUN

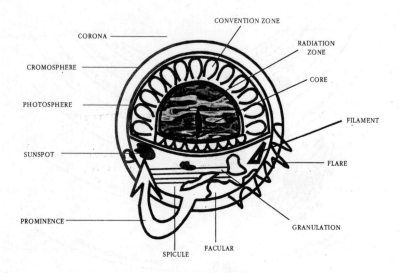

SOLAR ECLIPSE

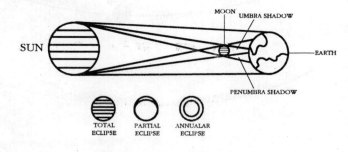

Diagram 6

EARTH AND MOON

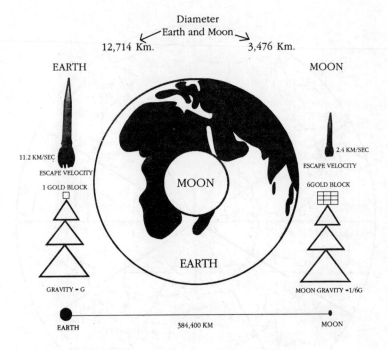

Gravity at Earth's Surface is about Six Times that at the Surface of the Moon.

Diagram 7

GROUP OF STARS OF NORTHERN HEMISPHERE

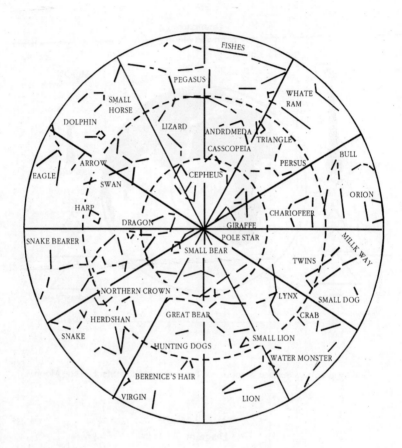

Constellations of the Northern Hempisphere Group of Stars

Diagram 8 (a)

GROUP OF STARS OF SOUTHERN HEMISPHERE

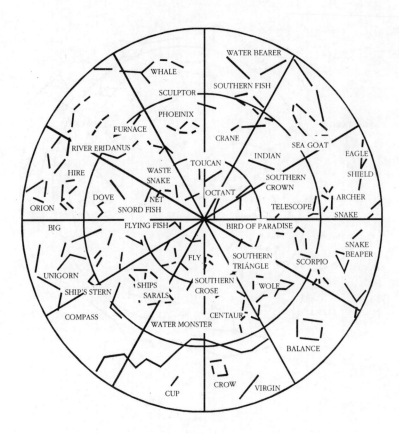

Constellations of the Southern Hemisphere Group of Stars

Diagram 8 (b)

ZODIAC SIGNS OF NORTHERN SKY

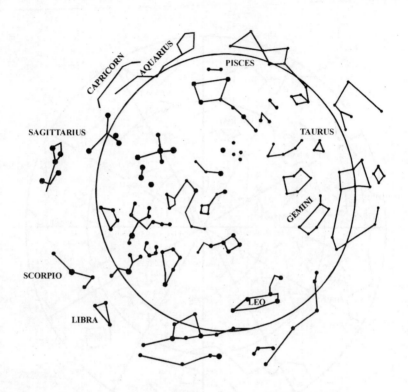

Diagram 9 (a)

ZODIAC SIGNS OF SOUTHERN SKY

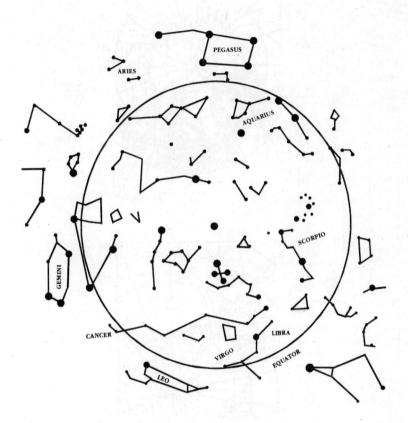

Diagram 9 (b)

NORTH AND SOUTH MAGNETIC POLE

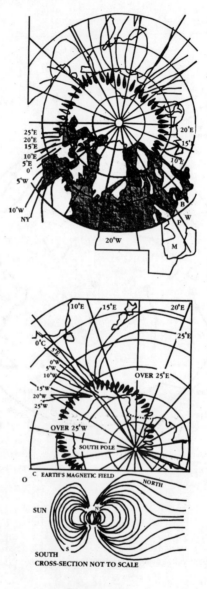

Diagram 10

Navagraha Mandala and its Yantras

In Vedic Period people got Health, Wealth and Power through Mantra, Yantra and Tantra.

NAVAGRAHA MANDALA
नवग्रह मंडल

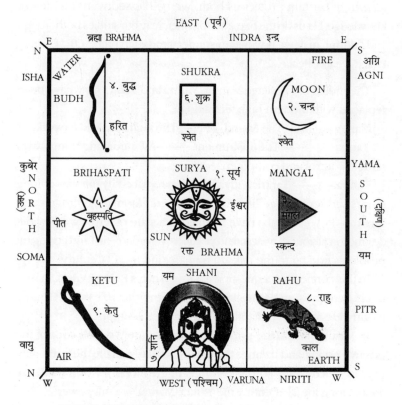

MANTRA FOR NINE PLANETS

Om Brahma Murari Stripurantakari Bhanuh Shashi Bhumi
Suto Budhashch, Gurushch Shukrah Shani Rahu
Ketvah, Servae Grahah Shantikara Bhavantu ||

Diagram 11

Saloka

> *Om Saha Navavatu, Saha Nau Bhunaktu,*
> *Saha Viryam Karavavahai |*
> *Tejasvinavadhitamastu Ma Vidvishavahai |*
> *Om Shantih, Shantih, Shantih ||*

Meaning: Let him protect us both, we be blessed with the bliss of knowledge. Let us do the brave act together, may our studies be thorough and faithful, may we not ever misunderstand each other. Oh ! Eternity Peace, Peace, Peace.

The Indian old heritage Mantra, Yantra and Tantra now have been replaced with modern high technology.

Mantra ----------- The Sound -----------Through Satellite Network.

Yantra ----------- The Instrument --------All automatic things with remote control and computerized things.

Tantra ---------- Tantric Vidya has been replaced by missiles of long term/short term range like Agni, Gauri etc. Atomic, Hydrogen and Thermo- Power bombs have resulted in a state of terror worldwide, destruction all round, widespread pollution, environmental and ecological problems adding to the risks to human kind in 21ˢᵗ Century.

In this connection a question arises, "What is Role of Vastu Shastra in 21ˢᵗ Century" Can Vastu Shastra play a significant role in 21ˢᵗ Century worldwide for the Humanity ?" The answer is simple.

In Vastu Shastra, the principle Mandalas are 9 which control the positive power and balance the house. Similarly, in life there are nine grahas which control our life source. In the modern world while we are entering the 21ˢᵗ Century the Yantra, Mantra are still powerful. You must have noticed that in Garhwal and Kumaon Hills where lightning is very heavy and common lots of people, animals, trees huts and houses are electrified. For effective earthing through lightning arrester, local people fix a Yantra in the main door of the house to protect their house/building and it is believed that this Yantra is really working. So, still the old tradition of Mantra, Tantra and Yantra is effective if properly studied and one should know how to apply it in modern life.

We are all born to lead successful lives but our conditioning leads us to failure. We are born to win but are conditioned to lose. We often hear that statement that this person is very lucky. He touches dirt and it turns to gold or that he is so unlucky that no matter what he touches it turns to dirt. This is not true. Nobody is lucky or unlucky, but the change in the position of stars which we call Nine Planets or Navagrahas change the timing of a person. These Navagrahas have definite effect on human beings in specific positions. When they all are well-placed, things go right. That is why while entering the house or at Graha Puja and Vastu Pujan, mantras are chanted so that these Navagrahas are auspicious to us, our house and our family members. Someone has rightly said that "our thoughts lead to habits, habit forms the character and character leads to destiny." Not only these nine planets have effect on human body but the two planets present in human body can make one's life positive or negative. These two planets are heart and mind. They play a vital role in building one's life. If these two planets are on the right path then life is also on the right path. If these two skip from the right track the life will also be strayed from the path.

Learned scholars like Varahamihir and Aryabhatta have long back mentioned about different planets having direct influence on human beings living on Earth. It is unfortunate that number of books written by these great scholars are not available now because our country has suffered from brutal aggressions from time to time. The findings of the Indian scholars are written in Surya Siddhanta, Pitamah Siddhanta, Vyas Siddhanta, Vasishth Siddhanta, Aarti Siddhanta, etc. A known Astronomer Varahamihir has mentioned that Surya Siddhanta is over 20 thousands years, B.C. old Similarly, other books which could throw light on the fact that the celestial bodies having effect on the human body are now not available, only a few are available. It might be difficult to prove this in crude mathematical terms. I would like to take this opportunity to present glimpses of this ancient knowledge to show that while following Vastu Shastra one has to take care of influence of different positions of nine planets in our life.

Sun

The Sun is very imminent and effective planet or Graha. Its influence can be seen on Earth and also on Moon. According to the Astrology the Sun is master of LEO. Highly place sun in a horoscope of any individual gives him state honor and also makes a worshipper and an intellectual etc. The planet Surya can help in making our life peaceful and contended. The sun according to Indian thoughts has to be worshipped by chanting Surya Stuti. The Surya Yantra is also helpful in getting blessings of sun. The placement of sun in Navagraha Mandala is in the centre the Brahmasthan. If we see the Surya Yantra the total comes to 15 on counting the figures from all directions or cross-section. Surya Gayatri is also helpful to have good effect of Surya. Surya gives energy to our body without which life is not possible. In human body, the effect of sun can be seen on stomach. Surya Sadhana is started on Sunday.

SURYA YANTRA

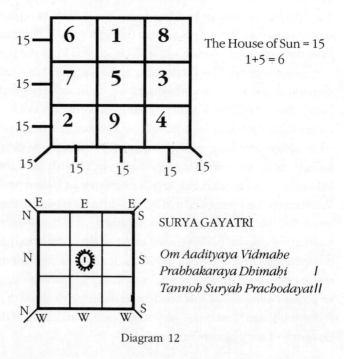

The House of Sun = 15
1+5 = 6

SURYA GAYATRI

*Om Aadityaya Vidmahe
Prabhakaraya Dhimahi   I
Tannoh Suryah Prachodayat II*

Diagram 12

Moon

Moon is very important from the Indian point of view. The moon has special effect on the human mind and the heart of an individual. The effect of moon is also seen in the manner of depression. A number of people commit suicide on full moon night, similarly flood tides and ebb tides are noticed on full night. The moon is the master of Cancer. Its position in Navagraha Mandala is in South-East Corner. The placement of moon in horoscope determines the imaginative and emotional aspect of any individual. The moon is also said to be responsible for rainfall, and agriculture and its attachment to the pulse is well-known. It plays an important role in the success of an individual. Chandra Sadhana is said to be useful for progress and family well-being. Chandra Sadhana usually begins on Monday especially on Somwati Amavasya. In Chandra Yantra the total of the figures comes to 18 on all directions. Moon affects human chest and water content in the human body. Som Gayatri is helpful in getting the blessings of moon.

MOON YANTRA

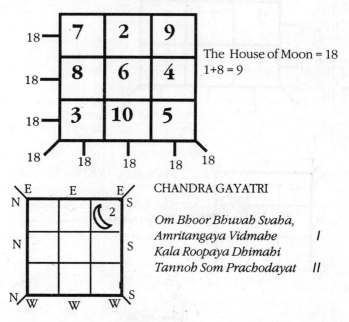

The House of Moon = 18
1+8 = 9

CHANDRA GAYATRI

Om Bhoor Bhuvah Svaha,
Amritangaya Vidmahe   *I*
Kala Roopaya Dhimahi
Tannoh Som Prachodayat   *II*

Diagram 13

Mars (Mangal)

In comparison to other planets, Mars is nearer to the Earth. It is placed in South in Navagraha Mandala. It is said to be the master of Aries and Scorpions. Mars is the Lord of Boldness. If Mars is in the right position, it not only gives wealth but also a person becomes powerful for management. Mars has effect on blood circulation in human body. To achieve good effects of Mars , Mangal Yantra is prepared and Mangal Gayatri is chanted. In human body it affects lungs and head. If we look at the Mangal Yantra, the total figure will come to 21 on counting them from all directions.

MANGAL YANTRA

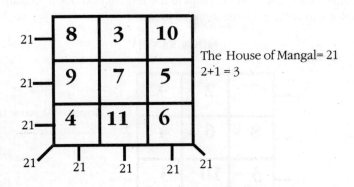

The House of Mangal= 21

$2+1 = 3$

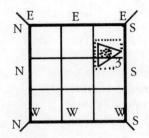

MANGAL GAYATRI

Om Aangarakaya Vidmahe,
Shakti Hastaya Dhimahi   I
Tannoh Bhaumah Prachodayat II

Diagram 14

Mercury (Budh)

This planet is closer to the Sun in comparison to the Earth and it is said to be the master of Virgo. This planet affects etiquette, poise speech presentation, learning capability, criticism limit and voice of a person. In Navagraha Mandala, its position is in the Ishan Kone i.e North-East Corner. Budh Sadhana is done to achieve good modulation effect of Mercury by offering Budh Yantra and chanting Budh Gayatri. If we look at the Budh Yantra, the total of figures will come to 24 on counting them from all directions. Good rays of Mercury can cure any skin infection. The color of Mercury is green. This is why green color is used in hospitals to heal as well as to provide soothing effect to the body. In human body, Mercury affects Hands and Arms.

BUDH YANTRA

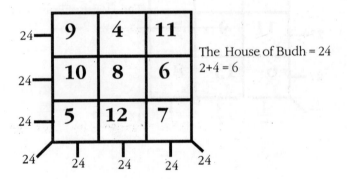

The House of Budh = 24
2+4 = 6

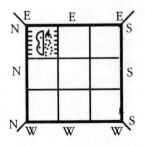

BUDH GAYATRI

Om Saumyah Roopaya Vidmahe,
Vaneshaya Dhimahi   I
Tannoh Saumyah Prachodayat II

Diagram 15

Jupiter (Brihaspati or Guru)

High placement of this planet makes a person intelligent, famous and always keeping him in the top priority in the society. It is said to be the master of sagittarius and Pisces. In the Navagraha Mandala, its position is in the North. People of this Sun Sign are very religious by nature. Guru Sadhana is started on Thursday in Shuklapaksha of any month. Evening time is recommended to start the Guru Sadhana. Guru Yantra is made and Guru Gayatri is chanted. If we see the Guru Yantra the total of all figures comes to 27 in all directions. It affects our thighs and feet.

GURU YANTRA

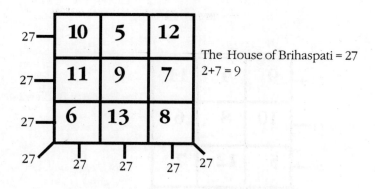

The House of Brihaspati = 27
2+7 = 9

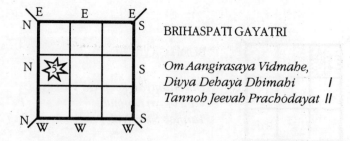

BRIHASPATI GAYATRI

Om Aangirasaya Vidmahe,
Divya Dehaya Dhimahi |
Tannoh Jeevah Prachodayat ||

Diagram 16

Venus (Shukra)

This planet is the most shiny planet. It completes full round around the Sun in eight months only. In Navagraha Mandala, its position is in the East and it is said to be the Master of Libra and Taurus. It increases love and affection for others. It affects Eyes of Human Beings. Shukra Yantra is made to achieve the good effect of Venus. In Shukra Yantra, the total of figures comes to 30 from all directions.

SHUKRA YANTRA

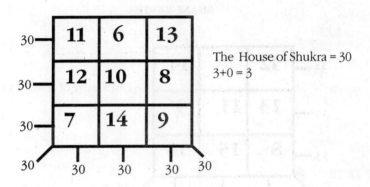

The House of Shukra = 30
3+0 = 3

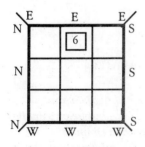

SHUKRA GAYATRI

Shukraye Vidmahe,
Shuklamber Dharah Dhimahi |
Tannah Shukra Prachodayat ||

Diagram 17

Shani (Saturn)

Saturn is considered the son of Surya. But Sun and Saturn are always anti to each other. Saturn has special importance in horoscope. Its position in Navagraha Mandala is in the West. It is the master of Capricorn and Aquarius Sign. Saturn is more powerful in comparison to other planets. In human body Saturn affects from Knees to Ankle. High placement of Saturn in horoscope brings fame, long life. If it is in wrong position, then it gives poverty and slavery etc. For the blessing of Saturn, Shani Yantra is prepared and Shani Gayatri is chanted. If we have a look at the Yantra, the total of the figures will come to 33 from all directions.

SHANI YANTRA

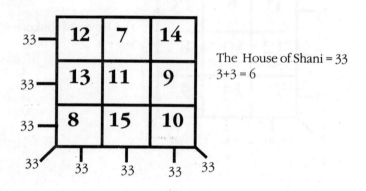

The House of Shani = 33
3+3 = 6

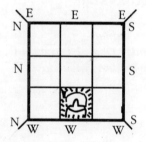

SHANI GAYATRI

Om Bhoor Bhuvah Svaha
Shanno Devirbhishtaye Vidmahe I
Neelanjanaya Dhimahi,
Tannoh Shanih Prachodayat II

Diagram 18

Rahu

It is a 'shadow' planet. It also moves round the Sun as well as other planets. Its position in Navagraha Mandala is in South-West corner which is the heaviest corner, in the Mandala in the shape of a crocodile. Rahu makes person's logical nature very powerful. In the horoscope, if it is highly placed then a person can be a good politician. But, if it is in the wrong position then the person is always tensed, he can't sleep soundly. Rahu Yantra which is prepared to have good result. The total of the figures comes to 36. Rahu Gayatri is chanted while offering prayer to Rahu. For pujan Saturday is recommended.

RAHU YANTRA

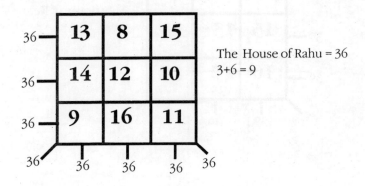

The House of Rahu = 36
3+6 = 9

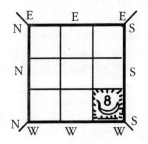

RAHU GAYATRĪ

Om Shiro Roopaya Vidmahe,
Amriteshaya Dhimahi   *I*
Tannoh Rahua Prachodayat II

Diagram 19

Ketu

This is also a 'shadow' planet. In Navagraha Mandala, its position is in the North-West corner. If in horoscope it is highly placed then the person is always saved from heavy accidents. If its position is wrong then a person can become a criminal. It is said to be the master of Pisces. For pujan of Ketu Gayatri is chanted. Tuesday, night time is recommended. In Ketu Yantra the total of figures comes to 39.

KETU YANTRA

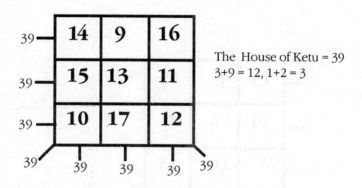

The House of Ketu = 39
3+9 = 12, 1+2 = 3

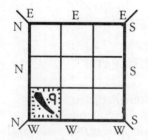

KETU GAYATRI

Om Padmputraya Vidmahe,
Amriteshaya Dhimahi   **I**
Tannoh Ketuh Prachodayat   **II**

Diagram 20

Our ancestors and present day scholars have been researching on the positioning and influences of planets on individual human beings. Anyhow, these studies remain incomplete and precise results are not always obtained due to insufficient and/or altering data. Science also has limitations. Suffice it to say that it is best not to temper with nature and to apply Vastu Shastra combined with Astrology in the 21st Century Modern World. Vedas and Upanishads are precious gifts given to us by that Supreme Power. Religion starts where Science ends.

Sloka

> *Vihay Kaman Yah Servan Pumansh Charit Nih Spriha |*
> *Nirmamo Nirhankar Sa Shanti Madhi Gachchati ||*

Meaning: A person who has given up all desires for sense gratification, who lives free from desires, who has given up all sense of proprietorship and is devoid of false ego—he alone can attain real peace.

Auspicious Months to Start the Construction Work

Astronomy is the foundation of Astrology and they together with calendar play an important role in different aspects of Vastu Shastra, particularly in the deciding the right time and day to commence the construction work.

Auspicious Months as explained in the Sloka

> *Griha samstaapnam chaitre dhanahaniramaahabhayam*
> *Vaishake shubhadam vindyaat jaishteetu maranam*
> *dhruvam*
> *Aashaade gokulam hanti shraavane putravardhanam*
> *Prajaarogam bhadrapade kulahooschayuje tathaa*
> *Kaarttike dhanlabhasyannnmargashirshe maha bhayam*
> *Pushechaagnibhayam vidyanamaghetu behuputravaan*
> *Phaalgune ratna laabhasyanamaasaanaam cha*
> *shubhaashubham*

Meaning: Building a house during the following months as explained in sloka;

Chaitra (March-April) will result in financial loss and fearfulness;

Vaishakha (April-May) will bring in good result;

Jaishtha (May-June) will lead to fear of death.

Aashaadhe (June-July)will result in loss of cattle wealth;

Shraavana (July-August) good for the welfare of the family.

Bhadrapada (August-September) will cause illness and diseases;

Ashwayuja (September-October) will result in unnecessary fight and enmity;

Kaarttika (October-November) will ensure acquisition of wealth;

Maargashirash (November-December) will cause fear of many things;

Pushya (December-January) result in fear of fire and other trouble;

Maagha (January-February) is good for the entire family;

Phaalguna (February-March) will ensure gain in wealth, richness etc.

Auspicious Days to Start the Construction Work

Auspicious Days as explained in the sloka

> *Bhanuvaree Krutam veshmam Vahminadahytae Chiraat*
> *Chaandrecha vardhate shuklesheyate krushna pakshate*
> *Bhaumavaare tadam sevaatallagne saptameepiva*
> *Dahyatee tadgruham shuunyam kartrumaranam mevacha*
> *Budhavaree dhanaishwaryam putra sampatsukhaavaham*
> *Guruvaarechiram teeshtekartaacha sukha sampadaam*
> *Chiram tishtesmamdavaare taskarebhyo mahaabhayam*

Meaning: Following is the effect of commencing building construction on different days:

- Sunday : Fear of fire.
- Monday of Shuklapaksha : Happiness and all round prosperity.
- Monday of Krishnapaksha : Should not start the work at all.
- Tuesday : Bad effects, fear of fire and death
- Wednesday : Gain in wealth and richness happiness, family welfare etc.
- Thursday : Long life, happiness and children will attain name and fame.
- Friday : Happiness and peace of mind, full of good activities and functions.
- Saturday : Even if the life of building will be

long the inmates will be full of debt, sorrow, misery, laziness and other bad effects.

Good Days

Monday, Wednesday, Thursday and Friday are good days to start the work, but it should be in Shuklapaksha of the particular months.

Krishnapaksha (from Purnima to Amavasya i.e. from full moon day to new moon day).

Shuklapaksha (from Amavasya to Purnima i.e. from new moon day to full moon day).

Chapter 16

Vastu and Astrology of Colors

Colors have the most powerful effect in influencing the human mind and body. It is also the least expensive, easiest and quickest means to use, to change or to create a decorating scheme. Colors can change the visual size and shape of a room as well as create an atmosphere and add warmth, vitality and beauty to a room and change the mood of the user.

The Color Radiations

Colors play a very important role in the human energy field and are closely related to the human form—its various energy axes and cosmic cycles and its environment. 'Doctors and Architects in France, found a set of slides with transparent colored filters of very high purity index related to Dr. Paul Nogier's method of identifying a particular color with an energy point or chakra, a particular organ and its functioning.'

Each of the harmful Bio-Electromagnetic radiation in a room is also characterized by a dominant color that affect us or disturb us. One can however, neutralize the affect with a complementary color (diagonally opposite color is complementary color). Color Therapy is used by various geomantists the world over.

Colors play an important role in two ways:

1. The relationship of colors to orientations.
2. Relationship of orientations and colors on the human body.

Thus , it is essential to take into consideration the total color radiation of the various axes in the frontal and dorsal parts of the body. When the body moves in space, or is oriented in any direction, the color radiation of the body should not be disturbed and should maintain a normal profile. The colors for each orientation were discovered by experimenting with the colors of the VIBGYOR respective in each orientation and observing how, where and in what color radiation in the body gets harmonized.

In Vedic period, all colors were taken out from vegetables and flowers, which were more permanent in shade, soothing to eye and had natural tint. Even now in many parts of the world instead of using synthetic colors, vegetables are used, particularly in textile printing and making design, miniature painting ceramics etc. Vegetable colors have no side effect on skin and eyes.

The ice age man buried his dead body in red caskets or painted their bones with red colors, because that the flow of red blood means the difference between life and death. Probably, they believed that the color itself was, therefore, life giving. The Egyptians used colors obtained from metal found in the Earth, plants, insects and fish.

At a very early stage in human history, a symbolic use of color was made. During early period, heart which was the seat of life and the blood was identified with life and the consciousness and was colored red. Yellow was possibly the color of fire, white that of day. If a room has poor daylight, it should be painted in light color and if a room gets good amount of natural light throughout the day it can be painted in some deep color. If a room has only a North window which admits cold light, we should not use blue color on the walls.

If a room gets enough direct sunlight it is not advisable to paint the walls yellow and peach. It is nearly always better to have the ceiling white because a white ceiling reflects heat and light into the room. A fluorescent tubelight in daylight or white color is harmful for human skin. It also changes the original tint of other colors. The ceiling temperature must be less than the human body temperature.

Color contrast in value is perhaps the most important factor on a composition or a design. A strong yellow on a black field is an excellent example of maximum visibility.

One must always bear in mind that no individual is completely white (Purity, Good) or black (Bad), but is an amalgam of the two 'Gray'. A sensible good blending can create a forceful creation.

Ancient Indian thinkers had rightly recognized the male and female forces, their need for each other for a harmonious co-existence and their coming together as equal partners in the process of creation. All the living creatures in the world are believed to be the children of nature, and the nature gives multi-million colors. A good healthy nation is only possible when we are surrounded with proper color and light arrangement. In darkness there is only one color i.e. black. Therefore, blending of proper light (Daylight or artificial light) with recommended color is very important.

White color depicts day and opposite to black which is symbolic to night and death. Since long times past we have been trained to recognise color in particular contexts and with specific events as we associate red with parades and games, blue with that of outstanding work, purple as of dignity and reverence, green with nature and healing, yellow with sunshine, pink to good health etc.

Colors affect our body and mind very much. The purest and the most thoughtful minds are those which love color. People wear different color stones as per astrology to activate their stars. These are the colors which play a vital role in activating our stars. Vastu suggests colors to be worn according to days and Astrology suggests color stones for different planets.

RECOMMENDED COLOR CLOTHES TO BE WORN ACCORDING TO WEEK DAYS AND PLANETS

SUNDAY	Surya (Sun)	Pink, Copper.
MONDAY	Som (Moon)	White/Sky Blue.
TUESDAY	Mangal (Mars)	Red Family
WEDNESDAY	Budh (Mercury)	Green Family
THURSDAY	Guru (Jupiter)	Yellow Family
FRIDAY	Shukra (Venus)	White
SATURDAY	Shani (Saturn)	Black

A particular color can activate or can control human glands of different parts of body functions. Such as for a good appetizer for the good habit, or to give excitement for the low blood pressure patient a red family color atmosphere is recommended. Similarly, blue color is to stop overeating habit. For a high blood pressure patient a light and limited soothing color atmosphere is recommended for hygienic reasons.

In a hospital white color is used for hygienic reasons, but for healing, doctors use green color in operation theatre. For a good healthy/tasty food a golden yellow, or tinted brown color is recommended.

A color attains its true appearance in a good daylight. Pleasing decoration in home can be acquired by using a variety of colors. A bedroom is intended for rest and the colors, therefore, should be delicate tints or tones—soft, calm and restful. A living room, however, can be enlivened with brightly colored objects. The baby's room should have pure bright color because babies can see only bright colors.

Every color has its unique qualities and purposes. Imagine a color wheel. Each color is a location on the wheel. No color is better than another. Each has its inherent lessons, its positive and challenging traits.

Color Equivalents

Red

Desire, vitality, power, the urge to win, to have success, intensity of experience, action, doing, love of sports, struggle, competition, force of will, leadership, strength, courage, passion, eroticism, earthiness, practicality, desire for possessions, sense of adventure, the survival instinct. A majority of young children and teenagers especially boys, have bright red auras.

Orange

Creativity, the emotions, confidence, ability to relate to others in an open and friendly manner, sociability, intuition or gut feeling. The ability to reach out and extend one's self towards others. Many talented sales people, entrepreneurs, and people who deal with the public have orange auras.

Yellow

Sunny and enthusiastic, cheerful, bright, great sense of humor and fun, optimism, intellectuality, openness to new ideas, happiness, warmth, relaxation. Uninhibited expansiveness, release of burdens, problems and restrictions. talent for organization, hope and expectation, inspiration. People with yellow auras encourage and support others by naturally being so themselves; they radiate like the sun and they also may have a great ability to analyze complex concepts.

Green

Perseverance, tenacity, firmness, patience, sense of responsibility and service, self assertiveness, high ideals and aspirations, dedication, puts high value on work and career. Ambitious desire for respectability and personal attainment, deeply focused and adaptable. Green is also the color of growth and of dedicated parents, social workers, counsellors, psychologists, and other persons focusing on creating positive changes in the world.

Blue

Depth of feeling, devotion, loyalty, trust, desire to communicate. The person so endowed puts great importance on personal relationships. Empathetic. May be a dreamer or have artistic ability. Possibly tends to put the needs of others before his own and may have the ability to meditate, and live in the moment. He may be emotionally sensitive, intuitive, inwardly focused, may enjoy solitude, non-competitive, be receptive activities, be receptive and desire unity peace, love and affection in relationship with other. They need a calm and tranquil environment. You'll find many blue artists, poets, writers, musician, philosopher, serious students, spiritual seekers, and people looking for truth, justice and beauty in everything.

Violet or Purple

The person rich in purple aura tends to be Magical, original, tends to be unconventional, often has psychic abilities, unusual charisma and charm, the uncommon ability to make their dreams come true, or manifest desire in the material world, wish to charm and delight other and can easily connect with higher planes of consciousness with friends and . Playful, non-judgemental, tolerant of others' eccentricities, sensitive and compassionate with friends and foes. "Purple" appreciate tenderness and kindness in others. Not especially practical, they tend to prefer to live in a dream world of their own creation. You'll find many "violet or purple" entertainers, movie stars, free thinkers, visionaries, revolutionaries, and other otherwise singular and magnetic individuals. Dark violet aura could indicate the person's a need to take charge of their life, or perhaps, that he needs time to spiritually ground him/herself.

White

Spiritually motivated, with ability to be open and receptive to the divine, or spiritual world. Can merge with all that is probably unconcerned with worldly matters or ambition. Inner illumination, cosmic wisdom characterize the white energy. Young children, energy workers, and intense meditators often will show bright white in their auras.

Saffron

Sacrificing: No attachment with the wonders of the world, no love with materialistic things. In search of spirituality or God.

Chapter 17

Towards 21st Century

Fogging the Atmosphere

Moving, living and even breathing will be a problem in cities with vehicular pollution accounting for 72 percent of the air pollution in by 2001. destroying the atmosphere further are the thermal power plants which contribute 13 percent of the air pollution and assorted industrial activities that add another 12 percent.

With the number of vehicles increasing on the roads, out of which 40 percent are personal vehicles, the average road length available in the city is reducing everyday and vehicular pollution is increasing resulting in a disastrous situation. The number of people injured or killed in road accidents shot up by about 38 to 40 percent from 1990 by 2000.

Generator sets and mess-room of industrial units will add smoke to the skies, resulting in adding smoke and noise pollution. With the increase in number of hospitals and nursing homes another area of deep concern is the hospital waste , which is disposed off in the conventional manner of burning in the open air inspite of its being immensely hazardous.

Solid waste management plans are just not in place and with a population increase of 43 percent between 1991 and 1999, all existing projections defy solution, says Wil Gibson, Chief of Party, Tetratech USA Ltd.At least 8,203 million tonnes. of garbage was generated in 1997 and only 4,885 mt. was disposed. Present consumption patterns indicate an increase in garbage volumes to 11899 mt. by the year 2011. At present projections, this will leave 40 percent of the total garbage, scattered all over with no viable collection or recycling plan.

The existing 12 large landfill sites in Delhi have been totally packed with a mix of non-biodegradable and toxic waste as it is only a matter of time before this toxic soup reaches out to contaminate ground water sources.

One-third of population lives in slums and another one-third in unauthorized, unplanned or non-regularized colonies in non-conforming areas. Eighty percent of its industries too are located in non-conforming areas.

Energy Consumption

It is estimated that the total average energy consumed by man in the past 2000 years, has been consumed in the last one century only.

Agricultural Productivity

Since 1900 to 1940 the index agricultural productivity went up from a base of 100 percent to about only 125 percent. But after 20 years i.e. in 1960, this reached about 400 percent and after 40 years i.e. in 2000, it was somewhere around 800 percent plus.

Urbanization

In 1850, only four cities in the world had a population of one million plus per city. 50 years later 1900 the number of such cities had increased to nineteen, and in 1960 there were 141 such cities. But in 21st Century there will be more than 1200 such cities in the world.

Speed of Human Movement

In 6000 B.C., the fastest transportation available to man over long distance was the camel caravan averaging eight miles per hour. In 1600 B.C., with the invention of chariot the speed limit went upto twenty miles per hour. The first steam locomotive, introduced in 1825 could muster a speed of only thirteen miles per hour. In 1880, this could achieve a speed of 100 mph. However, only 58 years later in 1938, airborne man was cracking the 400 mph. line. Again, only twenty two years later, rocket planes approached speeds of 4800 mph. and today, men in space capsules are circling the earth at 18000 mph.

Development

If we divide 50,000 years of man's existence into 800 lifetimes of 62 years each—we will find that full 650 lifetimes of them were spent in caves. Only during last 70 lifetimes has the art of writing or reading emerged. Only during the last 6 lifetimes did masses of men ever see a printed world map. Only in the last two has anyone, anywhere used an electric equipment. And the overwhelming majority of advanced technology and electronic equipments we use in daily life today have been developed within the present lifetime.

What is evident from all the above examples is the fact that we are developing with an acceleration which itself is accelerating.

GROWTH AND DEVELOPMENT IN UNITS

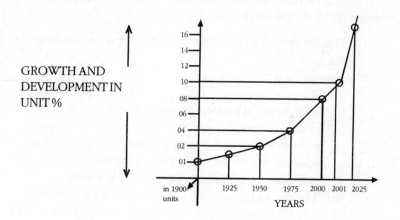

Diagram 1

Thus, if the actual growth between 1950 and 1975 was 2 units, the growth between 2001 and 2025 can be around 8 units. In other words, if a mature person in 1950 was to tolerate the social stresses generated because of changes of 6 units during his lifetime, (in next fifty years) an average adult in 2001 may have to face eight times more stresses i.e. 48 units during his life span of next fifty years. Needless to say, one will have to enrich his faculty of adaptability tremendously.

However, the acceleration of change is going to deeply penetrate in our private lives as well placing absolutely unprecedented strain on the family.

Family of the Future

In the start of civilization when the professions of human being ranged only from agriculture to cottage industry—human beings spent most of their times in and around their houses, i.e. with their families. Gradually, as the society started being industrialized, the concept of offices and factories cropped up and a significant proportion of people started spending quite a good number of hours outsides their homes. A few moved out of their native places and other outside their homes.

Career and status consciousness in the fair sex made life more mechanical and the time one spent with his family has decreased still further. Now the possibilities are three-fold :

1. The family will be dead except for the one or two years of childraising.
2. The family is for a Golden Age
   (a) With advances in information technology, homes and offices will become coincident. People may not have to move out of their homes because they can do most part of their jobs from their homes on E-mail, Website or Internet. As leisure spreads, the families will spend more time together and will derive great satisfaction from joint activity.
   (b) The very turbulence of tomorrow will drive people deeper into facsimiles. People will marry for stable structure and it will serve as one's roots anchoring him against the storms of change.
3. The future is more open than it might appear. The family may either vanish or enter upon a new Golden Age. It may break up and shatter only to come together again in weird and novel ways.

Let us discuss some possibilities which may revolutionize the concept of family altogether as compared to Vedic Age.

Concept of Motherhood

The birth technology is going to have the most upsetting effect on family. Let us consider a few possibilities:

- The extension of the test-tube baby concept may lead to babies which can be grown in a laboratory jar—what happens to the notion of maternity then ? And what happens to the self image of the female in societies which since the very beginning of man have taught her that her primary mission is the propagation and nurturing of the race?

- Further what happens to the cult of motherhood. Is the ofspring of a female not hers but that of a genetically "superior" Ovum, implanted in her womb from another women.

- Taking a step further—if a couple can actually purchase an embryo then parenthood becomes a legal and not a biological matter. Imagine a couple buying an embryo, raising it in-vitro, then buying another in the name of the first, as though for a trust fund. In that case, they might be regarded as legal "grandparents" before their first child is out of its infancy.

- Furthermore, if embryos are for sale can a corporation buy one? Can it buy then thousand ? Can it resell them ? And if not corporation, how about a non-commercial research laboratory ? If we buy and sell living embryos, are we back to a new form of slavery?

Dr. Beatrice Mintz, a developmental biologist at the Institute of Cancer Research in Philadelphia, has grown what are coming to be known as "Multi-mice"—baby mice each of which has more than the usual numbers of the parents. Embryos are taken from each of two pregnant mice. These embryos are placed in the laboratory dish and nurtured until they form a single growing mass. Then they are implanted in the womb of a third female mouse—which gives birth to a baby which clearly shares the genetic characteristics of both pairs of parents. If multi-mouse is here, can multi-man be far behind? Under such circumstances, what or who is the parent? Who is the mother and just exactly who is the father?

Birth of the Superhuman ?

Skin grafting techniques are commonly employed these days in plastic surgery and allied fields. In fact, if the top R and D people of surgery are to be believed very shortly human limbs can be developed in labs. What though, since the DNA code and working of brain has been understood *in toto,* it might be possible within next 50-100 years to develop human brain in laboratories. Brain transplants can come even sooner. Now, imagine a few scenrios commensurate with these developments in medicine and bio-sciences.

- A great scientist of NASA dies of certain malfunctioning in his body other than a brain disease. His brain is transplanted into the body of a rikshawpuller in Ethiopia. Now, who is that Ethiopian? What is his identity ? Does he become a scientist? And in that case who exactly has died—NASA scientist or the rikshawpuller? And what will be the relationship of the living person with the families of these two persons?

  Human mind functions almost like a computer, albeit, more efficiently. Now, with the advent of fifth generation computers and still more advanced such machines—where computers may be involved in the creation of better computers i.e. with better memory and speed—will it be possible to stimulate this process with human mind ? Will it be possible to develop human mind in lab and use it to develop superminds to be transplanted into super human beings? No wonder, that all the possible knowledge in the world is fed into such minds and they are given the task of developing new machinery and tools—will all the R and D labs of the world change their complexion to include such biological techniques.

  Ancient Egyptians used to keep their dead bodies inside pyramid properly preserved in the hope that some day it might be possible to inject back life in them. Medical researchers are actively involved in researches in which probably it will be possible to do so now. Say if someone has died of certain heart ailment which doesn't have any known treatment today—we keep his body at sub-zero temperatures with proper preservative chemicals applied and whenever the cure of that ailment will be known, we might apply it and the person will be alive waking up as if from a deep sleep. Now, this possibility can also create various complexities in family life.

  Say a person at the age of forty years dies of certain malfunction-ing—his wife and only daughter being aged thirty-eight years and ten years respectively. Now after, say thirty years, the man leaps back to life because of medical advances. Now, the person in question is aged forty years only while his wife and daughter are aged sixty-eight and forty years respectively. Now, how should a person behave with his wife and what will be his relationship with his daughter? What will happen, if say his daughter has achieved the age similar to that of his mother? The possibilities are enormous.

All of them can cause great social stresses. In fact, possibly, the whole set of human relationship will have to be redefined. Summing up, the final question arises, that when life and death can also be governed by human beings—what happens to our concept of God. And who, in that case, will control all these—the super human with super brains or the technocrats ? Finally, who is going to decide that who is to be converted into a super human. Will the concepts of "crime and punishment" change? Will the concept of "power and ego hazards" vanish? Will life become so mechanical as everyone does a set of jobs which is pre-programmed in his mind? If life becomes so mechanical then what right will we have to call ourselves human beings—will we not reduce to being machines? These possibilities need to be given further thought so that we are prepared to face them whenever they crop up. The answer lies with the Vedas and in the vedic knowledge.

Education in the Future

In the ancient Vedic times, fathers used to hand down to their sons all sorts of practical techniques along with clearly defined, highly traditional set of values. Knowledge was transmitted not by specialists congregated in schools, but through the family, religious institutions and apprenticeships. Learner and teacher were dispersed throughout the entire community. The key to the system, however, was its absolute devotion to yesterday. The curriculum of the past was 'the past'.

The mechanical age smashed all this : For industrialism required a new kind of man—man pre-adapted to world of repetitive indoor toil, smoke, noise, computer machines, T.V. and all type of gadgets, equipment, crowded living conditions, collective discipline etc. Men were to be regulated not by the cycle of the sun and moon, but by the factory whistle and the clock and so emerged the typical school of industrial era. The masses of students (raw materials) are assembled in a centrally located school (factory) to be processed by teachers (workers). Children arched from place to place and sat in pre-assigned stations (different stages of procession). Bells rang to announce change of times (shifts). The inner life of the school thus became an anticipatory mirror, a perfect introduction to industrial society. The most criticized features of education today—the regimentation, lack of individualization, the rigid system of seating, grouping, grading and marking, the authoritarian role of the teachers are precisely those that made mass public education so effective an instrument of adaptation for its place and time.

The schools, subtly instilled the new time-bias made necessary by industrialism. Faced with conditions that had never before existed, men had to devote increasing energy to understand the present. Thus the focus of education itself began to shift, ever so slowly, away from the past and towards the present.

In the technological system of tomorrow—fast, fluid and self-regulating machines will deal with the flow of information and insight. Machines will increasingly perform the routine tasks; men the intellectual and creative tasks. Machines and men both, instead of being concentrated in the gigantic factories and factory cities, will be scattered across the globe, linked together by amazingly sensitive, near instantaneous communications. Human work will move out of the factory and the mass into the community and the home. Machines will be synchronized, as some already are, to the billionth of second; men will be desynchronized. The factory whistle will vanish. Even the clock "the key machine of the modern industrial age" will lose some of its power over man.

The present administrative structure education, based on industrial bureaucracy will simply not be able to cope-up with the complexities and rate of change inherent in the system which is emerging. Today children are educated in a standard and basically unvarying organizational structure—a teacher led class, one adult and a certain number of subordinate young people, usually seated in fixed rows facing front, is the standardized basic unit of the industrial era school. As they move, grade by grade, to the higher levels, they remain in this same fixed organizational frame. They don't get any training of other forms of organization and for role versatility, and the practical experience in the role of there own life and for society.

In view of the accelerating changes, and the techniques and theories with very small span of life in future, the curriculum will have to be defined periodically and accepted by democratically run "Councils of Future" in the schools. Classes will have to be redesigned—classes with several teachers and a single student, students shifting from group work to individual or independent work and back, students organized into the task forces and project teams with varied organizational structure etc. To be precise the schools will have to focus on 'future'.

Or Another Scenario

When the birth techniques become so advanced that we can program the IQ, the attitudes and interest of a baby—that we can feed all possible knowledge of a stream in the memory of a new born then the school might get eliminated altogether. In fact, they will be replaced by workshops of professional who will update their skills by interacting with the people of the same profession who have evolved new techniques. Such workshops will also frame periodically frame new codes of conduct to be followed for intra-professional and inter-professional relationship. It's very much possible that one's career growth or expertise in any skill will depend more on the power which has been bestowed upon him before birth and less on what efforts he really makes in his lifetime. In fact, a multitude of prespectives can be imagined of in that case dealing all of which is probably out of scope of this chapter.

Or Trajectory Experiments

The future will unfold an unending succession of bizarre incidents, sensational discoveries, implausible conflicts and wildly novel dilemmas. The super industrial revolution can erase hunger, disease, ignorance and brutality.

Dr. F.N. Spiess, head of Marine Physical Laboratory of the Scripps Institution of Oceanography says man will move deep into the sea occupying it and exploiting it as an integral part of his use for recreation, minerals, food, waste disposal and transportation operations and, as population grows, for actual living space.

In United States more than 600 companies have a plan for ocean mining. The Japanese are already extracting 70 lac tones of coal each year from under water mines. A new word has already come in common use called "aquaculture"—the term for scientific cultivation of the oceans food resources— and will take its place alongside agriculture. The opening of the sea may also bring with it a new frontier spirit for life that offers adventure, danger etc. There are plans for artificial cities and play cities complete with hospitals, hotels and homes. General Electric has already designed and tested a synthetic membrane that extracts air from water while keeping the water out.

Or Climate Control

The advancement towards weather prediction and climate control accurately and ultimately climate control is the final goal. There are predictions that by the 21ˢᵗ Century there will be institutions like Weather Council at international level. In it representatives of various nations will hammer out weather policy and control people by adjusting climate i.e., imposing drought here are storm there to enforce there eddicts. This will provide man with a weapon that could radically affect agriculture, transportation, communication, recreation.

On the other side Earth's weather system is an integrated whole, a minute change at one point can trigger of massive consequences elsewhere. Even without aggressive intention, there is danger that attempts to control a drought on one continent could trigger a tornado on another. There are plans to produce sunshine or a facsimile of it at will. NASA is studying the concept of a giant space mirror capable of reflecting the sun's light downwards on night shrouded parts of the earth. It can easily be imagined that the use of orbiting mirrors will alter the hours of light for agriculture, industrial or even psychological reasons.

Changes for a Change or Need

We employ a variety of tactics to lower the levels of stimulation when they threaten to drive us above our adaptive range. For the most part these techniques are employed unconsciously. We can increase their effectiveness by raising consciousness. Heart palpitations, tremors, imsomnia or unexplained fatigue may well signal overstimulation, just as confusion, unusual irritability, profound lassitude and panicky sense that things are skipping out of control are psychological indications. By observing ourselves looking back over the changes in the recent past we can determine whether we are operating comfortably within our adaptive range or pressing its outlimits.

The transience level has risen so high the pace is so forced that historically unprecedented situation has been thrust upon us. This is why we may be approaching the upper limits of the adaptive range. No previous generation has faced this test. The answer to future shock in not non-change but a different kind of change. The only way to maintain any substance of equilibrium during the super industrial revolution will be to meet invention with invention to design new personal and social change regulators. Thus, we need neither blind acceptance nor blind resistance but an array of creative strategies for shaping effectively. The society meanwhile needs new institutions and organizational forms new buffers and balance wheels.

We form relationship with the "vicarious people" as we do with friends, neighbors and colleagues. As the time is passing our relationship with them is going on decreasing, the same is true of our ties with the vicarious spiritual people from vedic period who populate our minds. Events moving faster, constantly throw new personalities of celibrityhood. The same might be said for functional characters spewed out from the pages of books, from television screen, theaters, movies and magazines. No previous generation in history had so many fictional characters flung at it.

These vicarious leaders play a significant role in our lives. We learn from their models of behavior different style and try to adopt them. The accelerated flow has resulted in the instability of personality patterns among many real people who have difficulty in finding real life-style. What is happening is not merely a turnover of real people or even fictional characters, but more rapid turnover of the images and image structures in our brains. The result is that we are increasing the rate at which we form and forget our images of reality.

Today change is so swift and relentless in the techno society that yesterday's truth suddenly becomes today's fiction and the most highly skilled and intelligent members of society admit difficulty in keeping up with the deluge of new knowledge in extremely narrow fields.

At the rate at which knowledge is growing today, by the time the child graduates from the college the amounts of knowledge in the world will be four times as large. By the time the same child is 50 years old it will be 32 times as large and 97 percent of everything known in the world will have been learned since the time he was born. A good bit of new knowledge on the other hand is directly related to his immediate concurs, his job, his politics, his family life, even his sexual behavior.

In United States today the median spent time by adults reading newspapers is fifty-two minutes per day. The same man spends time in reading magazines, books, signs, instructions, labels on cans etc. Surrounded by print he receives between 10,000 and 20,000 edited works per day of the several times that many to which he is exposed. The same person spends several hours per day listening radio commentaries and TV, working on computer etc.

The Biological Factory in 21ˢᵗ Century

Our ancestors domesticated various plant and animal species in the past. But "micro-organisms" were not domesticated until very recently, primarily because man did not know of their existence. Today micro-organisms are already used in the large sale production of vitamins, enzymes, antibiotics, citric acid and other useful compounds. By 21ˢᵗ Century if the pressure for food continues to intensify—biologists will be growing micro-organisms for use as animal food and human food.

According to Arne Tiselius—the future of the industry will come from biology. The tremendous development of Japan since the war has not been only its ship building but its microbiology. Much of this food industry is based on processes in which bacteria are used. One would not be surprised if biological computers are made. Such computers will have electronic components modelled after biological components in the real brain. Man is already on the path towards integrating living tissue in the processes of physical mechanism.

Change roaring through society widens the gap between what we believe and what really is between the existing images and reality they are supposed to reflect. When this gap is moderate we can cope more or less rationally with change, we can react sanely to new conditions we have grip on reality; when the gap grows too wide we suffer psychosis or even death. Thus, to keep it update to relearn reality, his accelerative thrust outside finds a corresponding speed-up in the updating individual. Our image processing mechanisms are driven to operate at a higher and higher speed.

Conclusion

The human race in 21ˢᵗ Century is encountering changes with tremendous speed. A number of opportunities as well as challenges are lying in the lap of the future and unless we gear up to face those challenges—to grab those opportunities within a proper time frame—we are in for a massive adaptation breakdown. The social stresses which will be generated by the developmental forces might lead to the total collapse of human civilization and we will be doomed if don't prepare for them accordingly. On the contrary, proper channelisation of these forces and suitable adjusment in our values will make life much more easier, much more comfortable—a life really worth living, but one must know the art of living with the help of Vastu Shastra the gift of nature.

Conclusion

Chapter 18

Conclusion

Standard Tips as per Vastu Principle

Vastu Shastra covered each aspect of the built form—from the Urban scale down to individual decorative feature on columns. Ten building typologies have been mentioned in the Manasara. They are based on climatic suitability and are region specific for the different zones of the country. The method of building a house according to Manasara (followed in the North) and Mayamatam (Followed in the South) is as follows :

Site Selection

- Square or rectangular sites sloping towards the North or East are auspicious.
- Shape of plot with all angles of 90 degree is best. North-East Corner is auspicious.
- Plot projected towards North-East corner is very good, projections in other directions are bad.
- Roads on North and or East are best.
- Roads on South and West are good for business.
- Road or land on North and East having lower level than road in South and West are good.
- Road should not be round off any corner of the plot, in particular to North-East corner.
- River on North-East side of plot, and hills on South-West side of the plot is the best.
- The plot should be heavy in soil in South and West and light in North and East.
- Hill to the North or East and a depression or water body in the South-West are bad.
- The site should be free from potholes, ants and thorny trees and should not be in close proximity to public halls and temples. A depression in the middle of a site or being crossed by a road is considered a bad omen.

Orientation

- The ideal entrance is from the North or North-East or East.
- Opening from the West or South side are to be avoided for residence plot.
- Entrance to the house can be from any suitable side, considering the orientation in relation with surrounding condition.
- Maximum opening in terms of windows and ventilators should be provided in the North-East quadrant to allow positive sun-rays. Vastu further dictates that less windows should open to the West.

Placement of Rooms

- Master bedroom is recommended on the South-West part of the house.
- Guest bedroom be reserved in North or North-West corner zone.
- Childrens, bedroom, puja, meditation, yoga room is best in the North-East.

During Pregnancy

- Vastu suggests that the blessings of Vastu Purusha are sought throughout one's life. While getting married, the North-West direction, wherein preside the elements of air, is activated by occupying the zone. For conceiving, the western side of the house is favorable as it is considered to be the womb of the house. During pregnancy other than visiting your gynecologist regularly, you need an extremely vibrant environment and for that Vastu recommends keeping fresh flowers in the rooms hanging a picture of a smiling baby on the walls. You should sleep on the left of your husband and while stepping down from the bed, make sure that your right foot lands first on the floor. Avoid wearing dark colors like navy blue and black, and also warm colors such as red and bright orange as they represent excessive lunar and solar currents, respectively. A combination of these colors is acceptable in winter. Avoid sitting in dark and dingy rooms. Color of the room recommended bright color, ceiling white and wall off white or pink, natural light, good ventilation in the room, spending more time in the natural environment around garden and with fresh flowers are very stimulating for the mother and the child.

Kitchen

The kitchen is best in the South-East corner zone as that is the Agnisthan.

Construction of the House

- Use natural and local building materials.
- Use wood only after seasoning.
- Raise the plinth level by minimum 18" high from the existing road level.
- Keep the ceiling temperature below the human body temperature.
- Provide mud phuska treatment on the roof for water-proofing and make slope towards North-East for rain and drain water outlet.
- Construct staircase clockwise while coming up and keep steps in odd numbers.
- A living room, prayer room, temple room or W.C. is not recommended below a stair case.

Basement

- Basement is recommended in North, East or North-East side of the building.
- Excavation should start from North-East.

Setback and Open Space

- More open space should be left towards North and East.
- Keep Brahmasthan (Central Zone) a courtyard open, or, common place for family get together or a meeting place.
- Keep water bodies, fountain, borewell, underground water tank, in the North-East.
- Boundary wall on the South-West should be thicker and higher than North-East.
- Tall and snaded trees be planted in South-West side.
- Grass or seasonal flower plant be planted in East side.

Sitting and Sleeping Position

- Never sleep with head towards North direction.
- Never use steel/metal frame for bed.
- Wife should sleep on left side of her husband.
- Never sit below hanging beam either R.C.C. or steel girder.
- Never sit below the stair case.
- Never use steel/metal frame chair when you have to sit long hours.
- Avoid box type bed.
- If using box type bed, then do not store any type of metal or leather.

Tips on Bedroom Position

The tips on how to sleep is most important because a minimum 1/3 of your lifespan is spent on sleep. If we take the lifespan to be 60 years one sleeps, 20 years on his bed. So, Vastu advices, not to sleep with head towards North direction, because human head is considered North, magnetic principle is that same pole repels each other, thus a person sleeping with his head towards North Direction will have less blood circulation in his brain, the scientist has also proved that North pole has more magnetic effect than South pole and as human blood consists of iron, magnetic effect is more on human blood. All religions follow this principle and that is why Hindus/Sikhs place the dead body with head towards North before lighting the pyre (Fire), Mohameddans/Christians bury their dead body with head towards North.

Here are other directions to sleep:

- Growing children should have their head towards East while sleeping.
- Persons with low blood pressure towards East-South.
- A professional person towards South or South-West.
- A businessman with head towards West.
- A person having breathing problem towards West-North.
- A person having high blood pressure towards North-East.
- After retirement/old age high blood pressure towards North-East or East.

For specific problem like unwanted dreams, lack of sound sleep and so on please write to us in detail.

The bed should be of wood and not iron or brass frame or tubes as metal works as antenna. Avoid box type bed, if box one must use small hinges of brass and not long full sized hinges which too work as arial. Never store leather or metal in the box, store only bed sheet, blanket and clothes etc.

Keep T.V., music system, computer or any other electric gadget at least two metre away from the bed and after use particularly in night switch off from the mains because it gives—off harmful E.M.F. radiation otherwise. Your house electric wiring, particularly bedroom must be in conduit pipe and both end of conduit pipe must be earthed properly, because in PVC Pipe wiring gives off EMF radiation, which is harmful for humans.

Open all bedroom windows in the morning for about two hours.

Avoid synthetic material in the bedroom like Plastic Emulation paint on the wall; synthetic wall carpet, water proofing synthetic sheet on the roof because these choke the breathing of the room and we live in the room like a plastic bag.

The ceiling temperature of your bedroom should be less than your body temperature, otherwise you will get headache.

(For effetive results please consult Vastu Expert)

Bibliography

Bell, Daniel 1974, *The Coming of Post-industrial Society*, Heinemann, London.

Boulding, Kenneth 1968, *The Meaning of the Twentieth Century: The Great Transitions*, New York.

Dahrendorf, Ralf 1959, *Class and Class Conflict in an Industrial Society*, Stanford, Chap.7 and 8.

Durkheim, Emile 1933, *On the Division of Labour in Society"*, New York, Book 2, Chap. 2.

Lichtheim, George A 1963, *"The New Europe: Today and Tomorrow"*, New York, p. 194.

Porter, John 1968, *The Future of Upward Mobility*, American Sociological Review, Vol.33, No.1

Toffler Alvin, *The Future Shock*, 1970.

Toffler Alvin, *The Thirdwave*, 1980.

Power Shift, 1984, Bantom Book.

The World Encyclopaedia.

Prasanna Kumar Acharya, *An Encyclopaedia of Hindu Architecture*, Low Price Publications, New Delhi, 1998 (*Manasara Sr. no*, VII).

P.C.Bhatla, *The Gift of Life*, Ritika & Radhika Publications, New Delhi, 1998.

Olsborn Alex f, *Applied Imagination Principles and Procedure of Creative Thinking.*

P.C. Bhalla., *The Philosophy of Life.*

Hofstadesti Douglas R., *Meta-Magical Themes, Questioning for the Essence of Mind and Pattern.*

Swami Chinmayanandji, *Taittiriya-Upanishads.*

Rig Veda, Yajur Veda, Sam Veda and Atharva Veda

A.C. Bhaktivedanta Swami Prabhupada, *Books of His Divine Grace.*, The Bhaktivedanta Book Trust, Mumbai, 1997

Indian Monuments Through the Ages — Indian Society of Engineering Geology.

The Vedic Age, Bhartiya Vidya Bhawan, Mumbai.

Kautilya's Arthashastra.

Swami Chinmayanandji, *Tatva Bodh of Adi Shankaracharyaji.*

P.C. Bhatla, *Life and Living,* Ritika & Radhika Publication, New Delhi, 1988.

B.B. Puri, *Vedic Architecture and Art of Living,* Vastu Gyan Publication, New Delhi, 1998.

B.B. Puri, *Applied Vastu Shastra in Modern Architecture,* Vastu Gyan Publication, 1997.

B.B. Puri, *Mass Scale Housing for Hot Climate,* Oxford & IBH Publishing Co. Pvt. Ltd., New Delhi, 1993.

Index